The
Blue Riband
of the Atlantic

The
Blue Riband
of the Atlantic

Tom Hughes

CHARLES SCRIBNER'S SONS
NEW YORK

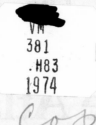

Contents

In memory of my father,
Thomas Scoffham Hughes
(1869-1952)

My special thanks go to Mr John McRoberts
for putting his photographic records at my disposal,
to Mrs Mary Thomas for her invaluable secretarial help,
and to Mr Leslie Reade for his vigilant scrutiny of my completed MS.

Illustrations

7

Foreword

THE NORTH ATLANTIC OCEAN, for hundreds of years the sole means of transport between Europe, Canada and the United States, holds an honoured place in maritime history. With the development of North America, the opening up of this vast continent to millions of settlers, expanding trade with the western world and the replacement of the sailing packet ships by the pioneer steamships, the sea lanes of the Atlantic Ferry, as it was known, were to become the setting for intense and unceasing international competition between enterprising shipowners. It began in July 1840 with the inauguration by the Cunard wooden paddle steamer *Britannia* of the first regular transatlantic mail and passenger service by steamship; it ended in February 1973 with the sale of the United States Lines liner *United States,* the fastest passenger liner in the world.

In the intervening years the struggle for supremacy on this, the most lucrative of all passenger liner routes, led to revolutionary developments in hull design and form, perfection in machinery installations and luxury in passenger accommodation. Shipowners, particularly in Britain, France, Germany, Italy and the United States, determined to commission the largest, fastest and most luxurious liners, invoked the assistance of the world's leading shipbuilders and marine engineers, whose genius, linked with the superb skill and craftsmanship of shipyard workers, was evidenced in a succession of magnificent ships, the beauty, grace and speed of which held the world spellbound, and upon whom in turn was bestowed the crowning accolade—the Blue Riband of the Atlantic. The North Atlantic Ocean will never see their like again; the world is the poorer for their passing. This is their story.

July 1973

One
1818—1839

The pioneers

SEVEN THERE WERE—seven small ships which pioneered the steamship way
across the North Atlantic to confound the many learned sceptics who had
pronounced that at that stage in steamship development it could not be
done. Whilst conceding that steamers could be operated on river services
or short coastwise runs, they argued that coal consumption problems alone
would rule out any chance of success on the long 3,000 miles voyage across
the Western Ocean. The seven pioneer steamers proved them wrong.

The first crossing of the North Atlantic by a ship fitted with an auxiliary
steam engine was achieved in May 1819 by the American paddle steamer
Savannah. Laid down in 1818 as a sailing ship in the shipyard of Crocker
and Fickett, Corlears Hook, New York, the *Savannah* was originally
intended for service between New York and Havre. While under construction she was bought by Captain Moses Rogers who, at one time, had
been master of the small paddle steamers, including the famous *Clermont*,
operating on the Hudson River, but who was then associated with the
recently formed Savannah Steamship Company, Savannah. The purpose
behind his purchase was to implement the company's objective: 'to attach,
either as auxiliary or principal, the propulsion of steam to sea vessels for
the purpose of navigating the Atlantic or other oceans . . . '.

A wooden ship with three tall masts and a long upward curving bow-
prit, the *Savannah* was launched on August 22 1818. After her launch she
was fitted with an auxiliary engine of 90 ihp built by Stephen Vail of
Morristown, New Jersey. This engine had one direct acting cylinder of
40 ins diameter and five feet stroke. Steam was supplied by two low-
pressure copper boilers and what was described as a 'smoke-pipe' was
installed. This was fitted at the top with a movable elbow which could be

11

deflected to direct the smoke and sparks away from the considerable spread of sails. Her two paddle wheels, 15 ft 3 ins in diameter, were so constructed that they could be folded up like a fan and stowed on deck. The main dimensions of the *Savannah* were: length overall 110 ft; length between perps 98.5 ft; breadth of hull 25.8 ft; breadth over paddle wheels 36 ft; depth of hold 14.2 ft; draft 13 ft; gross tonnage 320.

The *Savannah* completed successful trials in March 1819 off Staten Island and then proceeded to her home port. The original idea of operating her in coastal service was abandoned because of a trade depression, and eventually it was decided to offer the ship for sale in Europe. On May 19 1819 what was probably the first advertisement of a steamship sailing across the Atlantic appeared in the *Savannah Republican*. It read: 'The Steamship *Savannah,* Captain Rogers, without fail, will proceed for Liverpool direct tomorrow 20th inst.'

In the event she did not sail until May 24. She carried very little cargo. Most of the space available was taken up by the 75 tons of coal and 25 cords of wood which were required. There were no passengers. Twenty-four days later on June 17 she was reported off Cape Clear, Ireland, as a ship 'on fire' and the British naval cutter, *Kite,* quickly set out to help a vessel apparently in distress. However, on June 18 Captain Rogers found he had run out of fuel—an entry in his log book reading 'No cole (sic) to git up steam'. He put into Kinsale for fresh supplies and then proceeded to Liverpool where the arrival of the *Savannah* on June 20 caused a great sensation. Her passage from Savannah had taken 29 days 11 hours, during which her engines had been used for a total of 85 hours, and only when there was so little wind that speed had fallen to four knots. It has been contended that, as the *Savannah* was primarily a sailing ship fitted with an auxiliary engine little used, her claim to be the first steamer to cross the Atlantic is invalid. But in view of the fact that for many years North Atlantic steamers were to make considerable use of sail when occasion arose, not to include the *Savannah* would be ungenerous and unjust.

Fourteen years elapsed before a second steamship ventured to cross the North Atlantic. She was the Canadian paddle steamer *Royal William (1)* the construction of which was subsidised by the Government of Lower Canada with the objective of 'creating closer trade links between the old French Province by the St Lawrence river and the British provinces by the sea'. Maintenance and operation of the ship was carried out by the Quebec and Halifax Steam Navigation Company, specifically formed for this purpose. There were 235 shareholders among whom were a Halifax shipowner, Samuel Cunard, and his brothers, Henry and Joseph.

A wooden ship, schooner rigged, with three masts and a standing bowsprit, the *Royal William (1)* was built at Black and Campbell's shipyard, Cap Blanc, Quebec, to the design and under the supervision of James Goudie, a young Canadian who had learned his craft on the Clyde as an apprentice with a Greenock firm of shipbuilders named Simmons. The keel of the *Royal William (1)* was laid in September 1830, the launch taking place on April 29 the next year, an event regarded as of national importance. Lord Aylmer, the Governor-in-Chief, was present as representative of King William IV after whom the ship was named. The Mayor of Quebec declared the day a national holiday, and thousands gathered on the river banks to watch Lady Aylmer name the ship. A Guard of Honour and the band of the 32nd Foot regiment paraded at the slipway, and gunners of the Royal Artillery stationed at the Quebec Citadel fired a salute as the *Royal William (1)* moved down her slipway and took the water.

After her launching the ship was towed up the St Lawrence to Montreal where her side lever engines developing 200 hp were installed by the firm of Bennet and Henderson of that city. These engines comprised two cylinders of 50 inches diameter by 60 inches stroke to develop about 300 indicated horsepower. Designed speed was about eight knots. Incidentally, the crankshafts were forged in the Glasgow works of Robert Napier—a name to become famous in transatlantic Blue Riband history—and were shipped across to Montreal. Main dimensions of the *Royal William (1)* were: length overall 176 ft; length (between perpendiculars) 160 ft; length of keel 146 ft; breadth overall 44 ft; breadth between paddle boxes 28 ft; depth of hold 17.75 ft; draft 14 ft. Accommodation described as 'tasteful and elegant' was provided for 50 passengers in the cabin class and 80 in the steerage. Cost of the ship was estimated at £16,000.

On August 24 1831 the *Royal William (1)* steamed out of Quebec on the outset of her maiden round voyage to Miramichi, Prince Edward Island, and Halifax, Nova Scotia. She completed three similar round voyages before winter closed in on the St Lawrence and the *Royal William (1)* was perforce laid up. Hopes of resuming successful services in the spring of 1832 were not to be realised. An epidemic of 'Asian' cholera had spread to Canada bringing business in Quebec to a virtual standstill. The *Royal William (1)* made one voyage during the year but was so restricted by quarantine regulations that, on her return to Quebec in the August, her owners, whose financial losses had brought them to the verge of bankruptcy, had no alternative but to lay up the ship and offer her for sale.

So it came about that, in the spring of 1833, a group of six of the original shareholders (Cunard was not among them) bought the ship and operated her as a river steamer and on occasional excursions. These included a voyage to Boston, Mass, whence she sailed on June 4 to receive a great welcome on June 17 as being the first steamer flying the British flag to enter a United States port. This was but a 'flash in the pan'; on her return to Quebec her owners decided to sell the ship in England, and accordingly advertised her prospective sailing to London on August 1, the cabin passage being £20, exclusive of wines.

At 05.00 hours on August 4 the *Royal William (1)*, under the command of Captain John McDougall, steamed from Quebec for Pictou, Nova Scotia, where she remained for a few days taking on coal, stores, and being prepared for her Atlantic adventure, eventually sailing on August 17. Her clearance papers issued by the Pictou Customs read:

Royal William	363 tons.	36 men.
Whither bound	London.	
Carrying goods exported :—	254 chaldrons of coal (about 330 tons); a box of stuffed birds. Six ship's spars. One box, ten trunks. A quantity of household furniture. One harp.	
Seven passengers, all British.		

The *Royal William* (*1*) soon ran into heavy weather. Overtaken by a great storm off the Grand Banks, Newfoundland, her wooden hull badly strained, the ship began to leak; the starboard engine was disabled. It was fortunate for the passengers and crew that in their master (who hailed from Oban, Scotland) they had a seaman of great skill, perseverance and personal courage. He ordered all hands to the pumps, held to his course and kept the ship under way for ten days using the port engine. When the weather cleared, repairs were effected and on September 6 Captain McDougall put into Cowes, Isle of Wight, to take on new supplies of coal, provisions and fresh water. The *Royal William* (*1*) then proceeded to London where she arrived on September 12, some 25 days after leaving Pictou, delighting the watchers on the Thames waterside by 'steaming up to Gravesend in fine style'.

Captain McDougall is said to have claimed of the *Royal William* (*1*) that: 'she is justly entitled to be considered the first steamer that crossed the Atlantic by steam, having steamed the whole way across'. His claim is open to dispute in that in his own words it was necessary to stop the engines 'from 24 to 26 hours every fourth day to clear the boilers of salt'. Presumably sails were then hoisted, if only to keep the ship on course.

Like that of the *Savannah* the transatlantic voyage made by the *Royal William* (*1*) was an isolated event in her sea-going career. She never returned to Canada. Ten days after her arrival in the Thames the *Royal William* (*1*) was chartered by the Portuguese Government for employment as a transport, and a year later on September 10 1834 was sold to the Spanish Government for £10,000. She was refitted as a warship and re-named *Ysabel Segunda* to become the first steamer in the Spanish navy. It says much for Captain McDougall's reputation as a shipmaster and navigator that the Spanish Government invited him to remain in the ship with the rank and pay of Commander and other emoluments—an invitation he accepted.

The historic voyages of the *Savannah* and *Royal William* (*1*)—particularly the latter—had demonstrated that, while it was possible for steamers to cross the North Atlantic, a great deal more would have to be done in hull design and machinery installations before such voyages could become economic and practical. It was not until 1838 that there came the long awaited breakthrough. This was the splendid and memorable year when three newly formed British steamship companies almost simultaneously commissioned their pioneer ships on the Western Ocean.

The three companies were the British and American Steam Navigation Company of London, the Great Western Steamship Company of Bristol and the Transatlantic Steamship Company of Liverpool. At the outset five steamers were involved. Three of them were the first steamers specially designed and built for transatlantic service — the *British Queen* of the British and American Steam Navigation Company, the *Great Western* of the Great Western Steamship Company, and the *Liverpool* of the Transatlantic Steamship Company. The remaining two were small steamers normally engaged in coastal services between Britain and Ireland and specially chartered for voyages to New York while the bigger ships were completing. Their names were the *Royal William* (*2*) chartered by the Transatlantic Steamship Company, Liverpool, and the *Sirius* chartered by the British and American Steam Navigation Company, London.

And it is to the *Sirius*, which in a very real sense had greatness thrust upon her, that belongs the imperishable honour of being the first steamer to cross the Atlantic under continuous steam power. A wooden paddle steamer of 703 tons, the *Sirius* had been built in 1837 by Robert Menzies and Son, Leith, for the service between London and Cork, operated by the St George Steam Packet Company. Her machinery installation comprised side lever engines of 320 nominal horsepower with two cylinders 60 inches in diameter and 72 inches stroke. Steam at a pressure of five pounds per square inch was supplied by rectangular boilers which consumed about 24 tons of coal a day. A special feature of the machinery installation was the fitting of the new surface condensers, invented by Samuel Hall of Basford, Nottinghamshire, which enabled her boilers to be fed with fresh water. Designed speed was nine knots. The figurehead consisted of a dog holding between its front paws the Dog Star 'Sirius' after which the vessel was named.

Commissioned in August 1837, the *Sirius* maintained sailings on the London to Cork run until March 1838, when she was chartered by the British and American Steam Navigation Company pending the completion of the *British Queen* which had been delayed due to the bankruptcy of the engineering firm responsible for the machinery installation.

Under the command of Lieutenant Richard Roberts RN, the *Sirius* left Blackwall, London, on March 28 1838 for Passage Quay, Cork (later to be known as Queenstown). During her voyage down-channel she sighted the *Great Western* running her trials before entering service—one of the main reasons why the *Sirius* had been chartered. On arrival at Cork, she took on supplies of coal (450 tons) and embarked 44 passengers. Her crew totalled 37 including two boys, one stewardess and one 'attendant' whose duties were not specified. At 10.30 hours on April 3 the *Sirius* began her momentous voyage to New York. For her master it was to prove a hazardous passage not only because of the stormy weather — his log recorded heavy seas, gales, sleet and snow—but because at one stage his frightened crew were on the point of mutiny. But discipline prevailed and at 22.00 hours on Sunday April 22 the *Sirius* came to anchor off the Battery, New York. The total distance for the voyage was 2,897 miles, the best day's run was 220 miles and the worst day's 85 miles. Average speed was 6.7 knots. The *Sirius* steamed into New York harbour the next morning, April 23, to receive the first of those rapturous welcomes accorded to newly arrived transatlantic liners which were to become a tradition of this great port. On this particular day, April 23, the welcome was intensified when within a few hours of the arrival of the *Sirius* the *Great Western* which, commanded by Captain James Hosken, had left Bristol on April 8, five days after the *Sirius*, steamed into the harbour having completed the voyage to New York in 15 days at an average speed of 8.2 knots.

Commenting on the arrival of these two pioneer steamers the New York *Courier and Enquirer* of April 24 said: 'What may be the ultimate fate of this excitement—whether or not the expenses of equipment or fuel will admit the employment of these vessels in the ordinary packet service—we cannot pretend to form an opinion; but of the entire feasibility of the passage of the Atlantic by steam, as far as regards safety, comfort and despatch, even in the roughest and most boisterous weather, the most sceptical must now cease to doubt.'

The triumphant *Sirius* began her return voyage from New York on May 1, and after another stormy passage arrived at Falmouth at 20.00 hours on May 18. Loaded with honours, including the Freedom of the City of London, the Freedom of the City of Cork, and numerous presents, her master, Lieutenant Roberts, was appointed to the command of the *British Queen*. The *Sirius* having valiantly accomplished all that was required of her was withdrawn from Atlantic service and returned to her less adventurous, if more comfortable routine on the London-Cork coastwise run.

The *Great Western* began her homeward passage from New York to Bristol on May 7, carrying 68 passengers and 10,000 letters. If she had been denied the honour of being the first steamer to cross from Europe to New York, she had the satisfaction of having made the fastest passage. There is little doubt that the *Great Western* was the most outstanding of all the transatlantic pioneer steamers. Designed by Isambard K. Brunel specifically to meet the rigours of North Atlantic voyaging, the *Great Western* was an exceptionally strong wooden ship. She was built at the Bristol shipyard of William Patterson and launched on July 19 1837. When nearing completion she was towed from Bristol to London to have her engines installed; they had been constructed by Maudslay Sons and Field. They were of the side-lever type having two cylinders 73.5 ins in diameter and stroke of seven feet to give an indicated horsepower of 750. Steam at a pressure of five pounds per square inch was supplied by four iron boilers. Coal consumption worked out at 33 tons a day; designed speed was nine knots. A feature of her passenger accommodation was her main saloon some 75 ft long, 21 ft wide and nine feet high, claimed to be the largest and most luxurious room ever provided in a steamship. Principal dimensions of the *Great Western* were: gross tons 1,320; net 680; length overall 236 ft; length between perpendiculars 212 ft; length of keel 205 ft; moulded breadth 34 ft; breadth over paddle boxes 58.3 ft; depth of hold 23.3 ft; mean draft 16.7 ft.

After her successful maiden voyage the *Great Western* remained in her owner's service for the next eight years, during which she made no fewer than 64 round voyages between Bristol and New York. In a reference to this great ship, Sir John Rennie, a famous marine engineer, once said that the success of her maiden voyage across the Atlantic 'having exceeded the most sanguine expectations of her promoters and indeed of the whole world there seems no bounds to the extension of steam navigation'.

But the achievements of the *Sirius* and the *Great Western* did not bring to an end the flurry and excitement of 1838. London had supplied the *Sirius,* and Bristol the *Great Western.* Now it was the turn of Liverpool, where the Transatlantic Steamship Company were finalising plans. To make a beginning, the directors chartered from the City of Dublin Steam Packet Company, which had sponsored the new company, the paddle steamer *Royal William* (2), then maintaining passenger and mail services between Liverpool and Kingstown (Dublin). Built of wood in 1837 by the Liverpool shipbuilders William and Thomas Wilson, the *Royal William* (2)

16

The 1,320-ton wooden paddle steamer *Great Western*, designed by I. K. Brunel and a rival of the *Sirius*, was the first passenger-carrying ship to be built specially for the transatlantic service. (*National Maritime Museum, London*)

The *Britannia*, *Acadia*, *Caledonia* (shown here) and *Columbia* were all built on the Clyde in 1840, with identical horse-power and passenger accommodation. They were the first ships supplied following the Admiralty's acceptance of Cunard's tender for the conveyance of mails to North America.

The Cunard royal mail steamer *Britannia* leaving an ice-bound Boston harbour in February 1844. On her maiden voyage in 1840 she reached Halifax from Liverpool in 12 days and ten hours. (*National Maritime Museum, London*)

In 1843, the year of her commissioning, the *Hibernia* made a record eastbound passage for Cunard of nine days and ten hours, and four years later improved on this record by eight and a half hours. (*National Maritime Museum, London*)

The *Europa* did not have a very successful career with Cunard. Built in 1848 she collided with and sank the barque *Charles Bartlett* in the following year and was damaged in a collision with the *Arabia* nine years later.

The famous Collins Line Blue Riband holder *Arctic,* sinking after a collision off Cape Race. Although the Collins Line posed a serious threat to Cunard, it was never a commercially viable company and was beset by misfortunes.
(*City of Liverpool Museum*)

Faced with the ever-growing challenge from the American Collins Line, Cunard produced the 2,200-ton *Asia* and her sister ship *Africa*. When the Collins' *Atlantic* covered the New York-Liverpool route in ten days eight hours 20 minutes, the *Asia* replied with a passage which was one hour and 20 minutes faster. (*National Maritime Museum, London*)

Six years later, in 1856, the *Persia* joined the *Asia* in putting the Collins Line in the shade. She was the first ever iron paddle steamer, built expressly to regain the speed record, and this beautiful vessel was the main reason for the Cunard Line regaining supremacy on the Atlantic.

was the first steamship to sail from Liverpool to New York and was, in fact, the smallest steamship ever to steam the whole way across the Western Ocean. A special feature of her design was that the hull was divided into separate compartments by four transverse watertight bulkheads which, it was stated, 'have given much security and comfort to passengers'. Her propelling machinery, constructed by Fawcett and Preston, Liverpool, comprised side-lever engines of 270 nominal horsepower with two cylinders 48.5 inches in diameter by 66 inches stroke, which developed 400.1 hp. Her designed speed was 11 knots. 'Spacious' accommodation was provided for 80 passengers.

The *Royal William* (2) was advertised to sail from Liverpool direct to New York under the command of Lieutenant W. Swainson RN. The fare was 35 guineas 'including wines and all stores'. The confidence of the owners that their pioneer ship would accomplish the voyage was indicated in an additional note which, anticipating by many years the tourist trade to America, read: 'The *Royal William* will remain ten days at New York to allow travellers to visit the splendid scenery of the Hudson River and the celebrated Falls of Niagara. Her return from that port will therefore be postponed until July 29'.

As if sensing the importance of the occasion to the future of the port, Merseyside people gathered in thousands to cheer the *Royal William* (2) on her way out to sea on the evening of July 5. Contemporary accounts record how cannon were fired in salute to the gallant ship and how she was so deeply laden with 410 tons of coal 'that her paddles were buried six feet and it was possible by leaning over the bulwarks to wash one's hands in the water that surged at the vessel's sides' – a disquieting experience for her 32 passengers who had yet to face the unknown terrors of the North Atlantic. Their worst fears were quickly realised. The North Atlantic was uncharitable to the newcomer. Storms were encountered throughout the voyage which took 19 days to complete, during which the *Royal William* (2) consumed 351 tons of her precious coal supplies. Homeward bound the *Royal William* (2) left New York on August 4 and not July 29 as originally advertised. Favoured by better weather she made the passage in 14 days 12 hours.

Meanwhile the directors had been looking for a ship which would eventually replace the little *Royal William* (2). They found one in the *Liverpool,* then completing in the shipyard of Humble and Milcrest, Liverpool. A wooden ship of 1,150 tons, the *Liverpool,* launched on October 14 1837, had been ordered originally by Sir John Tobin, a Liverpool shipowner and merchant, who had a financial interest in the Transatlantic Steamship Company and agreed that they should buy the *Liverpool* from him for their New York service.

When commissioned in October 1838, the *Liverpool* brought a completely 'new look' to the North Atlantic. Not only was she the first Atlantic steamer to be fitted with two funnels, but in the elegance and decorative features of her passenger accommodation she was in many respects the forerunner of the great 'floating hotels' which in years to come were to dominate the Atlantic Ferry.

Commanded by Lieutenant Fayrer RN, the *Liverpool* began her maiden voyage from the Mersey to New York on October 20 1838. She carried

50 passengers, 150 tons of cargo and 563 tons of coal. It was not an auspicious first voyage. When his ship had been at sea for six days, the master became anxious about the rapid consumption of coal and put back to Cork to replenish supplies. On November 6, the *Liverpool* resumed her voyage, finally arriving at New York on November 23. The passage from Cork to New York was made in 16 days 17 hours at an average speed of 7.9 knots, but overall the *Liverpool* had been 26 days at sea.

A three-masted wooden ship, the *Liverpool* was propelled by side-lever engines of 468 nominal horsepower constructed by A. Forrester and Company of Liverpool, with two cylinders 75 inches in diameter by seven feet stroke. Steam at five pounds per square inch pressure was supplied by four rectangular boilers. Main dimensions of the ship were: gross register 1,150 tons, net 560 tons; length overall 240 ft; length between perpendiculars 223 ft; breadth of hull 30.8 ft; breadth over paddle boxes 56 ft; depth of hold 21 ft.

Unfortunately the splendour of the *Liverpool's* passenger accommodation was not matched by her performance at sea. In heavy weather she proved a very 'wet' ship, much to the discomfort of her passengers, and was much slower than the *Great Western*.

The seventh and the last pioneer steamer was the *British Queen*, described as 'a most beautiful specimen of London shipbuilding, and for elegance of mould, great strength and admirable proportion of parts, thought by many to be unequalled'. Ordered in 1836 by the British and American Steam Navigation Company from Curling and Young, Limehouse, London, the *British Queen*, at the time of her launching on May 24 1838, was the largest vessel in the world. A barque-rigged wooden ship with three masts, she was fitted with a splendid figurehead representing Queen Victoria – when first planned it had been intended to name the ship *Princess Victoria* – who succeeded to the throne whilst the ship was under construction, the name being then changed to *British Queen*.

The principal dimensions of this, the largest of all the pioneer steamers, were: gross register 1,862 tons; net 1,053; length overall 275 ft; length between perps 245 ft; breadth of hull 40.5 ft; breadth over paddle boxes 64 ft; depth of hold 27 ft; draft 17 ft. Accommodation was installed for 207 passengers. The *British Queen* was propelled by side-lever engines of 500 nominal horsepower with two cylinders 77.5 inches diameter by seven feet stroke. Steam was supplied at five pounds per square inch pressure, and, as in the *Sirius*, surface condensers were installed to enable her four boilers to be supplied with fresh water. Designed speed was 10.2 knots.

At the outset the contract for the machinery installation was given to Claude Girdwood and Company on the Clyde. This firm went bankrupt and the order was transferred to Robert Napier, also on the Clyde. At that time the Napier establishment was fully occupied with other orders. This inevitably led to delays in completing the contract for the *British Queen*. As a result, and much to the frustration of the owners, the vessel was not completed until the summer of 1839 – over a year behind her original commissioning schedule. By this time the *Great Western* and the *Liverpool* were firmly established on the Atlantic run.

It was not until July 10 1839 that the *British Queen*, commanded by Lieutenant Roberts RN, of *Sirius* fame, sailed from London to Ports-

mouth, where she embarked 220 passengers and loaded 800 tons of cargo
and 600 tons of coal to feed her hungry furnaces before she set out on
July 12 on her first transatlantic voyage. Fifteen days later, on July 27,
she arrived at New York. Her homeward voyage to Portsmouth was
scheduled to begin on August 1 and on that same day the *Great Western*
was due to sail for Bristol. It was inevitable that, learning of the almost
simultaneous departure of the two ships, New Yorkers should have
fastened on the idea of a 'race' between the two vessels, and crowds
gathered along the waterfront to cheer the ships on their way. Was this
the moment which saw the beginning of the mythical 'Blue Riband of the
Atlantic?' Bets were freely laid as to the outcome of the 'race'. In the
event the spoils went to the backers of the more experienced *Great
Western*, which arrived at Bristol on August 14. Twelve hours later the
British Queen steamed into Portsmouth harbour, completing a maiden
voyage performance of which she had every reason to be proud.

Of the seven ships which had pioneered the steamship way across the
North Atlantic only three remained – the *Great Western, Liverpool* and
the *British Queen,* and they could no longer be categorised as pioneers.
The steamship had 'arrived' on the Western Ocean. This in fact had been
recognised by the British Admiralty in November 1838 in their advertisement for tenders for the carriage of mails by steamship across the North
Atlantic – a contract which had been awarded to Samuel Cunard, a
Canadian shipowner virtually unknown in Britain. To the understandable
anger and dismay of the Great Western Steamship Company the tender
they had submitted had been rejected. Nor can they have found much
comfort in the fact that, when the time came for Samuel Cunard to return
to Canada, mail contract in his pocket and, as yet, no ships to implement
it, he booked a passage in the *Great Western*. That, perhaps, was the
unkindest cut of all.

Two
1840—1851

Cunard sets the pattern

AT 14.00 HOURS on Saturday July 4 1840 the Cunard Royal Mail wooden paddle steamer *Britannia* of 1,154 gross tons, began her maiden voyage from Liverpool to Halifax, Nova Scotia, and Boston, Mass. She was the first of four sister ships ordered by the British and North American Royal Mail Steam Packet Company (a formal title soon forgotten in the popular preference for Cunard Line) to comply with the terms of an agreement concluded with the British Admiralty to carry, for the first time, mails by steamship between Britain, Canada, and the United States.

For the *Britannia* her maiden voyage was a personal triumph. She completed the westward passage to Halifax two days ahead of schedule and in the record time of 12 days ten hours at an average speed of 8.5 knots. After disembarking passengers and landing mails and cargo she proceeded to Boston, where she arrived late on Saturday July 18. She had completed the full voyage—including detention at Halifax—in 14 days eight hours at an average speed of eight knots. The *Britannia* began her homeward voyage from Boston on August 1. After calling at Halifax she set a course for Liverpool, completing the crossing in ten days at an average speed of 10.56 knots. It was a remarkable performance, and the *Britannia* could lay just claim to being the fastest transatlantic liner in service. At that early stage in North Atlantic steamship history the term 'Blue Riband of the Atlantic' had not been conjured up. If it had, the *Britannia* would undoubtedly have been awarded this coveted honour.

As it was, she had set a target which her sister ships would find difficult to surpass. That they did so is a tribute to the skill and craftsmanship of their builders, and the wisdom of their owners. From the outset, this Cunard quartet were in a class apart from all other Atlantic steamers. They were the first steamships specifically built and engined on the Clyde for North Atlantic service. They were the first steamers to inaugurate regular all-the-year-round passenger and mail services across the Western Ocean. They were the first steamers whose plans stipulated the inclusion of a mail room, the care of which was the sole responsibility of a naval officer appointed by the Admiralty, and carried as a supernumerary member of the crew, and they were the first steamers to challenge collectively the fast American packet sailing-ships then dominating and crowding the North Atlantic lanes.

The first public announcement of the Cunard Atlantic service was published in the *Liverpool Mercury* on Friday July 3. It read:

'British and North American Royal Mail Steamships of 1,200 tons and 440 horsepower each, "Appointed by the Admiralty to sail for Boston calling at Halifax to land passengers and Her Majesty's mails:

Britannia ....Captain Woodruff
Acadia ....Captain Edward C. Miller
Caledonia............Captain Richard Cleland
Columbia............ *

'The *Britannia* will sail from Liverpool on the 4th July; the *Acadia* on the 4th August. "Passage including provisions and wine to Halifax, 34 guineas; to Boston 38 guineas. Steward's fee one guinea."

'The steamship *Unicorn* plies between Pictou and Quebec in connection with the above vessels carrying the mails and passengers.

'For passage apply to G. & J. Burns, Glasgow, J. B. Ford, 52 Old Broad St., London, or in Liverpool to D. & C. MacIver, 12 Water St.

'The *Britannia* goes out of Coburg Dock this morning (Friday) the 3rd inst., and all heavy baggage should be sent on board before that time. Tomorrow (Saturday morning) at 10. o'clock a steamer will be at the Egremont Slip, south end of Prince's Parade to take off the passengers.'

In this simple and straightforward manner, without undue elaboration, the first advertisement announcing the inauguration of regular mail and passenger steamship services across the North Atlantic was published. It was a historic event in that it presaged one of the major technical and commercial developments of the 19th century—the coming into being of what was to be known as the Atlantic Ferry.

Four men were behind the building of the *Britannia* and her three sister-ships. Three of them were shipowners and merchants, George Burns of Glasgow, David MacIver of Liverpool and Samuel Cunard of Halifax, Nova Scotia. The fourth man, without whose practical advice and faith in the project, the whole concept might never have come about—was Robert Napier, marine engineer of Glasgow.

It was Samuel Cunard who had started the whole affair when, in February 1839, in response to an advertisement issued from the Admiralty offices in London calling for tenders for a regular steamship service to carry mails across the North Atlantic, he had submitted a tender. In this, Cunard undertook to fulfil one of the Admiralty's requirements by pro-

---

* Captain E. Ewing was subsequently appointed first master.

25

viding three steamers by May 1 1840 for an annual sum of £55,000, and 'should any improvement in steam navigation be made during its continuance which the Lords of the Admiralty may consider as essential to the service, I do bind myself to make such alterations and improvements as their Lordships may direct'.

Cunard was awarded the mail contract. His next step was to find a reputable builder. Here he sought the advice of James C. Melville, secretary of the East India Company for whom Cunard was agent for Canada. Melville suggested Cunard could not do better than contact the firm of Wood and Napier, Clydeside shipbuilders and marine engineers, who had built tonnage for the East India Company. Robert Napier, the senior partner, was a well-known marine engineer who had designed and installed machinery in 14 ships for which John Wood had built the hulls.

Acting on this suggestion, Cunard got in touch with Napier, eventually meeting him in Glasgow in March 1839. The two men quickly got down to business and Napier agreed to build and engine the three ships for £30,000 each. While the contract was being drawn up, slight amendments were made. The tonnage of the proposed ships was increased from 800 to 960 tons, horsepower from 300 to 375 and the cost of each vessel from £30,000 to £32,000. This agreement between Cunard and Napier was ratified formally on March 18 1839 at the offices of Moncrieff and Paterson, Writers of Glasgow.

So far there had been only two people involved, Cunard and Napier. On his return to London, Cunard lost no time in submitting the plans to the Admiralty. On March 21 he was able to write to Napier to the effect that, 'The Admiralty and Treasury are highly pleased with the size of the boats. I have given credit where it is due to you and Mr Wood. I have pledged myself that they shall be the finest and best boats ever built in this country. You have no idea of the prejudice of some of our English builders. I have had several offers from Liverpool and this place (London) and when I have replied that I have contracted in Scotland they invariably say "You will neither have substantial work nor completed on time". The Admiralty agree with me in the opinion that these boats will be as good as if built in this country (England), and I have assured them that you will keep to time.'

On May 4 1839 the contract between the Lords of the Admiralty and Samuel Cunard was formally signed. The signatories were S. Cunard, John Brooke Pichell and Dalmeny.

Cunard lost no time in writing to his business associates in Halifax and Boston where the news created great excitement and enthusiasm. While Cunard was in London, Napier began preliminary work on the three ships. The more he went into the project the more he became convinced that the vessels as specified in the agreement would not stand up to the exacting requirements of the North Atlantic, especially in the winter. He also came to the conclusion that if the agreed Admiralty mail schedule was to be maintained all the year round, four larger and more powerful steamers would be needed. He wrote to Cunard pointing out that if they were to adhere to the original contract of March 18 1839 the result might well prove disastrous.

Napier's arguments were strengthened by a letter Cunard had received from his friend and business associate J. N. Stayner, Deputy Postmaster General of Quebec, who also argued that if the service was to prove successful, four ships not three, would be necessary to ensure fixed days of departure from Halifax as well as from Liverpool. Cunard sent this letter to the Admiralty with a request for an additional £5,000 to help in meeting the cost of a fourth ship, estimated at £43,000.

These developments brought about a major crisis for Cunard. He had already committed himself to the full extent of his available financial resources. In his dilemma he again turned to Melville, who advised him that the best thing he could do was to see Napier and explain his financial position openly and frankly. Cunard did so. Napier was sympathetic, but still held to his belief that the only way to ensure success lay in building four larger and more powerful ships. He told Cunard that he would be willing to help finance the project and to put Cunard in touch with other shipowners and merchants in Glasgow, who might be willing to subscribe to the necessary capital. Among them were two shipowners, George Burns and David MacIver, both of whom had considerable practical experience of coastwise steamship services.

On May 10 Cunard met George Burns who in later years was to record: 'It was not long before we began to see some daylight through the scheme, and I entertained the proposal cordially. That day I asked Cunard to dine with me, and also David MacIver, who was at that time residing in Glasgow as agent for the City of Glasgow Steam Packet Company. I propounded the matter to MacIver, but he did not seem to see his way clear; on the contrary, he went dead against the proposal, and advised that after dinner I had better tell Cunard that the thing would not suit us.

'As talking after dinner generally ends in nothing, so it did on this occasion. However, Mr. Cunard asked us to come down and take breakfast with him and Mr. Robert Napier the following morning in Mr. Napier's house. We went accordingly, and, after going into details, I told Mr. Cunard we could hardly take up such a large concern as the proposal before us would amount to, without inviting a few friends to join us; and that as it would not be fair to keep him in suspense, we would set him free to make any arrangements he thought best with his own friends. He replied, "How long will it take to ascertain what you can do?" I answered, "Perhaps a month;" and he said, "Very well then, I'll wait."

'That same day I set out and spoke first of all to Mr. William Connal, then at the head of a large firm engaged in the commission trade of produce and other things. Mr. Connal said to me, "I know nothing whatever about steam navigation, but if you think well of it, I'll join you." '

By May 14, such good progress had been made that a preliminary contract was drawn up and signed under which Samuel Cunard assumed George Burns and David MacIver as partners to the extent of one half in the mail contract and in the steam vessels to be employed in carrying the mails. The price paid by Burns and MacIver for this half interest was £25,000 and the right was given to them to take others into their share of the partnership.

George Burns then set about interesting some of his friends and business associates in becoming partners with him and Mr MacIver in their half share of the Cunard mail contract. Within a very short time no fewer than 31 men agreed to join the enterprise and, in June 1839, a contract of co-partnery was entered into between them and George Burns and David MacIver, under which a company was formed entitled 'The Glasgow Proprietary in the British and North American Royal Mail Steam Packets'.

Cunard was now in a position to instruct Napier to go ahead with his new proposals. The number of ships was increased from three to four, and their dimensions to 1,200 gross tons and 420 horsepower. The Admiralty were advised of the change in the situation, and Cunard also took the occasion to press the claims of Boston that the mail service should be extended to that port. The Government consented to the extension of the service and, in consideration of the larger fleet to be used, increased the annual remuneration from £55,000 to £60,000.

The keel of the first vessel, to be named *Britannia,* was laid down at Robert Duncan's yard, Greenock. Contracts for the other three ships, *Acadia, Caledonia* and *Columbia,* were given to Mr John Wood, Mr Charles Wood and Mr Robert Steele, all well-known Clydeside shipbuilders. Robert Napier was responsible for the machinery installation in all four ships.

Sister ships in every respect, their principal dimensions were: gross register 1,156 tons, net 619 tons; displacement at mean draught 2,050 tons; length overall 228 ft; length between perpendiculars 207 ft; breadth over paddle boxes 56 ft; depth of hull 22.5 ft; mean draught 16.8 ft.

They were three-masted barques, with two decks, square stern and clipper bow and single funnel. Total complement comprised 89 officers and crew. The officers' accommodation was on the upper deck and the passenger accommodation consisted of a dining saloon and cabins for 115 on the main deck. It was adequate but by no means luxurious.

The ships were propelled by side-lever engines of 440 nominal horsepower built by Robert Napier, with two cylinders 72 inches in diameter by 82 inches stroke which indicated 740 total horsepower. Steam at a pressure of nine pounds per square inch was supplied by four return flue boilers each with three furnaces. The total heating surface was 2,698 square feet, the grate area 222 square feet, and the coal consumption about 37 tons per day. The bunkers held 640 tons. The paddle wheels were each 28 feet in diameter with 21 fixed radial floats 8.75 feet in length and 2.8 feet wide. They made 16 revolutions per minute and normal speed averaged about 8.5 knots.

When the ships were first commissioned the single funnel was painted red with a black top. It was not until 1850 that the familiar three black rings were featured on the funnel. Again, at the outset, Cunard ships did not fly the gold lion house flag; instead they flew two pennants—a blue with a white saltire in the hoist flown over a red burgee. It was in 1850 that the pennants were changed to a single houseflag—a blue burgee carrying a large white star. Then, in 1880, with the formal establishment of the Cunard Steamship Company Ltd, the world-famous red flag, featuring a golden lion rampant (regardant and crowned) holding a globe was finally adopted.

The *Britannia* was launched on February 5 1840 in the presence of a vast throng of guests and spectators. They included Samuel Cunard who had made a special voyage from Halifax, Nova Scotia, to attend the launching and watch the naming ceremony being 'worthily performed' by Miss Isabella Napier, a niece of Robert Napier.

The event was described at length in the *Glasgow Courier* of February 6. The report began: 'We have now to notice an event which will probably turn out a very marked feature in the annals of this country, inasmuch as it is the commencement of a mode of communication between the old and new world, which brings them within one-half of the former passage, and thus strengthens the relation in which they stand to each other, as parent and child. The launch of the *Britannia* steamship which took place yesterday from the building yard of Messrs R. Duncan and Company, Greenock, was an event of general interest, and we, therefore, do not regret having left Glasgow for the purpose of being a spectator, and joining in the warmest expressions of congratulation on the occasion. The launch of a trim-built and seaworthy craft is, at all times, a pleasing and most gratifying spectacle, and never did we witness more intense interest on any similar occasion.

'It ought to be mentioned that the name of the vessel was pronounced by a lady, Miss Isabella Napier, and we cannot doubt that it was, on that account, the more cheerfully received. At the risk of being tedious, we should add a very brief statement of the ship's dimensions, her capabilities, and of the trade for which she is intended.

'The *Britannia* is the first of the North American Royal Mail Steamers. Her length from taffrail to figure head is 230 feet, the breadth of her beam is 34½ feet, and the depth of her hold (*sic*) 22 feet 6 inches. She is to be propelled by two engines, each 220 horsepower, and, when put to sea, will be succeeded by three other ships of the same dimensions and similar construction, all intended, as we have said, to carry the mails, passengers etc., between Liverpool and North America, a scheme, it will be remembered, which was originated by the Hon. S. Cunard, of Halifax, Nova Scotia, who, with a small party of influential gentlemen in Glasgow, is associated in this undertaking. The vessel's hull and machinery are constructed under the direction and superintendence of Mr. Robert Napier,

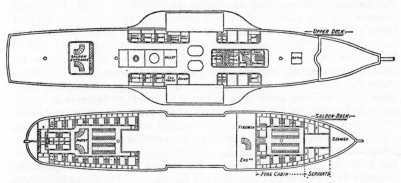

Plan of the saloon and upper decks in RMS *Britannia*, the first of the Royal Mail steamers. The accommodation, although adequate, was by no means luxurious.

of the Vulcan Foundry, Glasgow; and when we mention this gentleman's name as connected with such a work, we give a sufficient guarantee that, when completed, nothing better will be found in the Kingdom.

'The accommodation of the vessel is provided on an improved and magnificent scale, the cabin below deck being fitted up with spacious and well ventilated state rooms. The dining saloon will be unique, and we may safely say that, from the keel to the topmast, everything will be found substantial, and adapted to the course the vessel is to take.'

By June 16 the *Britannia* had been fitted out ready for commissioning. She steamed round from the Clyde to the Mersey and berthed in the Coburg Dock. On Friday July 3, having loaded baggage and mails, she was towed out of dock and anchored in mid-stream, almost opposite Laird's Shipbuilding Yard, Birkenhead. The next day her passengers were taken out to the ship by river steamer. There were 63 all told, 48 bound for Halifax, Nova Scotia, and 15 for Boston, Mass. In addition to Samuel Cunard and his daughter, they included the Bishop of Nova Scotia and family, the Earl of Caledon, Lieut-Col Monius and lady, Colonel Butler and his lady, Major Ruxton, his lady and family, Mr C. M. Rosberry, General Broughton, Mr Featherstonhough, Mr Russell, Capt and Mrs Winter, Capt J. Hunter, F. B. Ogden Esq, American Consul at Liverpool, W. Andrews Esq, American Consul at Malta, Mr and Mrs Noone, Mr John Cunningham, Mr Swaine, Mr S. Henshaw, Mr B. Ross, Mr Thomas Palmer, Mr L. C. Coltenmorley, Mr C. F. Kenworthy, Mr H. T. Jenkins, Mr and Mrs James Clarke, Mr Foord, Miss Haliburton, Miss Stewart, Mr Inglis, Mrs Inglis and family, Mr Colin Russell and Mrs Russell, Mr and Mrs Piquinet and family, Mr Charles Minturn, Mr T. J. Spence, Mr Frankland, Mr A. Mitchell, Mr McQueen, Mr Joseph Lawyer Shean and Mrs Hart.

Commanded by Captain Henry Woodruff RN, the *Britannia* began her maiden voyage at 14.00 hours. It was a wet, miserable day with a strong SSW wind blowing as the ship made her way down the Mersey and out to sea. Meanwhile the passengers were busy settling themselves down, seeking out Mr Taylor the purser, introducing themselves to Doctor Scott, the surgeon, and watching the officer in charge of mails, Lieutenant Roberts RN. At 18.00 hours the *Britannia* was reported off the Great Orme's Head, Llandudno, the North Wales seaside resort, and 'all was well'. According to his sailing schedule, Captain Woodruff was due at Halifax on July 20. In the event he reached the port on July 17, nearly three days ahead of schedule. The Halifax newspaper, the *Haligonian,* stated that 'the success of the *Britannia's* initial voyage, her noble proportions, figurehead and name alike suggested a new era of progress in transit, not only for our city but for the whole of the North American seaboard'.

The *Britannia* herself received the unusual honour of being accorded a gun salute from HM frigate *Winchester* on station at the Canadian port. After a stay of eight hours to discharge mails and disembark passengers, the *Britannia* proceeded to Boston. She arrived there at 22.00 hours on Saturday July 18, having completed the voyage from Liverpool in 14 days eight hours.

The *Britannia's* arrival in Boston was the occasion for another remarkable demonstration of enthusiasm. Despite the lateness of the hour she was escorted to her berth by the Revenue Cutter *Hamilton,* while shore batteries salvoed welcoming salutes. The next day, being a Sunday, a crowded congregation at the Federal Meeting House sat through a lengthy sermon by the presiding minister, the Revd Ezra Stiles Gannet in which he held forth on the benefits which would ensue from the arrival of the *Britannia* and the regular mail and passenger service between America and Britain she had inaugurated.

Cunard himself, the hero of the hour, is said to have received no less than 1,873 invitations to dinner; he was presented with a silver loving cup, 30 inches high, to the cost of which 2.500 Bostonians had contributed. The climax was reached on July 21 with a public procession 'headed by various mayors, consuls and other important people'. This was followed by a civic banquet at Maverick House, attended by 2,000 guests, including ladies—a most unusual precedent. The chairman, Mr Josiah Quincy, after proposing the health, happiness and prosperity of Mr Cunard, went on to refer to the fact that 'the memory of time and space—famous in their day and generation have been annihilated by the steam engine'. Yet another toast ran: 'Cunard's line of steam packets—the pendulum of a large clock which is to tick once a fortnight; the British Government has given £50,000 for one of the weights and may the patronage of the public soon add another'.

Among the guests was one of the outstanding New York personalities of the day—Mr Philip Hone, Mayor of that city in 1824. Philip Hone with his brother John had been included in the small group of businessmen who had been granted the right to auction cargoes imported in ships arriving in the port from all over the world—a system begun in 1815. The Hone business flourished to the extent that Philip was able to retire at a comparatively early age. Thereafter he devoted himself to the political and social life of the city. Between the years 1828 and 1851 Hone kept a diary—still extant—in which he commented on the civic, commercial and social life of the city. Hone numbered among his friends many New England businessmen, including Samuel Cunard. Indeed it is not unlikely that he was present as the personal guest of Cunard at the banquet held in Boston to commemorate the arrival of the *Britannia.* In a reference to the occasion in his diary he was to comment: 'My little friend Cunard made no speech because (as he said) he didn't know how.'

The *Britannia* began her homeward voyage from Boston on August 1, reaching Liverpool in little over ten days—her best steaming was 280 miles in one day. What made the homeward voyage more historic was the fact that although they did not sight each other, at some stage in the crossing she must have passed the *Acadia* which, under the command of Captain E. C. Miller, had left Liverpool for Halifax on her maiden voyage on August 4.

So, the first regular transatlantic mail service by steamship was in operation; but what was more important, it continued to be so. The *Acadia* was followed on September 9 by the *Caledonia* (Captain Richard Cleland), but the fourth ship, the *Columbia* (Captain E. Ewing), was not commissioned until 1841, making her maiden voyage from Liverpool on January 5 of that year.

Of the first four ships, the *Britannia* and *Acadia* proved the fastest and

31

shared honours in respect of speed, as the following records of voyages between Liverpool and Halifax shows:

Year	Month	Ship	Voyage	Distance (miles)	Passage (d h m)	Av speed (knots)
1840	July	Britannia	Liverpool to Halifax	2,534	12 10 0	8.50
1840	August	Acadia	,,	,,	11 4 0	9.45
1841	July	Acadia	,,	,,	10 22 0	9.67
1840	August	Britannia	Halifax to Liverpool	,,	10 0 0	10.56
1842	Sept	Acadia	,,	,,	9 15 0	10.97

The *Britannia* and her sister ships carried sail of which they made considerable use whenever the wind was in the right direction. The masters were in fact given strict instructions to conserve coal supplies of which it was estimated they burned 6,960 tons a year. At eight shillings a ton, coal was cheap in Liverpool—in Boston it cost 20 shillings a ton!

The extent to which sail was used is indicated in a log of a voyage made by the *Britannia* in 1848 kept by John McFall, a member of the crew. In this he stated:

'*Sat. August 12:* At 4.30 p.m. the mail came on board bound from Liverpool to Halifax and Boston. Proceeded to sea, moderate northerly breeze and fine. At 6.p.m. sent down the foreyard and struck the main and top mizzen masts.

Sun. August 13: Light breeze, fine. At 6.a.m. passed the Isle of Man. At 10.30 a.m. went to prayers, the service being read by the Rev. Dr. Neville, a passenger. Bore away to N.W, the wind hauling to the eastward. Sent up the foreyard, fore top gallant and the main top gallant studding sails.

Mon. August 14: *Britannia* making 9.50 knots.

Tues. August 15: Wind changed to dead ahead, so furled everything, sent down the fore and top gallant yards and housed the foregallant mast.

Wed. August 16: Strong westerly wind, rain, ship taking a deal of water over forecastle, had stunsails out.

Thurs. August 17: Strong winds continued. 11 p.m. made Sambro Light. 12 p.m. Moored alongside wharf Halifax.

Friday August 18: Left Halifax for Boston. Passed Acadia.'

The four ships maintained the service with great regularity and it was not until 1843 that any mishap occurred. On July 2 of that year the *Columbia*, on passage from Halifax to Boston with 85 passengers, ran aground in dense fog off Rock Lodge, New Cape Sable. The ship became a total loss but all passengers and crew were saved and mails and cargo salvaged. Fortunately the company had commissioned a fifth ship, the *Hibernia* of 1,422 tons, in April of that year and after the loss of the *Columbia* placed an order for another ship, the *Cambria*. The latter made her first voyage on January 4 1845, maintaining her schedule with such clockwork precision that she became popularly known as the 'Flying Cambria'.

With a designed speed of over 10 knots and more luxurious accommodation, both ships were faster and became more popular than the *Britannia* and her remaining two sisterships. Yet it was the *Britannia* which was to make world news. Frozen up in Boston harbour in February 1844, she was freed by the citizens who, at their own expense and aided by thousands of volunteers, cut a channel seven miles long and 100 feet wide through the ice (seven feet deep in places) to the open sea so that the ship would not be unduly delayed. As a result the *Britannia* was only held up for two days, finally sailing on February 3. When a grateful British Post Office offered to meet the cost of cutting the ice channel, the citizens of Boston declined to be reimbursed.

For seven years Cunard ships virtually held a monopoly of regular transatlantic steamship services. Despite the success of the ships it was widely known that they made little or no profit, and that the Cunard partners were constantly asking for increased mail contract subsidies. Figures sent to the Treasury for 1840-1842 had revealed a deficit of £63,954, and when in 1846 the Great Western Steamship Company of Bristol, whose appeals for a share in the mail contract had been rejected, withdrew from North Atlantic service, Cunard had no British competition to fear.

The first serious challenge to Cunard supremacy came from the United States, with the commissioning in 1847 of the paddle steamer *Washington*. Her building was the direct outcome of an Act passed by Congress without debate on March 3 1845 under which the United States Postmaster General was authorised to contract for mails to foreign countries 'wherever he thinks it is necessary for the public interest'. Contracts were to be made with railroads or with the American-owned shipping companies, preferably those using steamships. An important proviso was that 'upon demand and payment of their full value these ships must be handed over to the government to be converted into warships'.

On October 4 1845 the US Postmaster General, Cave Johnson, advertised for the carriage of ocean mails as authorised by the Bill. Tenders were invited for routes from New York to Liverpool, Bristol or Southampton, to the Continental ports of Antwerp, Bremen or Hamburg with a stop at Cowes, and to the Continental ports of Havre, Brest or Lisbon direct.

There were four bids for the European mails and eventually that of Mr Edward Mills, who put forward a tender of 300,000 dollars a year, was preferred. After considerable delay the contract was finally agreed under which Mills was to receive five annual payments of 400,000 dollars; for twice-monthly sailings to Bremerhaven and Havre alternately the payment was to be 350,000 dollars.

Mills himself was not a shipowner—a fact which had provoked a considerable amount of criticism—but once having secured his contract, he assigned it to the Ocean Steam Navigation Company, which was incorporated in May 1846 and of which Mills became the general agent. The first ship of the company was the *Washington*, a wooden paddle steamer of 1,750 tons, built by Westervelt and Mackay, New York, and engined by the Novelty Ironworks of Stillman and Allen. When she was commissioned, she was the largest ship afloat and was claimed to be the most complete and beautiful ever constructed—an opinion not universally held. In fact, on her arrival at Southampton, one British newspaper correspondent described her as 'about as ugly a specimen of steamship building as ever went through this anchorage and one which seemed rather to roll along than steam through the water'.

Nor was this correspondent writing with the jaundiced eye of a Britisher who had just seen Britain's long monopoly of the North Atlantic steamship trade wrested from her. Because, although it had been prophesied of the *Washington* that she would prove herself an excellent sea boat in all respects, with a speed surpassing that of any sea steamer yet put afloat, the event confounded the optimists. She had sailed from New York for Southampton and Bremen with 120 first- and second-class passengers on June 1 1847. On the same day the Cunarder *Britannia* left Boston for Liverpool. In a sense, this was the first ocean 'race' between American and British steamers. The *Washington,* on paper, was incomparably the better ship, bigger, newer and with twice the *Britannia's* power. The *Britannia* had been in service for seven years, yet she made the crossing two full days ahead of her rival. In July 1848 the *Hermann,* second ship of the Ocean Steam Navigation Company, crossed from New York to Cowes in 11 days, 21 hours and in so doing claimed to have gained the record for the fastest crossing on this route.

The inception of the Ocean Steam Navigation Company focused attention on the growing importance of New York as an alternative to Boston as a mail and passenger terminal. In consequence Cunard approached the British Government and was successful in obtaining a new mail contract under which the Company was to operate a service from Liverpool to New York one week, and to Halifax and Boston the next.

It was agreed that there should be eight ships in service by January 1 1848, and a ninth a year later. The new contract contained the usual provisions respecting the rates for transporting soldiers and military supplies, as well as the requirement that the vessels should be capable of carrying the largest calibre guns. The total annual payment for the services to Boston and to New York was now £145,000. It was agreed also that the vessels should leave Liverpool every Saturday (calling at Holyhead if required) for New York and Boston alternately, the Boston steamer sailing at Halifax and the New York one to do so if required by the Lords Commissioners of the Admiralty; and in respect of these augmented sailings the subsidy was raised to £173,340 per annum, at which figure it remained until the end of 1867.

For the adequate accomplishment of this agreement four new ships were to be built: *America* (1,826 tons), *Niagara* (1,824 tons), *Europa* (1,834 tons) and *Canada* (1,831 tons). In design they were an adaptation of their predecessors with a gross tonnage of 1,825 and engines of 2,000 hp, giving them a speed of $10\frac{1}{2}$ knots, but many improvements in accommodation were carried out; they carried 140 passengers. Construction cost for each ship was £80,000 plus. The two most popular were the *Canada* and *Europa,* both of which held the Atlantic record.

The first Cunard sailing from Liverpool to New York was made by the *Cambria* on January 1 1848; on the same day the *Hibernia* left New York for Liverpool. From the outset the new service proved a success. At the end of 1848, duties collected on Cunard cargoes handled at New York totalled 40,501 dollars, the figure for Boston being 29,508 dollars. At the end of 1850, duties collected at New York had reached 118,055 dollars, as against 62,970 dollars at Boston.

According to a tabular statement of the Customs duties paid by the Cunard Company from its inception in July 1840 to 1851 inclusive, published in the *Boston Evening Traveller,* in the seven months to 1840 the first three Cunard ships commissioned, *Britannia, Acadia* and *Caledonia,* made eight voyages, duties on cargoes totalling 2,940 dollars. In 1851, with the *Asia, America, Cambria, Canada, Europa* and *Niagara* making 23 voyages in all, the duties paid totalled 1,805,059.30 dollars. In the 11 years the Cunard ships made 235 voyages paying nearly 10 million dollars in duties.

It was small wonder that by now the port of Liverpool should have recognised the importance of the Cunard Company and the ships, described in the *Liverpool Albion* of February 18 1850 as a 'magnificent fleet which stands pre-eminent among ocean steamers'. Statistics published in the same issue showed that in 1849 the fleet had made 44 voyages from Liverpool—23 to Halifax and New York, 21 to Halifax and Boston. The average passages to New York took 13 days 16 hours (including detention at Halifax); the average passages to Boston (including calls at Halifax) took 12 days 22 hours. The *Canada* held the record for the fastest voyages, having crossed from Liverpool in July in nine days 22 hours followed closely by the *America* and *Europa.*

At the end of the company's first decade its supremacy was universally acknowledged. There was indeed no other service to be compared with it in the North Atlantic. It might well have continued so, but for the determination of an American shipowner to sweep the Cunard Company from the Western Ocean. His name was E. K. Collins.

Three
1851—1862
America throws down the gauntlet

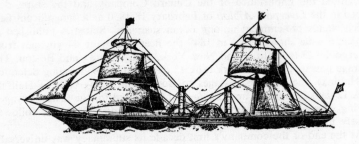

IN THE CHEQUERED HISTORY of the United States mercantile marine with all its peaks and depressions, no year was to prove more historic and memorable than 1850. This was the year when not only were the fast fleets of American-built and American-owned clipper and packet ships carrying all before them on the major trade routes of the world, but when at long last it looked as if American steamships would sweep the Cunard Line off the North Atlantic—and no patriotic American could think of anything better than that.

The failure of the paddle steamers *Washington* and *Hermann* of the Ocean Steam Navigation Company, operating subsidised US mail and passenger services between New York, Southampton and Bremen, to bring to an end Cunard supremacy had been a bitter disappointment to the American Government and people. However, in February 1847, Senator T. Butler King, an enthusiastic champion of steamship services, succeeded in getting Congress to approve a Naval Construction Bill which included an amendment authorising the Secretary of the Navy to contract with Mr E. K. Collins of New York for a projected mail steamship service from New York to Liverpool. Under the terms of this contract Collins was to build five large and fast mail steamers for which he would receive payments amounting to 385,000 dollars for ten years.

All America rejoiced at the news. Public reaction was well summed up by Senator Bayard when he declared in Congress: 'To enter the contest with England for the supremacy of ocean steam navigation required talent, energy and faith of the highest order known to our countrymen, for to fail would involve a loss not only of vast sums necessary to make the effort, but what is of far more value to every lover of his country's

36

The *Vanderbilt* created a sensation in 1857 when she steamed from New York to the Isle of Wight in nine days eight hours at a speed of 13.87 knots, easily a record for the Southampton route. (*National Maritime Museum. London*)

Scotia was the last paddle steamer to be built for Cunard. She was an elegant and luxurious ship and was universally acknowledged to be the finest specimen of a mercantile vessel then afloat; she was also a record-breaker in that she reduced the New York-Liverpool passage record to eight days 22 hours. (*National Maritime Museum, London*)

The first screw-propelled Atlantic liner to make a record crossing, the liner *Russia* was also the last of the Cunard ships to be graced with a clipper bow and figure head.

The *City of Paris* (I) in her dock berth at Liverpool. Built on the Clyde, she was the first Inman liner to secure the Blue Riband for her owners. Her closest rival was the Cunard liner *Russia*.

City of Brussels 1869

On only her second homeward voyage from New York to Queenstown, the *City of Brussels*, one of the famous Inman fliers, brought fame to her owners by attaining a record average speed of 14.66 knots. (*National Maritime Museum, London*)

reputation, it would ensure national disappointment more deeply felt from the fact that England had already been vanquished by our sailing ships and gracefully yielded to us the palm of victory since more brilliantly illustrated by the yacht *America* and the clipper ship *Witch of the Waves.*'

In Edward Knight Collins the United States had found the right man. Born in 1802 in Truro, Mass, he had begun his business career, which closely paralleled that of Cunard, in New York at the age of 15. When he was 20, he joined his father in the general shipping and commission business. On becoming head of the company, this enterprising young man expanded the firm's interests. In 1830 he established a service of full-rigged sailing ships to Vera Cruz and Tampico. Two years later he inaugurated the first regular New York-New Orleans packet line, and in 1835 entered the booming transatlantic packet ship trade from Liverpool with the establishment of the Dramatic Line whose ships included the *Shakespeare, Garrick, Sheridan, Siddons* and *Roscius,* all outstanding for their fast passages and the luxury of their saloon accommodation.

But Collins, even while highly successful with his sailing packets, had realised that with the coming of steam their future was uncertain. His determination to build ships to 'out-steam' the Cunard ships off the Atlantic was illustrated by his remark to a friend—'I will build steamers that shall make the passage from New York to Europe in ten days or less'.

With the American mail contract in his pocket, Collins immediately contacted business friends and associates, including two bankers, James and Stewart Brown, who looked after the New York branch of the international banking family, and established the United States Mail Steamship Company—always to be popularly known as the Collins Line.

Under the agreement Collins undertook to maintain a weekly mail service with five vessels between New York and Liverpool, each vessel to make 20 voyages a year, for which service the Company would be paid 19,250 dollars a voyage. At the current sterling rate of exchange this worked out at £4,010 8s 4d a voyage.

For the hull design and machinery installation of the ships Collins sought the advice and assistance of the leading American shipbuilders and marine engineers. For the hull design he went to George Steers who had won a world-wide reputation as the builder of the yacht *America*—her name was to be perpetuated in the America's Cup; the engines were designed and their installation supervised by two engineers, Messrs Faron and Sewell, seconded from the US Navy for this specific purpose.

No expense was spared in the building and the fitting out of the ships. The cost of each vessel (675,000 dollars) was so high that Collins was forced to approach the Government, who not only agreed to reduce the stipulated number of ships from five to four, but also increased the proposed mail payments per voyage from 19,250 dollars to 33,000 dollars. In return, the importance of speed was emphasised. When the matter of increased mail payments was being discussed in Congress, Senator Bayard declared, 'We must have speed, extraordinary speed with which they (the Collins ships) can overtake any vessel which they pursue and escape from any vessel which they wish to avoid; they must be fit for a cruiser with armaments to attack your enemy (if that enemy were Great Britain) in her most vital part, her commerce.'

Named *Atlantic, Pacific, Arctic* and *Baltic,* the four ships were all built and engined in New York—the *Atlantic* and *Arctic* by William H. Brown, and the *Pacific* and *Baltic* by Brown and Bell. The engines for the *Atlantic* and *Arctic* were built by the Novelty Ironworks of Stillman and Brown on the East River, those for the *Pacific* and *Baltic* at the Allaire Works.

The four ships were almost identical in appearance, their principal dimensions being: length overall 300 ft; length between perps 282 ft; length of keel 270 ft; breadth of hull 45 ft; breadth over paddle boxes 73 ft; depth of hold 31 × 4 ft; mean draught 19.8 ft; gross register 2,860 tons, net 1,559 tons; displacement 5,200 tons.

Their hulls were flat-bottomed, built of live oaks, planked with pitch pine, traced with lattice work of iron bars, and fastened with iron bolts. There were three decks (lower, main and spar with only decks fore and aft). The ships were built with rounded sterns and made history as being the first North Atlantic steamers to be given straight stems. Each carried three masts and a single black funnel with a red top (the reverse of the Cunard funnel colours). The black hulls were relieved by the red band.

Machinery installation comprised side-lever engines of 800 nominal horsepower. These had two cylinders of 95 inches diameter by 108 inches stroke developing an indicated horsepower of 2,000. The condenser air pump was 58 inches in diameter by 54 inches stroke. Steam at a pressure of 17 lbs per square inch was supplied by four rectangular flue boilers. These contained 32 furnaces in pairs, one above the other with a total grate area of about 495 square feet. Each pair of furnaces led into a common rectangular flue fitted with vertical water-tubes two inches in diameter. The total heating surface was about 16,500 square feet. Coal was delivered from the bunkers to the stokeholds by mechanically driven buckets. Daily coal consumption was 87 tons.

Larger, more luxurious and more powerful than their Cunard rivals, the four ships were acclaimed with delight by the rapidly growing professions of naval architects and marine engineers but, while the general public were willing to be suitably impressed by such technical 'mysteries', it was the striking innovations in the passenger accommodation which fired their imagination.

The years when an Atlantic voyage by steamship was considered a daring adventure had long since passed, largely as a result of the regular accident-free passages of the Cunard fleet. By 1850 such voyages were recognised as quite normal occasions and passengers were beginning to look for more luxury and more facilities, as in fact were provided in the packet ships and were notably absent in the Cunard steamers.

Collins, with long experience of packet ships and well acquainted with North Atlantic voyaging, quickly realised that in providing more luxurious accommodation he would score over the Cunard vessels. He realised it was no longer a novelty for male passengers to go out on deck if they wanted to smoke—as was the rule in the Cunarders, so in his ships he introduced a smoking room 'complete with spittoons'. He knew how uncomfortable it could prove to shave and wash in the narrow confines of a small stateroom and so he installed a barber's shop and bathrooms. From personal experience of miserable mid-winter Atlantic crossings with temperatures below freezing point, he installed a system of steam heating for the public rooms. He had every sympathy for harassed passengers who, when they wanted attention had to 'shout' for a steward, so he introduced a system of electric bells which enabled passengers without loss of dignity to ring for their stewards.

The *Atlantic* was the first of the Collins' fleet to be completed. Commanded by Captain West and carrying nearly 100 passengers (by no means a full complement) and 2,000 tons of cargo, she began her maiden voyage from New York to Liverpool at noon on Saturday April 27 1850. Thousands of New Yorkers gathered along the waterfront to cheer the liner on her way, confident that she would make a record passage.

The international battle for the Blue Riband of the Atlantic had begun.

Sadly enough for the jubilant Americans their hopes were not to be realised. Shortly after clearing Sandy Hook, at the entrance to New York harbour, the *Atlantic* steamed into drift ice which played havoc with her paddle wheel floats. Worse still, weather conditions prevented any attempts being made to repair the damage and Captain West had to reduce speed to prevent the floats being torn away from the paddles.

Then, on May 3, one of the ship's condensers broke down. Captain West was now in real trouble. He hove to for 40 hours while the engineers worked all-out to effect repairs. Their efforts proved unavailing and the ship finally proceeded at a much reduced steam and did not reach Liverpool until May 10, where, because of her great beam, special arrangements had been made by the port officials to provide dock facilities.

Interest and excitement over the arrival of the *Atlantic* in the Mersey was heightened by the fact that Cunard's newest liner the *Asia* of 2,226 gross tons had recently arrived from Robert Steele's shipyard on the Clyde and was even then in dock preparing for her maiden voyage to Halifax and New York scheduled to begin on May 18.

Although no eulogies were written about the exterior appearance of the *Atlantic*—a Scottish newspaper correspondent, perhaps with one eye on the reputation of the Clyde shipbuilders, described her as being 'undoubtedly clumsy'—there was unanimous praise for the luxury of her passenger accommodation. This praise was perhaps summed up in a descriptive article published in *The Illustrated London News* of May 18 1850 which stated:

'Her saloon is 67 feet long by 20 feet wide. Her interior fittings are truly elegant, the woodwork being of white holly, satinwood and rosewood etc., so combined and diversified as to present an exceedingly rich and costly appearance. In the drawing room the ornaments consist of costly mirrors, bronze work, stained glass, paintings etc. Between the panels connecting the staterooms are the arms of the different States of the Confederacy painted in the highest style of art and framed with bronzework. The pillars between are inlaid with mirrors, framed with rosewood and at the top and bottom are bronzed seashells of costly workmanship. In the centre of each are allegorical figures representing the ocean mythology of the ancients, in bronze and burnished gold. The ceiling is elaborately wrought, carved and gilded.

'The cabin windows in the stern are of painted glass, having representations of New York, Boston and Philadelphia painted on each. There is, in addition, another apartment equally beautifully arranged and ornamented for the exclusive use of ladies. Both apartments are heated by steam, an improvement now for the first time introduced in steamships. The dining room (60 feet long) is furnished in an equally elegant style with the drawing room. The staterooms which are light and airy are beautifully furnished and ornamented and combine every convenience that practical science and experience could suggest.

'It would occupy more space than can be spared to detail the magnificence of the furniture on the *Atlantic,*' the article concluded, 'the carpets are of the richest description; the table slabs are of Brocatelli marble. Each stateroom has an elegant sofa; the berths are of satinwood and the curtains of rich damask . . . '

The *Atlantic* was quickly followed by her sister ships. The *Pacific* began her maiden voyage to Liverpool on May 25, the *Arctic* on October 27 and the *Baltic* on November 16. Within a short time they had all established themselves and were beginning to show what they could do in terms of speed. The *Atlantic,* after her disastrous maiden eastward passage from New York which kept her in dock at Liverpool for 19 days while repairs were effected, redeemed herself by completing the maiden westbound run in ten days 16 hours, beating by 12 hours the record previously held by the Cunarder *Canada*—and all America rejoiced.

Then followed exciting years on the North Atlantic run which became the setting, above all other sea routes, for intense competition in which all the resources of, and new developments in marine engineering, shipbuilding and interior decoration were to play their part. Public interest in this competition was not entirely new. For many years Liverpool and New York had been involved in the tremendous rivalry between the shipowners operating the western ocean packet ships. The 'races' between these great sailing ships were a never failing source of excitement. Heavy betting on the outcome of their voyages was common and although there is no record of the expression having been used, it is not unlikely that it was from these 'races' that the idea of the 'Blue Riband of the Atlantic' germinated.

The entry of the steamship on the Atlantic scene brought one great difference which added to the excitement. With the designed speed of a steamer known, it was now possible for the public to estimate with a certain degree of accuracy just how long it would take to make the 3,000 miles voyage. No longer was the master of a ship dependent on favourable winds and his own skill in navigation to make a fast passage. Below decks he had machinery and engineers and firemen to help him. The time of his arrival had already been worked out for him on paper in the owner's office and, consistent with the safety of his passengers and his ship, he was expected to keep to that voyage schedule.

At the outset the Collins' ships did not have it all their own way. The Cunarders put up a fight for the Blue Riband honours. Thus, on June 16 1850, the *Europa* arrived in Liverpool from New York after a passage of ten days 12 hours 26 minutes—the fastest passage ever made from New York; but her triumph was shortlived. On June 26 the *Atlantic* docked at Liverpool after a voyage of ten days 12 hours—her best day's run being 319 nautical miles. In October 1850, the *Asia* sailing direct from New York to Liverpool (the first Cunard voyage in which Halifax had been omitted) made the passage in ten days seven hours. In December she achieved an even better passage as recorded in the log:

'This trip left New York December 18 mid-day; lost 55 minutes repairing wheel, arrived Liverpool December 28, 9.30 p.m. Best days steaming 328 knots, time 10 days 4 hours 5 minutes—2 hours 55 minutes less than fastest summer passage; 4 hours 5 minutes less than the U.S.A. ships' best eastward run and about 5 hours 20 minutes less than the remarkable summer run of the *Pacific* to New York.'

On December 28, the day the *Asia* arrived in the Mersey, the *Atlantic* sailed for New York with 28 passengers—the low complement was not unusual for a mid-winter voyage. Normally she would have reached New York in about ten days, that is January 6, but days passed without news of the ship. New York became a city of gloom which was only relieved when the Cunarder *Africa*, sister ship to the *Asia*, arrived in the port on February 15 with the good news that the *Atlantic* was safe. When about 1,800 miles west of Ireland she had broken her main paddle shaft. Her master, with only limited sail power at his disposal and facing strong westerly winds, had had no alternative but to put his ship about and return to Queenstown which he had reached on January 22. According to the *New York Herald* of February 16, when the news was announced crowds stopped in the streets and cheered, theatre performances were held up, church bells rang out and 'every New Yorker went to bed with a "thank God" on his lips'.

With a designed speed of 11.5 knots, the *Asia* and *Africa* were no match for the four Collins' ships with their designed speed of 11.75 knots. In the May of 1851, the *Pacific* crossed from New York to Liverpool in nine days 20 hours ten minutes at an average speed of 13 knots to gain the Blue Riband; in August, the *Baltic* voyaged from Liverpool to New York in nine days 18 hours at an average speed of 13.17 knots, and in 1852, the *Arctic* clinched the issue by crossing from New York to Liverpool in nine days 17 hours 12 minutes at an average speed of 13.25 knots—a record which was to stand for four years. In 26 round voyages between New York and Liverpool in 1852 the time taken by the Collins' ships was 19 hours 47 minutes less than the Cunarders.

It says much for Cunard and his partners that they refused to 'push' the *Asia* and *Africa* beyond their designed speed limits, despite criticism from the public and the Press epitomised in a doggerel verse published in *Punch*:

> 'A steamer of the Collins Line
> A Yankee doodle notion
> Has also quickest cut the brine
> Across the Atlantic ocean.
> And British agents no way slow
> Her merits to discover
> Have been and bought her—just to tow
> The Cunard Packets over.'

Financially the Cunard Line suffered a serious set-back. American patronage of Cunard ships had fallen by 50 per cent. Returns published

by the *New York Herald* in January 1853 gave the passenger carryings
by the two companies for the 11 months, January to November 1852, as:

	New York to Liverpool
Collins Line	2,420
Cunard Line	1,783

	Liverpool to New York
Collins Line	1,886
Cunard Line	1,186

One reason for the unusual fact that passenger traffic from New York
was greater than that from Liverpool was that this was the time of the
great rush to the Australian goldfields when packet ships from Liverpool
to Melbourne were sailing with anything up to 600 passengers—many of
them Americans.

In addition to the loss in passenger traffic the Cunard revenue from
cargo carryings fell heavily. As was to be expected, American shippers
supported the American ships and continued to do so despite the fact that
Cunard cut freight rates from £7 10s to £4 a ton. It was only in the carriage
of mails that Cunard scored over their rivals. In 1851 the Cunard ships
carried 2,613,000 letters compared with the meagre Collins total of
843,000.

It was, however, revenue from passengers and cargo which counted
and, although Charles MacIver, who in 1845 had succeeded his brother
David as a Cunard partner, was reported as having commented that:
'The Collins people are pretty much in the situation of finding that breaking our windows with sovereigns, though very fine fun, is too costly to
keep on', there must have been times during that first vicious Collins
onslaught when he wondered whether Cunard could hold on long enough
to weather the storm.

In fact, MacIver's caustic comment was nearer the truth than he
probably realised. Collins was finding the task of satisfying the American
public by keeping ahead of the Cunard Company a costly business. Heavy
fuel consumption, running repairs between voyages, were swallowing
up any profits made in passenger and cargo traffic. His ships were being
operated at a loss of 16,928.74 dollars (£4,232) per voyage. If the line was
to continue he would need more financial support from Congress. His
request for an increase in the mail subsidy was accompanied by a detailed
statement giving the financial position of the Company.

This read:

'New York and Liverpool U.S.M.S.S. Co.
No. 56 Wall Street,
New York,
December 15 1851.

Statement showing the actual expenses and receipts of the first 28 voyages
of the New York and Liverpool United States Mail steamships, *Atlantic,
Pacific, Arctic* and *Baltic.*

	Average each way Dollars	Sterling equivalent @ 4 dollars £
Expenses, wages of crew and provisions for same	8,845.04	2,214
Fuel	8,612.28	2,154
Repairs to machinery	4,571.90	1,143
Repairs to machinery (extras)	4,643.00	1,161
Ordinary expenses including carpenters and joiners, port charges, sailmakers, light and dock dues, passengers' provisions and waiters and other necessities	12,762.73	3,190.7
Insurance average on above voyages	8,904.64	2,226
Interest average on above voyages	8,438.00	2,109.5
Depreciation at 7 per cent per annum on do	8,438.00	2,109.5
	65,215.59	16,304.7

Receipts		
Passage money average as above	21,292.65	5,323.16
Freight	7,744.20	1,946.05
Mail money from Government	19,250.00	4,812.5
	48,286.85	12,081.71

Average deficiency per voyage 16,928 dollars (£4,232.18).'

The subsequent debate in the Senate was marked by considerable opposition, particularly from members representing the Southern States who deplored the Government's proposed extravagance to keep the Collins Line afloat. In the end a proposal that the mail subsidy should be increased from 385,000 dollars (£96,500) to 858,000 dollars (£214,500) a year was approved; the voting in the Senate was 27 to 19, and in the House 84 to 79. It was a close run thing. Commenting on the result, the *New York Daily Times* trumpeted 'Right and National pride have over-ruled a false and narrow economy. The supremacy of our steam marine has not been sacrificed to local and personal jealousies or to the insidious influence of a Foreign rival.'

Meanwhile the Cunard partners had been tackling the problem of recovering their lost traffic. The first results were seen when the Cunard partners commissioned the first two-funnelled Cunarder and their last wooden paddle steamer, the *Arabia*, built by Robert Steele of Greenock and engined by Robert Napier. The *Arabia* of 2,402 tons was a lovely ship and way ahead of her contemporaries; the luxury of her passenger accommodation was all that Atlantic passengers could desire. A feature of her main saloon was a cupola with stained glass panels giving extra headroom. Two small libraries and a children's nursery were facilities which were not to be found in the Collins ships. With a designed speed of 13 knots the stage seemed set for the long awaited British revival and triumph on the North Atlantic, especially when it was learned that on trials she had achieved a speed of 15 knots.

Unfortunately, when put into service, the *Arabia*, beautiful as she was, failed to come up to expectations. Her engines, so large that they had been installed in two sections, proved too powerful for her wooden hull. The result was that, not only with the safety of the ship and comfort of the passengers in mind, but also the cost likely to be involved in constant repairs—a lesson learned from Collins' experience—it was considered unwise and uneconomic to run her full out, and on her Atlantic voyages she seldom reached her contract speed.

The Collins Line continued on its all-conquering way. The prospects for the Company had never been so good, despite an increase of 10,984 dollars per voyage as a result of higher costs in the price of coal, voyage repairs and a recent increase in crew wages. Then in 1854 there came an unexpected 'bonus'. The outbreak of war between Britain and Russia led to the British Admiralty exercising their right under the mail subsidy contract to requisition Cunard ships for transport and other services to the Crimea. As a result, within days, 14 Cunard ships found themselves on war duties. The company's North Atlantic service was completely disorganised. Collins found himself, for the first time, with the virtual monopoly of Western Ocean passenger and cargo traffic to the extent that the British Government was forced to turn to Collins' ships for the carriage of mails.

But just when good fortune was attending the company and all seemed 'set fair', there came the first disaster which, in the event, was to mark the beginning of the end for Collins. On September 21 1854 the record-holder *Arctic*, commanded by Captain James Luce, left Liverpool for New York. On board were 233 passengers, including Mrs Collins and their two children. Six days later, on September 27, when about 60 miles south of Cape Race, she ran into dense fog and collided with the small French steamer *Vesta* of 200 tons. At first it looked as if the *Vesta* was doomed but her collision bulkhead held and, lost in the fog, she limped away finally to make port safely at St John's, Newfoundland. The *Arctic*, which had stood by to render assistance, was left alone and only then was it realised that she had sustained extensive damage and, in fact, was sinking fast. Every effort was made to keep the ship afloat. Captain Luce ordered the engines full ahead in the hope of making Cape Race and beaching his ship, but it was too late. When still 20 miles from land it became clear that the ship was on the point of foundering. Orders were given to launch the five lifeboats she carried—pitifully few for the 391 passengers and crew. Four boats were successfully got away but only two reached shore. There were only 45 survivors—Mrs Collins and her two children were not amongst them. Captain Luce went down with his ship, but managed to get clear and swim to wreckage to which he clung for two days before being picked up by the Cunarder *Cambria*.

The loss of the *Arctic* adversely affected the prestige of the Collins Line, particularly amongst the Americans who, conveniently forgetting their past pride in the record-breaking passages of the ships, now condemned the 'reckless speed' which, without full knowledge of the facts, they declared had been a contributory factor to the disaster. Atlantic travellers who had once poured scorn on the slower Cunard ships were now quick to point to the tribute paid to the Company during a current legal case in which the Cunard Line was cited as possessing the proud record of having made 7,000 transatlantic passages between 1840 and 1854 and having carried 100,000 passengers during which 'not a single passenger had been lost nor a pound of baggage damaged'.

It was a little unfortunate that the Company, most of whose ships were still requisitioned, could do little to capitalise on this return to popular favour. It was not until October 1 1856 that the Cunard partners were able to announce to the press: 'The Public are respectfully informed that it is intended to resume in January 1856, the weekly sailings of the steamships of this Company from Liverpool to the United States. The British Mail steamships will thereafter be dispatched from Liverpool every Saturday as formerly, alternately to Boston (calling at Halifax) and to New York direct.'

Curiously enough, in making this announcement, the Company apparently did not think it worth while to mention the fact that the outstanding feature of their post-war service would be the commissioning of a new mail steamer, the 3,600 ton paddle steamer, *Persia*, which was not only the largest and most powerful ship of her day but also the first iron-built mail paddle steamer to appear in the Atlantic.

Despite appeals by the Cunard partners the Admiralty had previously vetoed the building of iron steamers for the mail service on the grounds that such ships would be of little use if requisitioned for war service. However, due in part to the success of the French iron-clad naval ships in the Crimean campaign and in part to the success of the Cunard subsidiary iron steamers which, during the war, had perforce carried the Atlantic mails, the Admiralty had waived their veto with the result that Cunard and his partners had been able to go ahead with their schemes to counter the Collins competition.

The company had apparently anticipated that this restriction would be withdrawn, for plans for building the *Persia* had been under discussion for several years. In August 1853, Robert Napier, who had been entrusted with preparing specifications and who, as always, was anxious that any contract into which he might enter should be as perfect as possible, wrote to Charles MacIver:

'I am convinced, unless the greatest care, attention and judgment are exercised in the getting up of this large vessel with a limited power that there is a very great risk of failure in one thing or another. On the other hand if care is taken and we are not untrammelled as to dimensions etc., I have no fears but that a good result will be obtained, and I think from past experience had of my character in such matters you may have every confidence that I shall not propose or recommend anything to you that is at all likely not fully to answer its purpose.'

Napier, however, need have had no fears about the ultimate success of the *Persia*, for when she was commissioned in 1856 she was all that her owners and builders could desire. 'Stupendous!' *The Illustrated London News* called her, a sentiment echoed by the company of shippers and merchants and distinguished citizens, headed by the Mayor of Liverpool, who inspected the ship as she lay to anchor in the Mersey before starting on her maiden voyage in January 1856, and who listened with bewildered wonderment to technical descriptions of such features as the 'double bottom' and watertight compartments, while revelling about the sumptuous public rooms and staterooms, and marvelling at the vast kitchens and pantries 'exceeding most and equalling any of the culinary establishments of the most extensive and noted hotels in the Kingdom'.

Built and engined at Robert Napier's shipyard in Glasgow, the *Persia* was a two-masted vessel with two funnels. Her principal dimensions were: length overall 398 ft; length between perps 376 ft; length of keel 350 ft; breadth of hull 45.3 ft; breadth over paddle boxes 71 ft; depth of hold 29.8 ft; mean draught 20 ft; gross tonnage 3,300 tons, net 2,079 tons; displacement about 5,850 tons.

The iron hull was subdivided into seven watertight compartments. The cargo holds were fitted down the centre of the ship with coal bunkers on either side and a double bottom below. The hold spaces for 1,100 tons of cargo were made watertight, and in the event of an accident to the hull would, it was stated, keep the ship afloat.

There was luxurious accommodation for 250 passengers and the ship carried eight lifeboats. Side-lever engines of 950 nominal horsepower were installed to give a designed speed of 13 knots. Coal consumption worked out at 143 tons a day.

Commanded by Captain Charles Judkins, the *Persia* began her maiden voyage from Liverpool to New York on January 26 1856. Three days earlier, on January 23, the Collins liner *Pacific* had sailed for New York with 45 passengers, and the public, recalling that during her trials on the Clyde the *Persia* had achieved a speed of 16 knots, immediately fastened on to the idea of a race between the two ships. Fourteen days later, with her bows stove in, the *Persia* arrived at New York. The *Pacific* had not arrived and, when it was learned that the reason for the *Persia's* crumpled bows was that in the course of a stormy passage she had collided with an iceberg, fears for the safety of the overdue *Pacific* increased. Days and weeks passed with no news of the ship. Finally, that brief and poignant epitaph of lost ships, 'Never heard of', was posted against her name.

This second disaster shook public faith in the Collins Line to a disastrous extent and when, later that year, opposing interests united to attack Congress on the question of the Collins Line subsidy and won to the extent that the subsidy was reduced from 858,000 dollars per annum to 385,000 dollars, the company received a financial blow from which it was never to recover.

In direct contrast, the accident to the *Persia* which had caused no casualties was hailed as providing proof of the safety of iron ships linked with the splendid craftsmanship of her Scottish builders. When, in July 1856, she gained the Atlantic record by crossing from New York to Liverpool in nine days one hour 45 minutes at a speed of 13.8 knots, the public delight knew no bounds. The Blue Riband was back in Britain!

It was in September of that year that Delane, the famous editor of *The Times* of London, crossed to New York in the Cunarder *Niagara*. His record of the voyage provided an interesting commentary on Atlantic travel at that time. In his diary Delane recorded there were 150 passengers, 'the majority Americans, some Canadians, some English, some French,

Spanish and Germans'. Then he went on to say how he had secured a place at the Captain's table and how to his great delight he was told that 'although I had only paid for a single berth I was to have a stateroom to myself'.

No doubt he was glad of this privacy before the end of the voyage because the *Niagara* ran into very bad weather. Delane, although 'determined to resist as long as possible', and to this end and in the belief that 'rapid succession of meals during the day is the best preventative of sea sickness', took 'lunch at one, dinner at four, tea at eight and supper at ten, seemed to spend a large part of his time either lying down before getting up or lying down after getting up'.

Still, when the weather improved he got out on deck, played whist in the evening, listened to plenty of 'good Yankee stories' and one evening thoroughly enjoyed an impromptu concert which, enhanced by bowls of punch, 'lasted till long past midnight'. On Sunday he attended Church service at which 'a Free Kirk Minister officiated', and on Monday he attended a lecture given by a Spiritualist passenger who was rather 'stuck up by being asked whether they (the Spirits) ate and drank, and if so whether it was spiritual beef and mutton . . . '.

So the voyage proceeded, giving Delane opportunities of meeting his fellow passengers and thus writing in his diary: 'It is remarkable as an evidence of the general well going of the United States that we have on board five men all very rich who are not yet passed middle life, and all the architects of their own fortune.'

'Architects of their own fortune'—that was a phrase which might well have applied to E. K. Collins. He was a doughty and courageous fighter; despite the private domestic sorrows and business misfortunes which had overwhelmed him, he did not give up the struggle. In reply to the Cunard *Persia* and to replace the *Arctic,* he had placed an order with Mr George Steers, New York, for a wooden paddle steamer which would retrieve the fortunes of his company. Named *Adriatic,* she was the last wooden paddle steamer built for the North Atlantic passenger and mail run. Her principal dimensions were: length overall 351.7 ft; length between perps 343.8 ft; length of keel 330 ft; breadth of hull 50 ft; breadth over paddle boxes about 79 ft; depth in hold 32.8 ft; mean draught 20 ft. Her engines of 1,300 nominal horsepower were constructed by Stillman and Allen, Novelty Ironworks, New York. Coal consumption worked out at 145 tons a day and designed speed was 13 knots. Two classes of accommodation were installed, 316 first class and 60 second class. The number of lifeboats was increased to 16—a significant development in safety precautions.

Launched on April 8 1856, it was not until November 23 1857 that the *Adriatic* was commissioned, when she sailed on her maiden voyage to Liverpool with 38 passengers. The voyage took ten days, and on her arrival in the Mersey she was acclaimed by those who watched her proceeding up-river as 'the finest and fastest steam vessel built up to that date'.

But the effort had come too late. The decision of Congress to reduce the mail subsidy from 853,000 dollars a year to 385,000 dollars made it impossible for Collins to operate the ships which were very costly to run, on an all-the-year-round basis. In February 1858, after the *Adriatic* had made only two voyages, the company suspended operations. On April 1 a public auction was held at the company's pier in New York when only one bid was made, and the *Atlantic, Baltic* and *Adriatic* were sold for 50,000 dollars (£12,500).

Thus, Collins' connection with the Atlantic sadly came to an end. Of the three ships, the *Adriatic,* after being laid up for three years was bought by the Galway Line. When this company went out of business in 1864 she was laid up at Birkenhead and was finally sold to serve as a store ship at Bonny on the coast of West Africa, where she ended her career in 1885.

The *Atlantic* and *Baltic* were employed as transports in the American Civil War, the latter ship taking Major Anderson and the surrendered garrison of Fort Sumter to New York. Later, both ships maintained sailings in the North American Lloyd Line service from New York to Bremen and Southampton. The *Atlantic* was finally withdrawn from service and broken up at Cold Springs. The *Baltic,* converted into a sailing ship, made a number of fast crossings in the Californian trade and was finally broken up at Boston in 1880.

Four
1855—1861
Interlude for
an interloper

Overwhelmed by misfortune at sea followed by financial disaster, the Collins Line had foundered. The Cunard Line had survived the fiercest competition it had yet encountered, although economically badly bruised and battered in the process. As Mr Charles MacIver had shrewdly forecast, Mr Collins had found that 'breaking Cunard windows with sovereigns' was too costly to keep up.

The *Persia* had regained the Blue Riband of the Atlantic for the Cunard company and for Britain. Despite the fact that more shipowners had established passenger steamship services on the Western Ocean, notably the British Inman Line (1850) and the German Hamburg Amerika Line (1856), there were no immediate signs on the horizon that Cunard's new-found supremacy was likely to be challenged.

The liquidation of the Collins Line had led to vociferous recriminations inside and outside Congress, whilst an indignant American public smarted under what they considered to be an affront to their national pride. It was left to one American, Cornelius Vanderbilt, to make one last, defiant gesture. Hailing from Staten Island, 'Commodore' Vanderbilt, as he was popularly known (he had no claim to this naval rank beyond the fact that he had once been master of a Hudson River ferry steamer) was one of that group of ruthless businessmen who, in the 1850s, were the driving force behind the building up of New York into a great and prosperous city and a centre for American trade and commerce with the world.

Of Dutch descent, Vanderbilt, while still a young man, had foreseen the immense possibilities of steamship services. To make a beginning he had established a Hudson River ferry service to and from New York. Riding roughshod over all competition by cutting fares to an almost uneconomic level, he had finally secured a virtual monopoly of the traffic and had amassed a private fortune in so doing. Then he had capitalised on the rush from the US eastern seaboard to the Californian goldfields by setting up the Vanderbilt Line of steamers to carry prospectors, including immigrants from Europe, and supplies from New York to Aspinwall (Panama), the first section of the route to the goldfields. His venture had prospered.

Vanderbilt next turned his attention to the North Atlantic but here he was not so successful. He put in several bids to Congress for the carriage of mails, but found the Collins Line so firmly entrenched that he could make no headway. Finally he decided to operate a North Atlantic service without the financial benefit of a mail subsidy. With this objective he withdrew steamers from his Panama service and inaugurated the Vanderbilt European Line, maintaining sailings from New York to Southampton (Cowes) and Havre.

At the outset sailings were maintained by the 2,000-ton steamer, *North Star,* which on April 21 1855 left New York on her first transatlantic voyage, and the 1,736-ton *Ariel* which began her Atlantic service on May 20. These wooden paddle steamers had been built for Vanderbilt by his nephew Jeremiah Simonson, New York. Machinery, including the new type of overhead beam engines, was constructed by Secor and Braisted at their Allaire Works, New York. A feature of both ships was their luxurious passenger accommodation.

The *North Star* had, in fact, been originally ordered by Vanderbilt for his personal use as a private yacht. In May 1853, with his family and friends, he had voyaged in her to Europe, visiting England, St Petersburg (Leningrad) and Mediterranean ports. On her return the New York newspapers are reported to have stated that the *North Star* had 'astonished John Bull, was admired by the Russian Court, gazed at by the Sultan and frightened the Pope'.

Encouraged by the success of his transatlantic service, Vanderbilt ordered from Jeremiah Simonson his largest and most ambitious ship and named her after himself. Launched on December 17 1855, the *Vanderbilt* was one of the most magnificent paddle steamers to grace the Atlantic ferry. A two-masted brig with two funnels, her machinery included overhead beam engines of about 950 nominal horsepower; designed speed was 13 knots.

The *Vanderbilt* began her maiden voyage from New York to Southampton and Havre on May 5 1857. One month later the Ocean Steam Navigation Company which held the US mail subsidy on the New York-Bremen route ceased operations. Vanderbilt at last realised, in part, one of his ambitions. He was given a contract to carry American mails to Bremen and accordingly extended his services to the German port.

But it was after the collapse of the Collins Line that Vanderbilt made his great bid to bring the Blue Riband back to the United States. On her third eastbound voyage in August 1857, the *Vanderbilt,* under the command of Captain Peter C. Lefebure, made the passage from New York to Southampton (the Needles) in nine days eight hours at an average speed of 13.87 knots. This was undoubtedly the fastest passage ever made over the Channel route, but was six hours behind the record passage of nine days one hour 45 minutes set up by the *Persia*. In April 1860 the *Vander-bilt* set up a new record for the Channel route by crossing from South-ampton (the Needles) to New York in nine days five hours at an average speed of 13.9 knots.

It had been a gallant challenge but not quite good enough. The Blue Riband remained with Britain.

With the outbreak of the American Civil War in 1861, Vanderbilt, with a characteristic flamboyant gesture, presented the *Vanderbilt* to the Federal Government for service as an armed merchant cruiser against the Southern States. The other ships of the fleet were requisitioned for transport work. After the war the service was never revived, Vanderbilt turning his atten-tion to the railroads—a more profitable venture.

Five
1862—1876
The battle
for supremacy

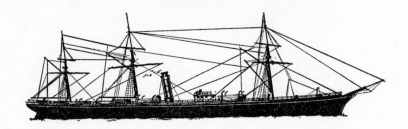

Part one

THERE NOW SET IN for Britain's shipbuilders, marine engine builders and shipowners maintaining North Atlantic passenger liner services, that incomparable Golden Age when for 41 years they were to dominate the Western Ocean scene. For 41 years the Blue Riband of the Atlantic was to be held by ships flying the Red Ensign, the symbol of Britain's merchant navy, years when shipping companies such as Cunard, Inman, Guion, National and White Star were to compete for supremacy.

It was to be an age marked by the development from iron to steel for the construction of hulls, from paddle-wheels to single- and twin-screw propellers, from simple to compound engines. They were years when passenger accommodation scaled new heights of luxury and when the American packet ships, so long champions of the North Atlantic, that most competitive of all international shipping routes, were finally eclipsed.

It had begun in 1856 with the commissioning by the Cunard Line of the iron paddle steamer *Persia* (3,300 tons) which regained the Blue Riband from the Collins Line 'flyers', and with it the patronage of the fickle Atlantic passenger to whom the prestige factor was all important. The *Persia* held the record for seven years but at a frightening economic cost to her owners. To maintain her reputation for fast voyages and to keep her popularity she burned enormous quantities of coal, consumption working out at 143 tons to 150 tons a day. This extravagance was the more serious because the Cunard Line was fast being overhauled by the Inman Line. From the time of its establishment in 1850, this Liverpool-based

Commissioned in 1872 the liner *Adriatic* (1) was a unit of the original White Star fleet which virtually revolutionised passenger travel conditions on the North Atlantic.

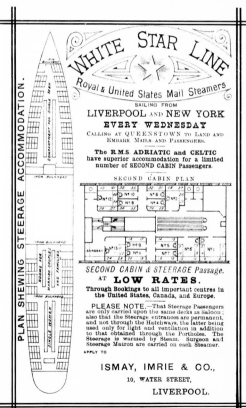

Of particular interest on the accommodation plan (right) is the layout of the steerage accommodation.

The Inman liner *City of Berlin* which, at the time of her commissioning, was the largest and longest passenger liner of the Atlantic Ferry. She was the first record-holder to achieve an average speed of over 15 knots.

The development of the North Atlantic passenger liner is well illustrated by this photograph of the White Star liner *Britannic (1)* lying to anchor in the Mersey. Built at Belfast (as were all White Star liners) the *Britannic*, with her sister ship *Germanic*, will always be numbered among the great 'pairs' of Blue Riband holders.

The White Star liner *Germanic*, one of the outstanding liners in maritime history. Her claim to fame rests not only on her Blue Riband voyages but also on the fact that, after her sale by the IMM in 1910, she continued her sea-going career for the next 40 years under the Turkish flag. She was scrapped in 1950.

company had operated steamers in which the 'new' system of screw propulsion had been installed. One benefit was that coal consumption was reduced to about half that of the paddle steamers. The challenge became acute when in 1858 the Inman Line, which had maintained services from Liverpool to Philadelphia, decided to make New York their main US terminal point. Yet another worrying problem was that, in 1852, Inman, appalled at the conditions in which emigrants voyaged in the packet ships, had made provision in his fleet for a steerage class. Specially designed for the emigrant trade, his was the first steamship company to do so.

The Cunard Line had left the emigrant business to the packet ships for two reasons. In the first place, the carriage of mails involved the operation of fast 'express' ships, which the Admiralty stipulated must be paddle steamers. This in turn involved the carriage of so much coal that there was little space left below decks for cargo, let alone emigrants. Obviously the Inman threat could not be ignored and the Cunard partners tackled it in a characteristic way. They placed orders with Robert Napier and Sons, Glasgow, for two liners—the *Scotia,* a paddle steamer of 3,871 gross tons, for the mail service, and the *China,* a single-screw propelled steamer of 2,539 tons, built to carry 160 'cabin-class' passengers and 771 in steerage accommodation. Although she had a designed speed of 13.9 knots it was not intended that the *China* should attempt any record passages, nor did she ever do so. She left Liverpool on her maiden voyage to New York on March 15 1862 and soon proved a money-making proposition.

It was the *Scotia,* however, the last and finest Atlantic paddle steamer, which fired the public imagination. Built at a cost of £170,000 she was a much bigger ship than the *China.* Her principal dimensions were: length overall 400 ft; length between perpendiculars 397 ft; breadth of hull 47.8 ft; breadth over paddle boxes 76.5 ft; depth of hold 30.5 ft; mean draught 20 ft. She was fitted with side-lever engines; indicated horsepower was 4,900 and designed speed 14.4 knots. Coal consumption was 164 tons a day compared with a figure of 82 tons for the *China.* There was accommodation for 300 cabin-class passengers who were charged a single fare of £26 and £50 for the return passage. No steerage accommodation was provided but there was hold space for 1,400 tons of cargo.

Launched on June 25 1861, the *Scotia* was completed in the spring of 1862. She ran her trials on March 5 when, despite bad weather conditions, she attained a speed of 16.51 knots. When she arrived in the Mersey from her builders' yard on the Clyde, this lovely and elegant two-funnelled liner —the finest, strongest and fastest ship of her day—won instant acclaim.

It was unfortunate that 1862 was not a propitious year in which to commission a steamship on the Liverpool-New York run. The outbreak of the American Civil War in 1861 had inevitably led to a drastic fall in transatlantic passenger traffic. As a result, after her arrival in Liverpool, the *Scotia* lay idle in dock for two months. It was not until May 10 that, with Captain Charles Judkins on the bridge, she began her maiden voyage for New York carrying only half her full complement of 300 passengers.

The general public were quite confident that the *Scotia* would bring Atlantic records tumbling down. Events proved them wrong. The *Persia* had other ideas; she held on tenaciously to her Blue Riband, and it was not until December 1863 that the *Scotia* succeeded in wresting it from her by completing a record passage from New York to Queenstown in eight days three hours at an average speed of 14 knots. In June 1864 she made doubly sure of the Blue Riband by making the westward voyage from Queenstown to New York in eight days four hours 34 minutes at an average speed of 14.54 knots. The *Scotia* had vindicated herself and for the next three years was the unchallenged queen of the Western Ocean.

Those years were to witness a remarkable quickening of competition on the North Atlantic, marked by the inauguration of the development of liner companies which in later years were to be contenders for the Blue Riband. In Britain, in addition to the Cunard and Inman Lines, the National Line (the directors included a young man, Mr T. H. Ismay, who was to found the White Star Line) and the Guion Line were now maintaining services from Liverpool. This latter company had been founded by Stephen Barker Guion, an American citizen and a partner in the firm of Williams and Guion, owners of the Black Star Line of sailing packets running between New York and Liverpool. Stephen Guion looked after the interests of the company at Liverpool.

When the packet ship emigrant trade began to lose ground to the steamships, Guion decided to form his own steamship company (formally called the Liverpool and Great Western Steam Ship Company) and placed orders for four ships with Palmers' shipyard at Jarrow-on-Tyne. Although Guion and his fellow directors were Americans, under a ruling made in 1846 by the Queen's Bench, London, as all the ships were built in Britain, for purposes of registry they were British 'subjects' and must fly the British flag.

Across the English Channel in Western Europe, the Hamburg-Amerika Line, founded on June 1 1856, was well established. The Norddeutscher Lloyd Line had begun services to New York in 1858, while in 1861 the Compagnie Générale Transatlantique (French Line) extended operations to the New York run. These three companies all included in their New York run a call at Southampton, at that time a very small cloud on the horizon so far as the Liverpool-New York route was concerned. There was no challenge from that direction to the rivalry between the Cunard and Inman Lines.

Meanwhile, the British Admiralty had waived their ruling that no screw-propelled steamers could operate on the Cunard mail service. Thankful for this dispensation the Company lost no time in placing an order for a single-screw liner to work in conjunction with the *Scotia*. The contract for the ship—to be named *Russia*—was given to J. & G. Thomson, Clyde-bank (forerunner of John Brown and Company, who many years later were to build the Blue Riband liners *Lusitania* and *Queen Mary* and also the *Queen Elizabeth* [1] and *Queen Elizabeth* [2]).

The last Cunarder to be graced with a clipper bow and figure-head, the *Russia* was one of the most elegant ships commissioned for North Atlantic service. The symmetry of her exterior lines were matched by the lavishness of her accommodation for 235 cabin passengers—no provision was made for the emigrant trade. A single-screw steamer of 2,960 tons, she was 358 feet long, with a beam of 43 feet, and depth of 28 feet. Her engines of 3,100 indicated horsepower gave her a designed speed of 14.4 knots; coal consumption was 90 tons a day. Commissioned in 1867, she began her first voyage from Liverpool to New York on June 15. Five months later, in November, she took the eastbound record from the *Scotia* by crossing from New York to Queenstown in eight days and 28 minutes at an average speed of 14.22 knots. It was the *Russia's* first, and last, Blue Riband voyage; perhaps more notable was the fact that she was the first screw-propelled ship to make a record voyage.

When commissioned the *Russia* found herself in direct competition with the Inman liner, *City of Paris (1)*, which had made her North Atlantic debut on March 21 1866. Built by Tod & McGregor, Glasgow—as had been the majority of Inman ships—the *City of Paris (1)*, of 2,651 gross tons, was a worthy rival to the *Russia*. Her principal dimensions were: length overall 359 ft; length between perpendiculars 346 ft; breadth 40.4 ft; depth 26.6 ft. She was a single-screw steamer, indicated horsepower was 2,600 and designed speed 13.5 knots; coal consumption was 105 tons a day.

There was little to choose between the two ships when it came to speed. Thus, in November 1867, after the *Russia* had made her record eastbound voyage, she was followed in the same month by the *City of Paris (1)* which set up a westbound record by crossing from Queenstown to New York in eight days four hours one minute at an average speed of 13.77 knots. Her claim to the record provoked endless arguments, reflecting the increasing intense public interest in the North Atlantic liner scene. There were many who were quick to point out that, although the *Scotia* in June 1864 had taken a longer time to complete a similar westbound voyage (eight days four hours 34 minutes), she had achieved an average speed of 14.54 knots which was considerably faster than the 13.77 knots of the *City of Paris (1)*. Also the *Scotia* had taken the longer North Atlantic route of 2,851 miles compared with the 2,700 miles completed by the *City of Paris (1)*.

However much owners (perhaps with tongue in cheek) might publicly deplore the fact, the North Atlantic had once more become the setting for 'races' between rival ships. One between the *Russia* and *City of Paris (1)* which created great excitement took place in 1868. Both ships sailed from New York for Queenstown and Liverpool on February 10, the *City of Paris* at 13.35 hours and the *Russia* at 14.40 hours. Their subsequent daily progress was:

	Russia	*City of Paris (1)*	*Weather*
Feb 11	245 miles	242 miles	Heavy head seas
Feb 12	282 „	295 „	„ „ „
Feb 13	314 „	316 „	Moderate breeze
Feb 14	323 „	323 „	„ „
Feb 15	333 „	342 „	*Russia*—strong gale
			City of Paris (1)—fresh breeze
Feb 16	338 „	346 „	*Russia*—gales
			City of Paris (1)—fresh breeze
Feb 17	232 „	338 „	*Russia*—gales
			City of Paris (1)—fresh breeze
Feb 18	349 „	346 „	Moderate
Total mileage	2,416 „	2,548 „	

The *Russia* completed the voyage to Queenstown in eight days 20 hours five minutes; the *City of Paris (1)*, which had taken the longer course, in eight days 19 hours 23 minutes. After a brief stay at the Irish port, both ships proceeded to Liverpool. The *Russia* made good the slight deficiency during the coastal run, her time for the complete voyage being nine days 13 hours 17 minutes against nine days 13 hours 50 minutes for the *City of Paris (1)*. They were not record voyages but they conclusively demonstrated the small margin in speed between the two liners.

All argument as to the ship which held the Blue Riband was settled in 1869 with the appearance on the North Atlantic of the Inman liner, *City of Brussels* (3,081 tons), also built by Tod and McGregor, and the first North Atlantic liner, apart from the *Great Eastern*, to be fitted with steam steering gear. On her second homeward voyage in December 1869 she crossed from New York to Queenstown in seven days 22 hours three minutes at an average speed of 14.66 knots. By so doing the *City of Brussels* not only put the Blue Riband issue beyond doubt, but also gained the distinction of being the first steamship to bring an Atlantic passage down to less than eight days. The Cunard Line had no immediate answer to that—in fact 15 years were to elapse before they were to take up the challenge again.

The Inman Line was riding high. Not only had the *City of Brussels* secured the Blue Riband but also the company's combined fleet had attained a commanding lead in the carriage of passengers to America. Published returns for 1870 of passengers from the United Kingdom landed in New York were:

Company	Number of voyages	Cabin passengers	Steerage	Total
Inman	68	3,635	40,465	44,100
National	56	2,442	33,494	35,736
Guion	55	1,115	27,054	28,569
Anchor	74	1,637	23,404	25,041
Cunard	70	7,638	16,871	24,509

These returns were of especial interest to three Liverpool shipowners, Thomas Ismay, George H. Fletcher and William Imrie who, despite the intense competition, were about to launch a new steamship company on the Liverpool-New York route. For this purpose, on September 6 1869, they had officially registered in London the Oceanic Steam Navigation Company (always to be known and publicised as the White Star Line). At the same time they had placed orders with the Belfast shipbuilders, Harland and Wolff, for four steamers of 3,707 gross tons to be named *Oceanic, Atlantic, Baltic* and *Republic*.

As directors of the National Line, Ismay and Fletcher had practical knowledge of the North Atlantic liner trade. They had made a long and detailed study in conjunction with Harland and Wolff of the Cunard and Inman fleets and determined what improvements could be effected in hull design, machinery installation and passenger accommodation to produce the finest and fastest liners afloat. Their plans materialised in the *Oceanic (1)* and her sister ships, all identical in appearance and dimensions. The building cost of each ship was £120,000 (600,000 dollars).

The pioneer ship of the fleet was the *Oceanic (1)*. Her principal dimensions were: length 420.4 ft; breadth 40.9 ft; depth 31 ft; gross tonnage 3,707. A single-screw ship, she was fitted with two sets of compound engines built by Maudsley Son & Field of London, to give a designed speed of 14 knots. There were 12 boilers and 24 furnaces, which consumed 60 tons of coal a day, compared with 110 tons in her nearest rival the *City of Brussels*.

Accommodation was provided for 166 saloon passengers and 1,000 emigrants in the steering class. Single fare for saloon passengers was 18 guineas or 16 guineas according to the type and position of the stateroom. The return fare was 27 guineas. Single fare for steerage passengers was six guineas with half-price for children.

But where the *Oceanic* and her sister ships triumphed over their rivals was in the 'new look' they brought to the accommodation for saloon passengers. Never before had comfort and facilities on such a scale been incorporated in a single ship. The greatest break with traditional planning was the decision to transfer all saloon accommodation from the after end to midships where the vibration and discomfort set up by the screw propeller would be less noticeable. The dining saloon, 80 feet in length, occupied the full width of the ships, the large portholes on either side giving the room a lightness and airiness which delighted passengers as did the separate chairs replacing the long benchlike seats at the tables.

The staterooms were fore and aft of the dining saloon. They were not only twice as big as the usual size, but all 'outside rooms' had portholes. Wash basins with fresh running water were installed, while a special feature was the introduction of what were known as 'bridal cabins'. Public rooms included a drawing room for ladies, and for the men a comfortable smoking room with a coal-burning fireplace.

No great fuss was made about the steerage facilities, but at least they were adequate. Single male emigrants were housed forward of the first class saloon and cut off from it by 'massive iron doors'. Married folk and their families were accommodated aft of the saloon as were single women, thus making sure, as far as possible, that the proprieties were observed.

Launched on August 27 1870, the *Oceanic* arrived in the Mersey from her Belfast shipyard on February 26 1871, where she caused a sensation with her four tall masts rigged for a wide spread of canvas, her long black hull, the iron deck rails which had replaced the traditional high wooden bulwarks, and the single buff funnel with black top, for so many years a distinguishing feature of the White Star ships.

Commanded by Captain Digby Murray, the *Oceanic* set out on her maiden voyage from Liverpool to New York on Thursday March 2. Despite the blaze of publicity which had attended her commissioning, it was not an auspicious beginning. Out of a possible 1,166 passengers only 64 people had booked passages and even they must have begun to have doubts when, within a few hours of leaving the Mersey, the ship's main engine bearings became overheated. As a result, she put into Holyhead, North Wales, for temporary repairs. These proved ineffective and the *Oceanic* made an ignominious return to Liverpool.

It was not until March 16 that she set out again. This time all was well and she arrived at New York to a rapturous welcome. During her stay in port over 50,000 people visited the ship, 'the wonders of which exceeded all expectations'.

Experience of the *Oceanic's* performance at sea had indicated that a number of alterations were necessary to make her an economic proposition. She returned to her Belfast birthplace where some of the top hamper was removed, two more boilers installed, bunker capacity enlarged and a turtle-backed forecastle added. She was, however, fated never to make a record-breaking Atlantic voyage.

This distinction was left to the *Adriatic (1)*, a slightly larger ship of 3,888 tons which began her maiden voyage from Liverpool to New York on May 4 1872, and made the passage from Queenstown in seven days 23 hours 17 minutes at an average speed of 14.41 knots. In so doing she joined the select company of 'maiden voyage' record-holders. Then, in January 1873, the *Baltic (1)* which had been in service for 16 months made Blue Riband history by crossing from New York to Queenstown in seven days 20 hours nine minutes at an average speed of 15.12 knots—the first time such an average speed had been attained.

This White Star triumph was soon to be overshadowed by the tragic loss of the *Atlantic* three months later. She was one of the most successful units of the pioneer fleet and had sailed from Liverpool on March 20 under the command of Captain James Williams. She had embarked 811 passengers, officers and crew totalled 141, and in her holds were 1,836 tons of cargo.

Five days out of Liverpool, the *Atlantic* ran into fierce gales which caused her to reduce speed to five knots. On March 31, by which time the ship would normally have been safely berthed in New York, the chief engineer, Mr John Foxley, reported that there were only 127 tons of coal remaining in the bunkers, and the ship had still 460 miles to run. Captain Williams decided to put into Halifax for fresh supplies and accordingly changed course. At 03.50 hours the *Atlantic* crashed on to Meagher's Rock on Maris Head, Prospect Cape, some 20 miles from Halifax.

There was no hope for the ship and little more for her passengers and crew. Of the 952 souls on board, 585 were drowned; those who were saved owed their lives to the gallantry of one of the liner's quartermasters, named Owens, who lashed a line around his waist and, swimming through the raging surf, managed to establish a link between the broken ship and Meagher's Rock.

The events which led up to the tragedy and the consequent heavy loss of life had the inevitable adverse effect on White Star passenger carryings. For a time the public lost confidence in the company—once again the Blue Riband counted for nothing. A great deal was heard about Cunard's remarkable immunity from such disasters, and critics were quick to recall the record of the Cunard Commodore, Captain T. Cook, who, when in command of the *Russia,* was said to have navigated her for 100 round voyages, a total of over 600,000 miles, in all weather conditions and without accident or breakdown, carrying 26,076 passengers in perfect safety.

The setback to the White Star popularity could not have come at a more inopportune time. The year 1873 was marked by a boom in emigration from Europe which increased to 378,000 compared with 338,000 in the previous year and 287,000 in 1870. This was an added incentive to competing liners to order new tonnage which at least would equal the high standards set by the White Star Company. Of these competitors, only the Inman Line concerned itself with the Blue Riband. With this objective the company contracted with Caird and Company, Greenock, for the *City of Berlin* in the design of which they incorporated many White Star innovations including a midships dining saloon. When commissioned on April 29 1875, she was the largest and longest liner in Atlantic service. The Inman Line had retained the long clipper-type stem and counter stern, an attractive feature of all their ships, so that her overall length was no less than 520 ft. Her length (between perps) was 489 ft, breadth 44.2 ft and depth to spar deck 34.9 ft; gross tonnage was 5,491. The *City of Berlin* was fitted with two-cylinder compound engines, indicated horsepower was 4,799 and designed speed 15 knots. Accommodation was provided for 202 cabin-class passengers and no fewer than 1,500 in the steerage.

Within a few months of her commissioning the *City of Berlin* deposed the White Star record holder *Adriatic* when, in September 1875, she crossed from Queenstown to New York in seven days 18 hours two minutes at an average speed of 15.21 knots. The following month she consolidated her position with a record homeward passage, her time from New York to Queenstown being seven days 15 hours and her average speed 15.41 knots. It was a splendid achievement, but the *City of Berlin* was not to enjoy her well-deserved Blue Riband for long.

Determined to remain in the forefront and in so doing restore some of its lost prestige, the White Star Line had placed an order with Harland and Wolff for two sister ships, the *Britannic (1)* and *Germanic,* destined to be one of the most famous 'pairs' in North Atlantic history. The two ships were 455 ft in length with a beam of 45.2 ft and depth of hold 33.7 ft. Gross tonnage was 5,004 and accommodation was provided for 220 first-class passengers and 1,500 in the steerage. Machinery installation comprised four-cylinder compound type engines, the high pressure cylinders being each 48 inches in diameter and the low pressure 83 inches. Steam at 75 pounds pressure was supplied by eight double-ended boilers. They consumed about 110 tons of coal a day to give a designed speed of 15-16 knots. They had four masts, rigged to carry sail, and were the first two-funnelled White Star ships. When first commissioned, the *Britannic (1)* (it had originally been intended to name her *Hellenic*) had been fitted with an experimental type of 'dropping' propeller with a universal joint on the shaft. The idea was that it could be lowered into water of greater density and so increase the speed of the ship. The innovation was not a success and after several voyages the *Britannic (1)* returned to Belfast, and a normal type propeller was fitted.

Launched on February 2 1874, the *Britannic (1)* left Liverpool for New York on her maiden voyage on June 25 1874. She took some time to get into her stride—her newfangled propellers were one reason—and it was her sister ship *Germanic,* launched on July 15 1874 and commissioned May 20 1875, which made the first of the many record voyages they were to achieve, and which gained for them a great reputation for consistency of speed and regularity of performance.

The *Germanic* dispossessed the *City of Berlin* in February 1876 by crossing from New York to Queenstown in seven days 15 hours 17 minutes at an average speed of 15.78 knots. In June of the same year the *Britannic* (*1*) lowered the westward record by one hour 27 minutes and followed this up in November by completing the Queenstown-New York run in seven days 13 hours 11 minutes at an average speed of 15.25 knots.

Public interest was now centred on competition between the two ships, and a great deal of excitement they provided. In April 1877, the *Germanic* crossed from Queenstown to New York in seven days 11 hours 37 minutes, at an average of 15.5 knots, and in the following August the *Britannic* achieved a similar passage in seven days 10 hours 53 minutes, at an average of 15.25 knots. Eastward, the *Germanic* crossed from New York in February 1876 in seven days 15 hours 17 minutes, at an average of 15.75 knots, a record surpassed by the *Britannic* in December 1876 when she came home in seven days 12 hours 41 minutes, at an average speed of 15.95 knots.

Six
1877—1897
The battle for supremacy

Part two

THE BLUE RIBAND was held again by the White Star Line, and all the indications were that it would continue to be held by them indefinitely. The Inman Line was temporarily out of the 'race' and the Cunard Line, no longer monopolising the British mail contract—it was shared between Cunard, Inman and White Star—was apparently content to watch the contest from the sidelines, and concentrate on commissioning comfortable but slower 13-knot passenger liners. The National Line was maintaining a steady course of catering mainly for the emigrant trade. There remained only one possible contender—the Guion Line—and, in fact, it was from this source that the challenge was to come. After maintaining North Atlantic services for 13 years, during which the company had built up a steady patronage, the directors decided to order their first ship, designed and engined to gain the Blue Riband. With this aim, in 1879 they broke away from their traditional shipbuilders and placed an order with John Elder and Company, Fairfield, Glasgow, which in 1878 had been taken over by that master-shipbuilder William Pearce; the fact that Pearce had business links with the Guion Line (at one period he was chairman) may go a long way to explain the Guion sudden change of policy.

Modelled to a large extent on the lines of the all-conquering *Britannic (1)* and *Germanic,* the new liner was named *Arizona*. A single-screw iron ship of 5,164 gross tons, she was 450 feet in length, 45 feet wide with a depth of 35.7 feet. She had four masts, of which the fore and main were square rigged, and two funnels (black with a red band) between the main and mizzen masts. Altogether she looked what she proved to be, an extremely strong and powerful ship. Where she differed from other North Atlantic passenger liners was in her machinery installation. This comprised a compound engine with three crankshafts each of which had one cylinder, the high pressure of 62 inches diameter was in the centre; the low pressures were each of 90 inches with a stroke of 5.5 feet. She was supplied with seven boilers and 39 furnaces. Indicated horsepower was 6,300 and designed speed 16.25 knots. On her trials she delighted owners and builders alike by achieving 17.3 knots. Daily consumption of coal at 125 tons a day was very heavy compared with the 85 tons of *Britannic (I)* and *Germanic*.

The *Arizona* sailed on her maiden voyage from Liverpool to New York on May 31 1879. Within two months she had secured the eastbound record by voyaging from New York to Queenstown in seven days eight hours 11 minutes at an average speed of 15.96 knots. In the same July she crossed from Queenstown to New York in seven days ten hours 22 minutes at an average speed of 15.73 knots. This was the shortest time yet recorded for this passage although the *Arizona's* average speed did not beat the 15.81 knots average set up in February 1876 by the *Germanic*.

The *Arizona's* fame, however, was not to rest solely on her Blue Riband honours. Homeward bound from New York for Liverpool in November 1879, under the command of Captain Jones, she ran head-on into an iceberg when off the Newfoundland Grand Banks in dense fog. Although her bows were stove in for a considerable length, her forward bulkheads held. Her master cautiously ordered the ship to go astern and after the ice which had fallen on the crumpled deck was cleared, it was found that not only had the *Arizona* not suffered mortal damage, but there was no loss of life, not even any serious casualties. She put into St John's, Newfoundland, where a wooden bow was fitted to enable the liner to proceed on her voyage to Liverpool. At the subsequent inquiry, the master was held to blame and his ticket suspended. Curiously enough the owners and the *Arizona* emerged with enhanced reputations; a perverse Atlantic travelling public decided that if a ship could collide with an iceberg and complete her voyage virtually unscathed she must indeed be the 'strongest and safest ship afloat'. As a result she was always well patronised.

Encouraged by the success of the *Arizona*, in 1881 the Guion Line ordered a companion ship from the Elder shipyard. Named *Alaska*, she was slightly larger than the *Arizona*, her principal dimensions being: length overall 500 ft; breadth 50 ft; depth 38 ft; gross tonnage 6,392. Her machinery installation, although more powerful, was similar to that in the *Arizona*. Her designed speed was 17 knots. Again, as in the *Arizona*, the machinery installation took up so much space that there was little room left down below for steerage accommodation, only 140 passengers being carried in this class.

The *Alaska* entered service on October 29 1881, when she left Liverpool for New York. In the April of 1882 she made Blue Riband history by crossing from Queenstown to New York in seven days six hours 43 minutes at an average speed of 16 knots. She surpassed this record in June 1882 when she completed the homeward run from New York to Queenstown in six days 22 hours at an average speed of 16.8 knots—the first time that an Atlantic voyage had been made in under seven days.

The Guion Line was in command of the Western Ocean routes. Nowhere was there greater delight than in the United States because, although the *Arizona* and *Alaska* like other ships in the Guion fleet operated under British registry, most of the directors and shareholders were American citizens, as were the masters of the ships. American pride in the Guion achievement was unbounded when it was learned that the company had ordered a third ship to run in harness with the two record breakers. The policy behind this decision was that developments in shipbuilding and engineering had reached a point where three fast ships could maintain services between Liverpool and New York previously maintained by five.

Like the *Arizona* and *Alaska,* this third ship named *Oregon* was built at the Fairfield yard. She was in fact simply a larger edition of her two distinguished predecessors. Her principal dimensions were: length overall 520 ft; length (between perpendiculars) 501 ft; breadth 54.2 ft; depth 40 ft; gross tonnage 7,375. Her machinery installation excited the admiration of marine engineers the world over. She was fitted with three-cylinder compound engines (one high-pressure cylinder of 70 inches diameter and two low-pressure cylinders, each 104 inches in diameter). The designed indicated horsepower was 12,500 and designed speed 18 knots. Coal consumption was 310 tons a day.

When commissioned on October 7 1883, the *Oregon* was the largest merchant steamer afloat. On her third westward voyage she secured the Blue Riband from the *Alaska* by crossing from Queenstown to New York in six days ten hours ten minutes, and in April 1884 made the run from New York to Queenstown in six days 16 hours 57 minutes at an average speed of 17.48 knots.

This was the *Oregon's* last record voyage under the Guion houseflag. Her owners had run into heavy financial weather and, unable to keep up the instalment payments for the liner with the shipbuilders, they returned her to the Fairfield yard. William Pearce found himself with an extravagant Atlantic record-breaker on his hands but fortunately he soon found a possible purchaser. Shortly before, a newly constituted Cunard board of directors had announced their intention to restore the company's fading image on the Atlantic Ferry by ordering 'two fast and luxurious steamers'. For this purpose they had gone to the Fairfield yard and were even then drawing up plans for the two ships with Pearce and Admiralty officials. Pearce suggested that the *Oregon* would prove a useful companion to the two ships. The Cunard directors, realising that it would give them a 'flying start', agreed to buy the ship. Thus it came about that the 'three-ship' express service envisaged by the Guion Line was to be finally implemented by the Cunard Line, one of their main competitors.

The *Oregon* made her first voyage wearing Cunard colours on June 7 1884 and, excelling her Guion performance, secured for her new owners the Blue Riband. In the August of that year she crossed from Queenstown to New York (Sandy Hook) in six days nine hours 42 minutes at an average speed of 18.14 knots. Homeward bound she completed the passage in six days 11 hours, her average speed being 18.52 knots. It was the first time since the record voyage made by the *Russia* in 1869 that the Cunard Company had led the way.

But if 1884 was to be marked by the Cunard Line re-imposing its authoritative image on the North Atlantic, it was also to be marked by the commissioning of the liner *America* which upset all calculations by winning the Blue Riband convincingly on her maiden voyage to become a 'nine days' wonder'. Owned by the National Line, Liverpool, a company which since its inception in 1863 had built up a splendid reputation in the emigrant trade, the *America* was built by J. & G. Thomson, Clydebank. She was a lovely clipper-stemmed ship fitted with two tapering masts and two extremely tall white funnels with a black top. One of the first record-breakers to be constructed of steel, the *America* was 441 ft 8 ins long, 51 ft wide and 36 ft deep; her gross tonnage was 5,528. Her engines were of the usual three-crank compound type, her designed speed being 18.75 knots. Coal consumption at 190 tons a day was considerably less than that of the Guion record breakers. An unusual and new feature of her cabin passenger accommodation was a great glass dome over the dining saloon providing extra height and light; it was an innovation to be adopted by other North Atlantic steamship lines.

The *America* began her maiden voyage from Liverpool to New York under the command of Captain Grace on May 28 1884, and completed the passage from Queenstown in six days 15 hours 22 minutes at an average speed of 17.6 knots. Homeward from New York she excelled herself by crossing to Queenstown in six days 14 hours eight minutes at an average speed of 17.8 knots. The *America* had joined the select company of Blue Riband holders. Ironically enough her owners, whilst duly gratified, quickly discovered that the presence of a record-breaker in their fleet was to be a source of embarrassment. The fact was they could not fit the *America* into their sailing schedules, maintained as they were by much slower ships. To make any profit out of the *America* a companion ship of similar speed would be necessary, so to solve the problem they chartered the Anchor liner *City of Rome*.

This three-funnelled liner, widely acclaimed as one of the most beautiful ever to grace the Western Ocean, had already been built by the Barrow Shipbuilding Company for the Inman Line. When commissioned on October 13 1881, she had failed to come up to her designed speed. After several voyages she was returned unceremoniously to her builders, who sold her to the Anchor Line.

The National Line plan to operate the *America* and *City of Rome* in a joint 'express' service was not satisfactory. In any event the *America* had only held the Blue Riband for two months, as she had been quickly deposed by the *Oregon*. What was more to the point was that the National Line directors, fully aware of the quickening pace of competition, had the sense to realise that any attempt to strive against the major Blue Riband companies could well result in financial suicide. With more wisdom than they had shown in ordering the *America*, they decided to get rid of her and in 1887 sold her to the Italian Government who converted her into a naval cruiser, renaming her *Trinacria*.

By this time the Cunard Line had firmly established itself as the leading North Atlantic liner company despite a serious setback when, on March 14 1886, the *Oregon,* nearing the end of a voyage from Liverpool to New York, had sunk after colliding off Fire Island with the wooden *Charles Morse*. There were 641 passengers and 255 crew on board the *Oregon*.

Fortunately the Norddeutscher liner *Fulda* was on the scene, and all passengers and crew were transferred to the German ship before the *Oregon* sank. It was the first major loss the Cunard had experienced since the grounding of the *Columbia* off Halifax, Nova Scotia, in 1843 but, once again, no lives were lost. The Cunard reputation for safety of life at sea remained unimpaired.

The sinking of the *Oregon* had put an end to the 'three-ship' express service, but the *Umbria* and *Etruria* more than compensated for this by their fast and regular voyages between Liverpool and New York. Not since the White Star *Britannic (1)* and *Germanic* had such a splendid pair of sister ships put to sea.

The last two single-screw big passenger liners built for Atlantic service, the *Umbria* and *Etruria* were identical in outward appearance, a distinguishing feature being their three masts, fitted to carry sail, and two enormous funnels which, while giving an impression of great power and speed, were in truth not particularly handsome. Principal dimensions were: length overall 520 ft; length between perps 501 ft; breadth 57 ft 3 ins; depth to upper deck 41 ft; depth to promenade deck 49 ft; gross tonnage 8,120. There was hold space for 1,450 tons of cargo and room for 2,600 tons of coal in the bunkers.

The machinery installation included three-crank compressed engines, with one high-pressure cylinder 71 inches in diameter, and two low-pressure cylinders 105 inches in diameter. The engines developed 14,700 indicated horsepower to give a designed speed of 19.5 knots. Coal consumption was 315 tons a day. Manning the engine room were 11 engineers, one electrician, and 109 firemen.

The ship was built of steel throughout and special attention was given to safety requirements. The hulls were divided into ten watertight compartments, most of the bulkheads were carried up to the upper deck and fitted with fireproof and waterproof doors.

At that time the Admiralty was completing plans under which, in the event of war, they would be enabled to requisition the largest British merchant liners for conversion into auxiliary cruisers; a subvention being paid to the owners concerned. The *Umbria* and *Etruria* were among the ships chosen and throughout their construction the Admiralty officials kept in close touch with the owners and the builders, John Elder & Co (now reconstituted as The Fairfield Shipbuilding and Engineering Company).

The splendour of the accommodation provided for the 550 saloon passengers reflected the progressive changes in design and furnishing which had taken place since the White Star *Oceanic* had pioneered luxury Atlantic travel by steamship in 1871. The *Umbria* and *Etruria* could well be said to have inaugurated the concept of the 'floating hotel' which from then on was to become an obsession with the competing lines on the Atlantic Ferry. The leitmotive in the furnishing of the *Umbria* and *Etruria* was to bring to sea all the affluence of the Victorian society. There were heavily carved tables and chairs, brocaded sofas and easy chairs, velvet curtains and hangings, bric-à-brac filling every forlorn niche, stained glass cupolas and, those indispensable hallmarks of the upper class home, a piano *and* an organ given a place of honour in the music room.

The *Umbria* was the first of the two liners to be commissioned. She was launched on June 25 1884 and the builders, conscious of the fact that this was their first Cunard order, went all out to complete her by the end of September. As a result the owners, who had originally scheduled the ship for service in the spring of 1885, were able to advance her first sailing to November 1884. The *Umbria* left her Clyde birthplace on October 4. She achieved a speed of 21 knots on her trials, and then proceeded to Liverpool. On November 1, commanded by Captain Theodore Cook, she began her maiden voyage to New York. She did not break any records, and in fact took some time to find her sea-legs.

The *Etruria,* launched on September 20 1884, was completed in March of the following year, sailing from the Clyde on March 24 for Liverpool, where she arrived on March 26. There a surprise awaited her: for some time the British Government's relations with Russia had been strained owing to a dispute over the extension of a Russian railway to the Afghanistan frontier. War was not improbable and, as a result, the Admiralty exercised their right to requisition the *Etruria* and the *Umbria* with other merchant cruisers. Fortunately a settlement was reached but, as a precautionary measure, the Admiralty retained the *Umbria* for six months, but released the *Etruria* which, on April 25 1885, commanded by Captain McMicken, began her first Atlantic voyage from Liverpool to New York.

For the next four years the two ships were to emulate the *Britannic (1)* and *Germanic* as champions of the Western Ocean and again, as with the White Star 'pair', when it came to fast voyages there was little to choose between the two liners, although in the event the *Etruria* proved slightly faster. Both ships won the Blue Riband, their fastest passages being:

			Days	hrs	mins	Av speed (knots)
Umbria	westward	May 1885	6	5	31	18.86
Etruria	westward	May 1887	6	4	42	19.25
Etruria	eastward	March 1887	6	4	36	19.90
Etruria	westward	May 1888	6	0	58	20.00

They proved a worth-while investment and, like the *Britannic (1)* and *Germanic,* improved on their voyage performances years after they had passed out of the company of record holders. In a tribute to these two profitable Cunarders it was once said: 'No ships ever gave their owners less uneasiness and none have done such an extraordinary quantity of good work. They are monuments that cannot lie to the skill of the design and faithfulness of the labour that went to their accomplishment.'

Meanwhile the Inman Line had run into financial difficulties. The failure of the *City of Rome* to come up to her designed speed requirements – and her subsequent return to her builders – had disrupted the company's services. The situation was aggravated when, on January 7 1883, the *City of Brussels* had sunk after a collision at the entrance to the River Mersey with the steamer *Kirby Hall*. Fortunately, only ten lives were lost. By 1886, the position was so serious that drastic measures had to be taken to keep the company afloat. Efforts were made to attract additional capital by means of a public loan, but the public showed no interest.

On October 18 1886 a general meeting was held at which it was decided that the Company should go into voluntary liquidation linked with the possible purchase by another company. This decision was in fact a formality in that negotiations were in progress with the International Navigation Company, owners of the American Line, Philadelphia, and the Red Star Line, Antwerp. Negotiations were concluded quickly and, after operating for 37 years on the North Atlantic, the Inman Line ceased to exist as an individual company. The fleet and few remaining assets were taken over by the newly-formed Inman and International Steamship Company (popularised as the 'I & I' line. Although controlled and financed by Americans, the Inman ships continued to fly the British flag and no change was made in management and services.

The new owners quickly showed that they were determined to restore the old company to the front rank of Blue Riband holders, and in 1887 placed orders with J. & G. Thomson, Clydebank, for two large and fast liners which would 'eclipse anything afloat'. It was not a bombastic promise, for in their design, construction, machinery installation and passenger accommodation, the two ships, *City of New York (III)* and *City of Paris (II)*, outclassed all North Atlantic liners then in service. Their main dimensions were: length overall 560 ft; length (between perps) 527.6 ft; breadth 63.2 ft; depth 39.2 ft; gross tonnage 10,499. Accommodation was provided for 540 first-class passengers, 200 second-class and 1,000 in the steerage class.

They were the first 'express' liners on North Atlantic service to be propelled by twin screws and the machinery installation comprised two sets of triple expansion engines of 18,500 indicated horsepower to give a designed speed of 20 knots. Close attention was given to safety precautions. Each ship had 15 watertight compartments separated by strong transverse bulkheads rising from the keel to the saloon deck, some 18 feet above the load water-line. Another innovation was the introduction of 'water chambers' which, it was hoped, would lessen rolling in a heavy seaway.

Modelled on similar lines to the *City of Rome,* the two ships provided a superb example of the skill and craftsmanship of Clydeside shipbuilding. With their clipper stems and short bowsprits, their figureheads, the long sweeping lines of their black hulls, three raking funnels, three pole masts and ornate rounded sterns, they presented an unforgettable sight as they went about their seagoing business. Watchers on the Liverpool and New York waterfronts were lost in admiration.

Nor did the beauty of these first two 'I & I' liners stop short at their exterior appearance. It was well matched in the comfort and facilities provided for passengers. The lavish richness of the first-class accommodation exemplified the insistence of the owners that cost should be the last consideration in the fitting-out of the ships.

A contemporary account of the luxury which awaited the first-class passenger embarking in either of the ships presents a fascinating picture of 'high society' on the Atlantic Ferry in the late 1880s. It read: 'The accommodation throughout is superb. The staterooms are large, lofty and well ventilated by fans and patent ventilators, which always admit fresh air, but exclude the sea. There are single and double beds which can be closed by day, as in a Pullman car, converting your room into a cosy little sitting room. Instead of the rattling, noisy jugs, you turn a tap and get a supply of hot or cold water; you touch a button and your steward instantly appears without a word being spoken. Neat wardrobes enable you to banish your portmanteaux or trunks to the baggage room; you turn a switch and you get an electric light; and if you want a nap or wish to retire early, you can turn it off in a moment.

'If you have plenty of spare cash and are willing to part with some of it, there are 40 rooms on the saloon decks, arranged in 14 suites. Each suite comprises a bedroom with a brass bedstead, wardrobe too; a sitting room with sofa, easy chair and a table, a private lavatory and in most cases a private bath. Here you can entertain your friends or enjoy a game in privacy. You can have the luxury of a morning bath and a promenade some 400 feet long.

'To diminish sea-sickness, you dine in a saloon near the middle of the ship beautifully decorated with naiads, dolphins, tritons and mermaids, lofty and bright. The arched roof is of glass 53 ft by 25 ft, and its height from the floor of the saloon to its crown is 20 ft. Besides the long tables in the centre there are a number of small ones placed in alcoves on both sides for the use of families or parties of friends; revolving armchairs replace the benches, and electric lights the candlesticks with their lashings. If you enjoy a cigar or a pipe a luxurious smoking room, 45 ft long, is provided; its walls and ceiling are panelled in black walnut and its couches and chairs are covered with scarlet leather. There is an elegant "drawing room" beautifully furnished and elegantly decorated. The library with its 900 volumes is lined with oak wainscotting, with the names of distinguished authors carved in it in scrolls, and its stained glass windows inscribed with quotations from poems referring to the sea.

'Provision is made for Divine Service on the Sabbath Day; at each end of the saloon is an oriel window built under the glass dome in the dining saloon. The casement of one of these serves for a pulpit. The opposite one contains an organ. Many famous organists and vocalists have taken part in the services as well as in musical entertainments given on week days for charitable objects. In truth the ships are fitted with an unequalled luxury and magnificence and are said to have each cost two million dollars.

'The second class passengers are placed in the after part of the ship where they have a dining room, smoking room, piano, etc. The steerage passengers are also well provided for, having no less than 300,000 cubic feet of space' – a curt dismissal which, if he had been alive, would have grieved William Inman, who had established the company in 1850 with the express object of looking after the needs and comfort of emigrants travelling steerage class.

First to be commissioned was the *City of New York (III)* which, launched on March 15 1888, began her maiden voyage from Liverpool to New York on August 1 of that year. She was followed by the *City of Paris (II)* on April 3 1889. They immediately attracted a big following, particularly among Americans visiting Europe, which was considerably helped by the opening in 1889 of the great Paris Exhibition. At the outset Blue Riband records eluded them but, during 1889, both liners reduced the Atlantic passage to under six days – the first ships ever to do so.

The Guion Line, established in 1866, entered the Blue Riband arena in 1879 with the *Arizona*, an iron-built single-screw ship fitted with compound engines. The *Arizona* made North Atlantic history in November 1879 when she crashed head-on into an iceberg and lived to tell the tale. (*City of Liverpool Museum*)

Companion ship to the *Arizona*, the Guion liner *Alaska* was commissioned in 1881. She was the first Blue Riband ship to reduce the passage from New York to Queenstown to less than seven days.

The lovely *America* owned by the National Line of Liverpool. Built of steel, the *America* joined the company of Blue Riband holders on her maiden voyage in 1884. She proved uneconomic to operate and was sold in 1887 to the Italian government.

Ordered by the Guion Line to operate with the *Arizona* and *Alaska*, the *Oregon*, when commissioned in 1883, was the largest merchant ship afloat. Although she proved a record-breaker, the Guion Line was in financial trouble and returned her to her builders. They sold her to the Cunard Line who operated her without change of name.

On both sides of the Atlantic the excitement which had attended the entry of the two ships into service had scarcely died away when it was reawakened by the commissioning of the White Star sister ships *Teutonic* and *Majestic*. Built by Harland and Wolff, Belfast, this famous White Star 'pair' have many claims to an honoured place in the book of Atlantic records. The last ships to be ordered by the White Star Line with the expressed objective of capturing the Blue Riband of the Atlantic, they were the first White Star liners to be propelled by twin screws and the first White Star liners specifically built to meet Admiralty requirements for rapid conversion into armed merchant cruisers in the event of war. Under the arrangement the owners received an annual subvention of 15/- per gross ton.

Construction of the ships began early in 1887. Their principal dimensions were: length 565.8 ft; breadth 57.8 ft; depth to main decks 39.4 ft; gross tonnage, *Teutonic* 9,984; *Majestic* 9,965. Machinery installation comprised three-cylinder triple expansion engines with an indicated horsepower of 17,000; designed speed was 20 knots. When first commissioned they had accommodation for 300 first-class passengers, 175 second-class and 850 steerage. There was also hold space for 4,000 tons of cargo.

By now the transatlantic travelling public was beginning to look for splendour of accommodation as well as speed in the liners of their choice and in this respect the *Teutonic* and *Majestic* were no disappointment. Indeed, the owners went one better than the I & I line by introducing 'period' styles in the main public rooms. Thus, in the *Teutonic,* the first-class dining saloon (described by one enthusiastic journalist as a 'banqueting hall') was decorated in the Renaissance style – 'Bas-relief figures of tritons and nymphs in gold and ivory gambol around and the ceiling is decorated in a corresponding style. A feature of the embossed leather walls of the smoking room were the inset panels which were oil paintings depicting ships representative of the Middle Ages.'

In their outward appearance the two liners broke away slightly from White Star tradition. They retained the straight stem and counter stern characteristic of the fleet, but the four masts, fitted to carry sail, were replaced by three tall pole masts while the two funnels, larger than usual, were widely spaced. The *Teutonic* and *Majestic* may not have been as elegant as the *City of New York (III)* and the *City of Paris (II)*, but for all that they were impressive examples of the shipbuilder's art.

The *Teutonic* was the first to be completed. She was launched on January 19 1889 and handed over to the White Star Line on July 25 of that year, when she proceeded to Liverpool. One week later on August 1 she left for Spithead, under the command of Captain Henry Parsell, to take an honoured place at the Naval Review as an armed merchant cruiser. In this capacity she was inspected by the Prince of Wales (later King Edward VII) and the German Emperor (Kaiser Wilhelm II) who evinced a close interest in the ship and expressed approval of all he had seen.

Returning to the Mersey, the *Teutonic* began her Atlantic service on August 7 when she sailed for New York. Her sister ship the *Majestic*, which had been launched on June 29 1889, joined her in this service on April 2 1890.

So far as the general public was concerned, the stage was now set for one of the greatest Atlantic Blue Riband contests of all time - a challenge the more exciting in American eyes because, although the *City of New York (III)* and *City of Paris (II)* were registered under the British flag, they were virtually American in ownership.

At that time the two I & I liners held the record. The two White Star 'giants' had yet to prove themselves, and there was always the chance that the previous record holders *Umbria* and *Etruria*, whose voyage performances were steadily improving, might come in from the 'outside' and recapture the Blue Riband. Not since the 1850s when the Cunard and Collins Lines had fought for supremacy had there been such interest and excitement kept alight by predictions in the world's press as to the possible result - predictions deprecated by the shipowners involved.

During a speech at a banquet held on board the *Etruria*, lying to anchor in the Mersey, on July 4 1890 to commemorate the 50th anniversary of the founding of the Cunard Company, Mr David Jardine, the Cunard chairman, criticised what he called 'rubbishy' articles in the papers about ocean racing . . . 'I do not believe,' he said, 'that either on our Cunard steamers or on those of any other Line which sail from Liverpool there is such a thing as racing . . . So far as Cunard commanders and engineers are concerned they are instructed that so far as racing is concerned they are not to recognise the fact that there are any other steamers on the Atlantic. I believe it is the same in other companies, for the responsibility is too great to allow any racing to be run.'

Mr Jardine's condemnation made little difference. One month later, on August 7, the *City of New York (III)*, commanded by Captain Watkins, and the *Teutonic* by Captain Irving, sailed from Liverpool for New York within one hour of each other, and all Britain and the United States awaited the outcome. Both liners arrived at Queenstown simultaneously to embark additional passengers and mails. The *City of New York (III)* cleared the Irish port some 35 minutes ahead of the *Teutonic*. It was a useful lead in time, but in this event it availed the ship little. At dawn the next day the two liners were still in sight of each other, but gradually the White Star challenger forged ahead, finally arriving at New York (Sandy Hook) at 4.20 am on August 13 to claim the record. A disconsolate *City of New York (III)* arrived four hours later.

This was the measure of the keen rivalry between the four ships which, over the next two years, were to share the Blue Riband honours. Memorable passages were:

Liverpool (Queenstown) to New York (Sandy Hook)

Year	Ship	Time of passage D	h	m	Average speed (knots)
1889	*City of New York (III)*	5	23	07	19.9
1889	*City of Paris (II)*	5	22	50	—
1889	*Teutonic*	5	21	20	—
1889	*City of Paris (II)*	5	19	18	20.0
1891	*Teutonic*	5	19	05	—
1891	*Majestic*	5	18	08	20.11
1891	*Teutonic*	5	16	31	20.35
1892	*City of Paris (II)*	5	14	24	20.7

New York (Sandy Hook) to Liverpool (Queenstown)

Year	Ship	Time of passage			Average speed
		D	h	m	(knots)
1889	*City of Paris (II)*	6	0	29	—
1889	*City of Paris (II)*	5	22	50	19.5
1891	*Teutonic*	5	21	03	19.8
1892	*City of New York (III)*	5	19	57	20.1

Competition on the Liverpool-New York run between the four liners came to an end in 1892 with the transfer of the *City of New York (III)* to American registry – a development for which American citizens, proud of the two liners, had been agitating for some considerable time. On May 10 1892 Congress passed a special Act authorising the transfer of the ships from British registry. In turn the British Government agreed to release the two ships from their obligation to serve as armed merchant cruisers in time of war.

Then, in October, the United States postal authorities concluded an agreement with the I & I company to carry American mails for which they were to receive an annual subsidy of £15,000. It was also arranged that, to expedite the mail service, the *City of New York (III)* and *City of Paris (II)* should be transferred from Liverpool and placed on the South-ampton-New York route – a sad blow to Merseyside prestige.

On February 23 1893 at a ceremony on board the *City of New York (III)*, attended by the President of the United States and members of his Cabinet, the two ships were formally transferred. After the British flag had been lowered, the United States flag was broken at the mainmast to a full salute from the guns at the nearby naval yard at Brooklyn. The prefix 'City of' was discarded and the ships were renamed *New York* and *Paris*. At the same time the opportunity was taken to change the title Inman and International to International Navigation Company, later to be known as the American Line, from which the present Blue Riband holder, the liner *United States,* can trace a direct descent. On February 8 1893 the *City of New York (III)* began her last voyage from Liverpool, followed by the *City of Paris (II)* on February 22. The *New York* made her first sailing from Southampton under the American Line houseflag on March 11 1893; the *Paris* on March 25.

The genuine sorrow on Merseyside over the death of the Inman Line – for 43 years an honoured name on the Atlantic Ferry – was tempered a little by interest in the imminent arrival in the port of the first of two new Cunarders, the order for which had been placed in August 1891 with the Fairfield Shipbuilding and Engineering Company, Glasgow, and which were to be named *Campania* and *Lucania*. In a reference to the two ships at the Cunard annual meeting on March 30 1892, Sir John Burns, the chairman, had said he thought shareholders would have 'no cause to com-plain of the new liners' magnificent equipment, great strength and speed'. He earnestly trusted 'that their financial results both individually and collaterally would not disappoint expectations'.

The largest and fastest merchant ships in the world, their construction excited world-wide interest, so much so that at one period complaints were made by journalists that neither the owners nor the builders were as forthcoming with information about the ships as they might have been.

The first Cunard twin-screw steamers, they had a straight stem, elliptical stern, two pole masts and two great funnels, some 130 feet in height from the keel and with an external diameter of 21 feet. Main dimensions of the ships were: length overall 620 ft (600 ft between perpendiculars); breadth 65 ft 3 ins; depth from upper deck 43 ft; gross tonnage 12,950 tons. The machinery consisted of two sets of triple-expansion engines, each in separate rooms, placed on either side of a dividing centre-line bulkhead fitted with watertight doors for communication. Steam at 165 lb/sq in pressure was supplied by 12 main double-ended boilers. Indicated horsepower was 30,000 and average speed 22.01 knots. There was bunker space for 3,200 tons of coal, 2,900 tons being consumed on the passage.

When commissioned the two ships had accommodation for 1,700 passengers – 600 first-class, 400 second- and 700 steerage. Crew complement totalled 416, made up of 61 deck department, 195 engine room and 160 catering personnel.

Claims that they were the 'most magnificently appointed passenger liners in the world' were well justified. First-class accommodation was particularly sumptuous; it included 'single' staterooms, a dining saloon 100 feet in length and 64 feet wide, situated amidships, drawing room and smoking rooms complete with 'real fireplaces', library and a magnificent grand staircase. Another feature was the 'period' style furnishing and decor in the public rooms – 'Elizabethan', 'Italian Renaissance', and so on. As one journalist describing the *Lucania* put it – 'the wandering millionaire had his little wants provided for at a price which, though it may make ordinary folks stare, is not at all unreasonable for what he gets'. It is perhaps not surprising that Cunard had to foot a bill for £650,000 for each ship.

Construction of the ships had begun in September 1891 and the *Campania* was the first to be completed. Launched on September 8 1892, she ran her trials on March 17 1893, achieving an average speed of 23.25 knots. Her maiden voyage from Liverpool to New York via Queenstown began on April 22. She left Queenstown at 13.25 hours on April 23 and passed the Sandy Hook Lightship (New York) at 17.24 hours on April 29, covering a distance of 2,899 miles in five days 17 hours 27 minutes. Liverpool-bound passengers disembarked six days after leaving New York – yet another record.

All that remained was to see what the *Lucania* would do. Her construction had been delayed by a dispute by the ironworkers who had claimed special rates because of the 'heavy nature of their jobs'. The steel plates ordered for both ships were thicker and heavier than usual, which made riveting the more arduous. At one period 20 squads of men had stopped work.

The *Lucania* was eventually launched on February 2 1893. Her completion was held up while alterations were carried out in the stern section to minimise the possibility of vibration which had proved troublesome in the *Campania*. The *Lucania* finally left the Clyde for Liverpool on July 31 1894. On arrival in the Mersey she was drydocked at Laird's, Birkenhead, for hull cleaning preparatory to full speed trials. It was discovered that in her passage down the Clyde she had indented some hull plates which had to be taken off and re-shaped. To enable the ship to keep to her advertised sailing schedule, further trials were dispensed with. She left Liverpool for New York on the evening of September 2 and, after calling at Queenstown, passed Daunt's Rock at 13.43 hours. Five days 15 hours and 37 minutes later she triumphantly passed Sandy Hook Light (New York), beating the *Campania's* record.

From the time of their commissioning, the *Campania* and *Lucania* proved faster than the *New York, Paris, Teutonic* and *Majestic,* and thus established their claim as the fastest ships on the Atlantic run. Between them they held all records for a matter of four years with average speeds of over 21 knots and, in the case of the *Lucania,* with one passage from New York at an average speed of 22 knots. Many experts believed, in fact, that the ultimate in speed at sea, consistent with safety and economy in operation, had been reached.

No British companies appeared eager to challenge the Cunard record holders, and the last place from which people expected it to materialise was the Continent. There was, therefore, considerable astonishment, not unmixed with mortification, when it was learned that the two German North Atlantic liner companies, assisted financially by their Government, were planning to build liners large enough and powerful enough to challenge all comers.

The Battle for Supremacy

Record voyages – Atlantic liners
Liverpool to New York

Year	Month	Ship	Gross tons	Owners	Passage D h m	Distance (naut miles)	Av speed (knots)
1856	June	*Persia*	3,300	Cunard	9.21.41	3,070	12.0
1862	June	*Scotia*	3,871	„	8. 4.34	2,851	14.54
1867	Nov	*City of Paris*	2,651	Inman	8. 4. 1	2,700	13.77
1872	May	*Adriatic*	3,888	White Star	7.23.17	2,788	14.41
1875	Sept	*City of Berlin*	5,491	Inman	7.18. 2	2,829	15.21
1876	Nov	*Britannic*	5,004	White Star	7.13.11	2,820	15.44
1879	July	*Arizona*	5,147	Guion	7.10.22	2,800	15.73
1882	April	*Alaska*	6,400	„	7. 6.43	2,803	16.1
1884	Aug	*Oregon*	7,017	Cunard	6. 9.42	2,792	18.14
1885	May	*Etruria*	8,120	„	6. 5.31	2,821	18.93
1887	March	*Umbria*	8,120	„	6. 4.34	2,890	18.91
1888	May	*Etruria*	8,120	„	6. 2.27	2,872	19.65
1889	Sept	*City of Paris (II)*	10,500	Inman & International	5.19.18	2,788	20.0
1891	Aug	*Teutonic*	9,860	White Star	5.16.31	2,778	20.43
1892	Oct	*City of Paris (II)*	10,500	Inman & International	5.14.24	2,782	20.76
1893	June	*Campania*	12,950	Cunard	5.15.29	2,873	21.21
1894	May	*Lucania*	12,950	„	5.12.57	2,873	21.75
1894	Oct	*Lucania*	12,950	„	5. 7.23	2,779	21.81

New York to Liverpool

Year	Month	Ship	Gross tons	Owners	Passage D h m	Distance (naut miles)	Av speed (knots)
1856	June	*Persia*	3,300	Cunard	9. 1.45	2,732	12.53
1862	June	*Scotia*	3,871	,,	8.22. 0	2,700	14.06
1863	Dec	*Scotia*	3,871	,,	8. 3. 0	2,731	14.0
1867	Nov	*Russia*	2,960	,,	8. 0.28	2,731	14.22
1869	Dec	*City of Brussels*	3,081	Inman	7.22. 3	2,786	14.66
1873	Jan	*Baltic (I)*	3,707	White Star	7.20. 9	2,843	15.12
1875	Oct	*City of Berlin*	5,491	Inman	7.15.28	2,820	15.41
1876	Feb	*Germanic*	5,008	White Star	7.15.17	2,894	15.81
1879	July	*Arizona*	5,147	Guion	7. 8.11	2,810	15.96
1882	June	*Alaska*	6,400	,,	6.22. 0	2,791	16.8
1882	Sept	*Alaska*	6,400	,,	6.18.38	2,800	17.17
1884	June	*America*	5,528	National	6.14. 8	2,815	17.05
1884	Aug	*Oregon*	7,017	Cunard	6.11. 9	2,853	18.52
1887	March	*Etruria*	8,120	,,	6. 4.36	2,890	19.9
1889	Aug	*City of Paris (II)*	10,500	Inman & International	5.23.38	2,792	19.52
1889	Dec	*City of Paris (II)*	10,500	,,	5.22.50	2,784	19.47
1891	Oct	*Teutonic*	9,860	White Star	5.21. 3	2,790	19.79
1892	Aug	*City of New York (II)*	10,500	Inman & International	5.19.67	2,864	20.1
1893	Oct	*Campania*	12,950	Cunard	5.12.51	2,821	21.33
1894	June	*Campania*	12,950	,,	5.12.32	2,908	21.94
1894	Sept	*Lucania*	12,950	,,	5. 8.38	2,810	21.84
1894	Oct	*Lucania*	12,950	,,	5. 8.38	2,836	22.0

Seven

1897—1907

The German
break-through

SEPTEMBER 1897 was to prove one of the most dramatic and memorable months in the growing competition for the North Atlantic passenger liner trade. It was a month of challenge and of triumph; of challenge to the Cunarders *Campania* and *Lucania* which, since their commissioning in 1893, had shared the honours of being the fastest liners on the Western Ocean route; of triumph for the Norddeutscher Lloyd's new liner *Kaiser Wilhelm der Grosse*, the first German liner specifically designed and built in a German shipyard to win the coveted Blue Riband of the Atlantic.

Excluding the six years between 1850 and 1856 when the American-built Collins Line steamers had carried all before them, British shipping companies and British shipbuilders had dominated the western ocean. For 40 years all the Blue Riband holders had been built in British yards—for the most part on the Clyde; in shipbuilding and marine engineering Britain led the world. It was to this country that other industrial nations, in particular Germany, sent their young ship designers and marine engineers to work with British craftsmen, study their methods and 'know-how' and to apply these skills when they returned to their own countries.

The Germans had proved apt pupils, in particular Robert Zimmerman who had spent 11 profitable years at shipyards at Greenock, Jarrow and Barrow-in-Furness. At Barrow he had been assistant to William John, the designer of the Inman liner *City of Rome,* by common consent one of the most beautiful ships ever commissioned. The fact that in the matter of speed she did not meet Inman Line specifications and was returned to the builders, may well have been a useful lesson to Zimmerman when, as naval architect with the Vulcan Shipyard at Stettin, he was responsible for the design and construction of the *Kaiser Wilhelm der Grosse*.

Like the Hamburg Amerika Line, with whom they worked in close association, the Norddeutscher Lloyd were no strangers to the North Atlantic business. They had been operating steamship services between Bremen and New York since 1857—the call at Southampton was inaugurated on March 22 1859. For 20 years the company had concentrated on the emigrant trade from Germany and Central Europe, carried in ships of medium size and speed—all built in Britain. There was a change of policy in 1877 when Herr H. H. Meier, founder of the company and a shrewd shipowner, appointed Herr J. G. Lohmann managing director of the company, an appointment in which luck had played no small part in that Lohmann's two predecessors had died in quick succession.

However, there is little doubt that Lohmann was the man needed to direct the company's business. Young and enthusiastic, he had kept a close watch on the performances of the Cunard, Guion, Inman and White Star 'express' ships, in particular the prestige gained by the company which held the Blue Riband. The enormous success of the Guion liner *Arizona*, when commissioned in 1879, finally convinced him that the future of successful passenger and mail services on the North Atlantic lay in providing passengers with greater speed and safety 'combined with special elegance and comfort during the voyage'.

The first move came in 1880 when the board decided to place contracts for a fleet of 12 ships which, if not potential record breakers, would be highly competitive with the fleets of rival companies. They would maintain services between Bremen, Southampton and New York, popularly known as the 'Channel route', and it was hoped that they would break the stranglehold of the Liverpool-based companies.

It had been the original intention of Lohmann and his fellow directors to place the orders with German shipbuilders, but they were overruled by their president, Herr Meier, who insisted that any contracts should be given to 'a British yard where they had experience of building such ships'. The board bowed to his ruling—indeed they had little option. The contract for the first ship, to be named *Elbe*, was given to John Elder & Company, Fairfield, Glasgow, where reigned that genius of ship designers William Pearce, whose latest product, the *Arizona*, had so captivated Lohmann.

The *Elbe*, a single-screw steamer of 4,897 gross tons with a designed speed of 17.5 knots was completed in 1881, and on June 24 of that year began her maiden voyage from Bremen to Southampton and New York. It was later stated that the profits made on her first five voyages covered nearly 20 per cent of her first cost—Meier's acumen had been well justified.

In the circumstances it was not surprising that the company should have gone to the Fairfield yard for their next ten ships, all bearing the names of German rivers and all improvements on the *Elbe*. Meanwhile there had been considerable technical progress in German shipbuilding, so much so that the Hamburg Amerika Line, which had also initiated a new passenger liner programme, had not hesitated to place certain orders in Germany. These had included the *Augusta Victoria* (7,661 gross tons) and the *Fürst Bismarck* (8,430 gross tons), both built at the Vulcan Yard, Stettin, and both popular on the Hamburg-Southampton-New York run.

Reassured by this practical evidence, Herr Lohmann and his fellow directors of the Norddeutscher Lloyd at long last realised their cherished ambition of seeing their ships built in the Fatherland. As a beginning the Vulcan Yard, Stettin, were given contracts to build three liners for the company's 'express' transatlantic service—the *Kaiser Wilhelm II* (6,990 gross tons) ordered in 1889, and the *Spree* and *Havel* (6,950 gross tons each) in 1890. The last two ships with a designed speed of 19 knots as against the 16 knots of the *Kaiser Wilhelm II* were an immediate success.

By this time the two German lines were dominating the Western Ocean passenger trade. This was proved in the official returns for transatlantic passenger traffic landed at New York between the years 1881 and 1891. These showed that the Norddeutscher Lloyd Company had led the way with 738,668 pasengers, followed by the Hamburg Amerika Line with 525,900. The White Star Line came third with 371,193, followed in turn by Cunard (323,900), Inman (322,930) and Guion (273,836). Here was statistical proof that, when it came to passenger carrying, the Liverpool-based liners were dropping well astern of the ships maintaining the Channel route services. A greater challenge was to come.

By 1895 the overall age of the Norddeutscher Line fleet had reached the point where it would be necessary to replace some of the older units if the company was to remain competitive. With that characteristic boldness which had always marked his direction of the company, Herr Lohmann decided to commission two ships which, when completed, would be the largest, fastest and most luxurious in the world. By so doing the company would gain for themselves the lucrative cream of the traffic and win for themselves, and for Germany, the coveted Blue Riband of the Atlantic—then held by the Cunarders *Campania* and *Lucania*. It was an ambitious and imaginative concept, the more so as the Norddeutscher Lloyd Company was in no financial position to risk failure.

After long consideration the directors agreed to put the plan into operation. Perhaps with memories of the failure of the *City of Rome* to meet the required designed speed, the Company's request for tenders for the two ships included a most unusual proviso. This was to the effect that the potential owners would not accept either ship after the normal short sea trials but only when the ships had shown their paces by making one round Atlantic voyage. If the vessels failed to maintain their guaranteed speed the company had the right to reject them.

It was asking a lot of the builders, but two shipyards, possibly inspired by national pride, took up what was virtually a challenge to their expertise. They were the Vulcan, Stettin, and the Schichau Shipyard, Danzig. The Vulcan yard received an order to build a liner to be named *Kaiser Wilhelm der Grosse*; the Schichau yard got the contract for the *Kaiser Friedrich*.

Curiously enough, although intended to operate together in service, the two ships were not 'sister' ships nor did they resemble each other externally in any way. As an instance, the *Kaiser Wilhelm der Grosse* was to be given four funnels; the *Kaiser Friedrich* three. Other differences were:

Kaiser Wilhelm der Grosse		*Kaiser Friedrich*
Gross tonnage	14,349	12,481
Length	627.0 ft	581.7 ft
Beam	66.0 ft	63.9 ft
Depth of hold	35.8 ft	44.0 ft

First to be completed was the *Kaiser Wilhelm der Grosse*. Her launching on May 3 1897 was a great national occasion attended by the German Emperor. From the outset the Kaiser had taken a personal interest in the planning and building of the two great ships, not least in their potential use as auxiliary naval cruisers. For this purpose their upper decks were specially strengthened to carry guns.

Working at full pressure the builders completed the ship in the remarkably short period of just under four months and on August 29 1897 the *Kaiser Wilhelm der Grosse* sailed from her birthplace. Her maiden voyage was scheduled for September 15, which gave ample time for trials during the 600 miles voyage from her shipyard to Bremerhaven; but fate decided otherwise. Early on in her voyage the ship ran aground in the Kaiserfahrl and was not refloated until September 7. As a result, her sailing schedule was upset and, to their chagrin, the owners had to postpone the date of the maiden voyage from Bremerhaven until September 19.

This time all went well. The *Kaiser Wilhelm der Grosse* duly left Bremerhaven on September 19, arriving at Southampton the following afternoon to a rapturous reception. Reporting on the day's events, a correspondent of the *Marine Engineer* wrote: 'On September 20 I had the opportunity of going down from London by the passengers' special train to have a look at her. The start was an early one and the train was heavy, for a large number of London passengers were booked by her. We reached Southampton soon after 11 a.m. Here we were greeted by the news that the liner had passed the Weser Lightship at 7.10 the previous evening. This looked like a very long spell of aimless wandering round the town and docks. But a little later came the news that she had passed Dover at 9 a.m. This set people to work at various calculations with pencil and paper and it soon appeared that she was showing her paces to some purpose.

'It was next announced that the tender would go out to her at 2.30 p.m. This arrangement was adhered to and I may remark that the big ship was said to have passed Ryde at 2.20 p.m. thus having made the run from the Weser Light in 19 hours 10 minutes—distinctly a record. As the tender reached Netley the liner's four funnels appeared upon our starboard bow, and very soon the big ship dashed up, passed us and anchored off the hospital. We struggled alongside. An interminable time seemed to be consumed in making fast and getting the gangway rigged. Meanwhile there was a tremendous amount of cheering, band playing and waving of handkerchiefs.'

The watchers on the waterfront had good reason to wonder at their first glimpse of this great ship—the largest passenger liner in the world. They had never seen any ship like her. With her four buff funnels, arranged in pairs, her straight stem, long sleek hull, two pole masts and counter-type stern she looked every inch a challenger to the supremacy of the *Campania* and *Lucania*. Her accommodation, in particular for first-class passengers, set new standards in comfort and luxury—private suites, four private dining saloons opening out of the main saloon, writing and reading rooms and a special nursery for children.

The machinery installation comprised two sets of four-cylinder triple expansion engines aggregating 28,000 ihp. They were supplied by 12 double-ended boilers, coal consumption working out at 250 tons a day.

Designed speed was 22.5 knots. The great question was, would the liner's performance justify the proud hopes of her owners and the claims of her builders?

The maiden voyage was to prove that the *Kaiser Wilhelm der Grosse* was indeed a potential record breaker. Outward bound she made the voyage from Southampton (the Needles) to New York (Sandy Hook) in five days 22 hours 30 minutes at an average speed of 21.39 knots, the distance being 3,050 miles. The homeward run to Plymouth—a distance of 2,962 miles—she achieved in five days 15 hours 25 minutes at an average speed of 21.87 knots. These times set up new records for the Channel route. They had, however, been exceeded on the Liverpool-New York run by the *Campania* and *Lucania*; for example, in July 1897, after leaving Liverpool, the *Lucania* had completed the passage from Queenstown (Daunt's Rock) to New York (Sandy Hook) in five days ten hours 16 minutes at an average speed of 22.11 knots—a distance of 2,874 miles.

However, the German contender had shown that a great future lay ahead and it was not long before she left the world in no doubt of her capabilities and, equally important, her remarkable consistency. On her third homeward voyage in November 1897 she made the passage between New York (Sandy Hook) and Southampton (Needles) at an average speed of 22.35 knots, acquiring the double distinction of being the world's largest and fastest passenger liner. A contemporary account of this historic voyage records that the liner passed Sandy Hook at 4.47 pm on November 23, and passed the Needles at 3.10 pm on November 29. 'Her passage occupied five days 17 hours 28 minutes; she stayed 25 minutes alongside a burning ship, which makes her actual steaming time five days 17 hours 3 minutes.' Daily runs on this passage were:

Left New York November 23; run to noon November 24, 401 miles; to noon November 25, 520 miles; to noon November 26, 573 miles; to noon November 27, 528 miles; to noon November 28, 525 miles; to noon November 29, 507 and to 3.10 pm, 71 miles. Total 3,605 miles. Average speed 22.35 knots.

On May 5 1898 the London *Daily Chronicle* carried this news item: 'By running 580 knots on the last day of her westward Atlantic voyage the *Kaiser Wilhelm der Grosse* has won the blue ribbon of ocean steaming. As the westward day represents 25 hours, her average steaming per hour was a trifle over 23 knots.'

But her greatest distinction lay in the regularity of her performances. For five voyages in 1898 her average speed was greater than that on her maiden voyage the previous September. In 1899 her average speed on six successive passages to New York was 21.75 knots, and for six successive homeward passages 22.13 knots, to give a mean average of 21.94 knots. In November of that year (not the best of months for fast voyages) she crossed from Southampton (the Needles) to New York (Sandy Hook) in five days 17 hours 27 minutes at an average speed of just over 23 knots. This voyage incidentally included a call at Cherbourg, at that time not a regular occurrence in her schedule.

Commenting on these outstanding performances the London *Times* of August 24 1900 had this to say: 'When the *Kaiser Wilhelm der Grosse* made her first appearance it was hinted that she was being driven for all she was worth and that as a consequence she was being shaken to pieces and could not possibly keep up her rate of speed. Events have falsified this anticipation. She has throughout maintained the promise of her early voyages and has made uniformly rapid and safe passages.'

The supremacy of the *Kaiser Wilhelm der Grosse* had one immediate material effect on the fortunes of her owners. Within months, the Norddeutscher Lloyd Line became the most popular shipping company maintaining North Atlantic services. Prospective passengers clamoured to travel in the liner and, if no accommodation was available, were content to bask in the reflected glory of the great ship by voyaging in another ship flying the company's house-flag.

In 1897, when the *Kaiser Wilhelm der Grosse* made only four voyages, the company landed at New York 11,583 first- and second-class passengers and 24,562 steerage; the following year passengers landed comprised 17,895 first- and second-class and 58,223 steerage. The combined total of 71,118 represented nearly 24 per cent of all North Atlantic passengers disembarked at New York; for the first time the NDL first- and second-class totals exceeded those of the Cunard Line.

Competing companies on the North Atlantic had every reason for concern, especially as the Blue Riband holder's companion ship, the *Kaiser Friedrich*, was completing at Danzig. If she repeated the success of the *Kaiser Wilhelm der Grosse* the economic effect on rival companies could well prove disastrous. Fortunately for them—if not for her owners—the *Kaiser Friedrich*, launched from the Schichau yard on October 5 1897, failed as completely as the *Kaiser Wilhelm der Grosse* had succeeded. Externally the *Kaiser Friedrich* was a lovely ship; internally her passenger accommodation was spacious and luxurious. But when it came to record voyages her engines could not respond to the challenge.

On her maiden voyage which began from Bremen, via Southampton, on May 12 1898, she made the outward crossing in seven days 11 hours; homeward she took nine days two hours 30 minutes. Her second voyage showed a slight improvement—westward six days 12 hours; eastward six days 12 hours ten minutes. But that seemed to be the limit of the *Kaiser Friedrich's* capabilities. Figures for her third voyage showed an outward passage of six days 16 hours and homewards six days eight hours 55 minutes. Her fourth round voyage was worse as westbound to New York she took seven days to the minute; and eastbound she crossed in six days 21 hours 45 minutes.

It became obvious that the liner would never break any records nor indeed was she the right 'stable companion' for the speedy *Kaiser Wilhelm der Grosse*. The Norddeutscher Lloyd did not immediately reject her as she was a big ship, comfortable and popular with passengers. To withdraw her at the height of the season would have been foolish; in any case there was always the off-chance that she might improve on her speed. So she remained in service until June 1899, making in all nine round voyages before, under the terms of the building contract, she was returned by the owners to the Schichau yard, Danzig. From September 30 1899 until October 10 1900 she was chartered by the Hamburg Amerika Line, after which the Schichau yard laid her up at Hamburg. After a 12-year wait she was bought by the Cie-Sud-Atlantique and was renamed *Burdigala*.

The rejection of the *Kaiser Friedrich* meant that, while the company considered what they should do about a replacement, the *Kaiser Wilhelm der Grosse* had to 'go it alone'. Eventually an order was placed in 1901 with the Vulcan yard, Stettin, for a liner of 14,908 gross tons to be named *Kronprinz Wilhelm*. This decision was the more vital because by this time the supremacy of the *Kaiser Wilhelm der Grosse* had been threatened by the commissioning in the previous year of the Hamburg Amerika liner *Deutschland,* 16,703 tons. It was only natural that the continuing success of the *Kaiser Wilhelm der Grosse* should have been followed closely by other North Atlantic shipowners, in particular the chairman of the Hamburg Amerika Line, Albert Ballin. One of the most able shipping men of all time, Ballin soon realised that if his company was to compete successfully against the Norddeutscher Lloyd Line they would have to bring into service a liner which in size, luxury and speed would eclipse the existing Blue Riband holder.

There was one problem—finance. Large and fast ships cost a deal of money to build and to maintain and the economic effect on the company's resources had to be taken into account. Here, Ballin had a stroke of luck. The outbreak of the Spanish-American war in 1898 found the Spanish Navy seriously short of auxiliary cruisers and to make good this deficiency the Spanish Government purchased from the Hamburg Amerika Line two of their 'express' steamers for conversion into armed merchant cruisers. They were the *Columbia* of 7,363 gross tons, built by Laird's, Birkenhead, in 1889, and the *Normannia,* 8,242 gross tons, built in 1890 at the Fairfield yard on the Clyde. The withdrawal of these two ships upset the balance of the Hapag Services between Hamburg, Southampton and New York. On the other hand the purchase money enabled Ballin, who had made a round voyage in the *Kaiser Wilhelm der Grosse,* to go ahead with his plans. An order was placed with the Vulcan yard, Stettin, (builders of the NDL record-holder) for a ship 'which would outrival the *Kaiser Wilhelm der Grosse* and prove to be the finest liner in the world'.

This was no idle boast. Launched on January 10 1900 in the presence of the Kaiser, the *Deutschland,* as she was named, was indeed the largest and finest liner in the world. Like the *Kaiser Wilhelm der Grosse* she was fitted with four funnels arranged in pairs, but she was of 16,502 gross tons compared with the 14,349 gross tons of her rival. Other dimensions compared with those of the *Kaiser Wilhelm der Grosse* were:

	Deutschland	*Kaiser Wilhelm der Grosse*
Length	660 ft 9 ins	627 ft
Beam	67 ft 3 ins	66 ft
Depth to main deck	40 ft 3 ins	43 ft
Passenger accommodation—		
First-class	700	332
Second-class	300	343
Third-class	280	1,074

The *Deutschland's* machinery installation comprised two sets of six-cylinder quadruple expansion engines, the contract horsepower being 33,000 and the designed speed 23.6 knots. Steam was supplied to the engines by 12 double-ended and four single-ended boilers.

She was a much larger ship than the *Kaiser Wilhelm der Grosse* not only in gross tonnage but in length also. It was noticeable, too, that Ballin's objective was to attract first-class passengers and her accommodation was planned accordingly; Lohmann of the Norddeutscher Line had relied most on carrying more emigrants in the third or steerage class. In emphasising first-class 'luxury' rather than third-class comfort, the *Deutschland* was in effect the fore-runner of the great liners which in later years were to transform the Atlantic Ferry into the 'floating hotel' route.

Completed in the remarkably short time of five months, the *Deutschland* steamed proudly from the Stettin shipyard in June 1900. But like the *Kaiser Wilhelm der Grosse* she ran into trouble; despite the fact that there were seven tugs in attendance, she ran aground on the Nodder Bank. The salvage ship *Seeadler* and two naval vessels were rushed to assist her but it took a fortnight before they and the seven tugs managed to refloat her. Inspection of the hull showed no serious damage and the liner was able to keep to her scheduled maiden voyage date—July 4 1900. (By a curious coincidence this marked the 60th anniversary of the day when the first Cunarder *Britannia* had sailed from Liverpool to pioneer regular transatlantic passenger and mail services.)

After leaving Hamburg the *Deutschland* called at Plymouth on July 6 to embark more passengers. She then proceeded on her voyage to New York which she completed in five days 15 hours 46 minutes (Eddystone Light to Sandy Hook) at an average speed of 22.42 knots, the distance being 3,044 miles. Her homeward voyage was on a slightly longer course of 3,085 miles. Leaving her berth at Hoboken Pier, New York, at 9.30 am on July 18, she passed Sandy Hook at 11.35 am and was off the Eddystone Light, Plymouth, at 7.40 am on July 24. The passage had been achieved in five days 14 hours six minutes at an average speed of 23 knots. The *Deutschland* dropped anchor in Plymouth Sound at 8.30 am to land about 100 passengers and mails by tender. She then proceeded to Cherbourg where more passengers disembarked, and finally made her home port Hamburg where a rapturous welcome awaited the new Blue Riband holder.

It was in September 1900 that the *Deutschland* conclusively proved that, when it came to speed, she had the edge on the *Kaiser Wilhelm der Grosse*. Despite the vague denials by the respective owners it was the month of the great 'race' between the two fastest merchant ships in the world. Commanded by Captain Albers, the *Deutschland* left New York for Plymouth at 1.15 pm (American time) on Tuesday September 4. She arrived off the Lizard at 12.35 am (GMT) on September 10. The *Kaiser Wilhelm der Grosse,* commanded by Captain Engelhart, which had cleared New York some 90 minutes before her rival, was sighted off the Lizard at 4.45 am on September 10. 'The *Deutschland's* net gain on the *Kaiser* (Wilhelm) between New York and the Lizard was thus five hours and 50 minutes and this must be taken as the measure of her superiority in speed' was the comment of a contemporary newspaper.

But the master of the *Deutschland* was not content to leave the outcome of the 'race' at that. His voyage schedule included a call at Plymouth before going on to Cherbourg; the *Kaiser Wilhelm der Grosse* was proceeding direct to the French port. Keeping to his schedule, Captain Albers put into Plymouth to land his passengers and mails, then speeded across the Channel to Cherbourg where he arrived at 8.30 am, landed more passengers and mails, and was on his way to Hamburg three hours before the *Kaiser Wilhelm der Grosse* arrived at Cherbourg. The official times for the respective voyages were given as:

Deutschland—New York (Sandy Hook) to Plymouth (Eddystone Light) five days seven hours 38 mins. Average speed 23.38 knots. Distance 3,027 miles.

Kaiser Wilhelm der Grosse—New York (Sandy Hook) to Cherbourg five days 17 hours 27 mins. Average speed 22.4 knots. Distance 3,076 miles.

Deutschland's net gain Sandy Hook to Lizard—five hours 50 mins.

'The story of the race is the most exciting since 1894 when the *Majestic* raced the *Paris* and beat her,' reported the fledgling *Daily Mail*, London, 'Everyone knew that Captain Albers of the *Deutschland* and Captain Engelhart of the *Kaiser Wilhelm der Grosse* were bent on showing the best their ships could do, although both commanders denied that there was to be a set race. Both vessels for the first time this season took the winter course which is more northerly and about 90 miles shorter than the summer course. The '*Kaiser's*' hour and a half start served her well for the *Deutschland* on leaving New York had to make a big curve to counter-act currents and when she got out to sea the '*Kaiser*' had disappeared ahead. All night the *Deutschland* tore through the water at full speed making over 23 knots, and at five o'clock next morning the '*Kaiser*' was sighted.

'There was a stampede for the decks and hour by hour the excited passengers and crew kept their eyes on the chase. The *Deutschland* slowly but surely overtook her rival. In the early hours breakfast was neglected. As mid-day drew near and the '*Kaiser*' was more closely approached all thought of dinner was abandoned.

'At 11.30 a.m., cheers rang over the water for the *Deutschland* yard by yard had lessened the distance and drawn level with the galloping Nord-deutscher. Four miles apart, nose level with nose, the great liners struggled for the lead. It was the *Deutschland's* day. In one hour's time she was well ahead. By nightfall the '*Kaiser*' was out of sight behind and she never saw the *Deutschland* again.'

The daily runs (noon to noon) of the liners were given as follows:

	Deutschland	*Kaiser Wilhelm der Grosse*
First day	507 miles	498 miles
Second day	535 miles	514 miles
Third day	540 miles	519 miles
Fourth day	540 miles	520 miles
Fifth day	545 miles	520 miles
Last day	360 miles	505 miles
Average speed	23.38 knots	22.4 knots

Talking to newspaper correspondents after the arrival of the *Deutschland* at Plymouth, Captain Albers said the vessel 'had some speed in reserve'. One of the passengers, a Mr F. Higbee of the Red Cross Society, said that the stokers worked bare to the waist, were constantly sprayed with cold water and that it had been necessary to play the hose on the machinery almost constantly.

How much truth there was in this allegation is difficult to assess, but one incontrovertible fact was beginning to emerge. When driven at speed the *Deutschland* shook from stem to stern and was a most uncomfortable sea boat. Her tendency to vibrate had become evident during her trials in June 1900 and extensive experiments had been carried out to eradicate the trouble. These experiments formed the subject of a long technical paper read by Herr Otto Schlick at the spring meetings of the Institute of Naval Architects held in London on March 28 1901. It may have delighted the experts, but it brought no solace to the *Deutschland's* passengers.

Throughout 1901 the great ship continued to show her paces. In July of that year, taking the longer winter route, she crossed from New York (Sandy Hook) to Plymouth (Eddystone Light) in five days 11 hours five minutes at an average speed of 23.51 knots—an undoubted record. Again in 1903 she made the passage from Cherbourg to New York (Sandy Hook) in five days 11 hours 54 minutes at an average speed of 23.15 knots, but she was not a consistent performer like the *Kaiser Wilhelm der Grosse*; vibration problems persisted. On several occasions there were machinery breakdowns and although, in 1908, her boilers were renewed there was little improvement. Above all she was a lone member of the company's fleet, no other unit approached her in size and speed.

So in 1910, Ballin, possibly influenced by the outstanding successes of the Cunarders *Lusitania* and *Mauretania*, withdrew her from transatlantic service. The first and last Hamburg Amerika Blue Riband holder was returned to the Vulcan yard at Stettin. Here she was extensively overhauled and converted into a cruising liner with accommodation for 500 one-class passengers. Her 12-cylinder quadruple expansion engines which had proved so troublesome were replaced by eight-cylinder engines to give a comfortable designed speed of 18 knots. Shorn of two funnels and renamed *Victoria Luise*, she was engaged in cruises to Mediterranean ports, the West Indies and Norway until the outbreak of the First World War in August 1914. It may not have been such a glamorous career as making Atlantic records, but it brought a great deal of pleasure to rich voyagers seeking a leisurely way of life. But that career as a cruise liner was yet to come. At the turn of the century the *Deutschland* was the acknowledged holder of the Blue Riband—the fastest merchant ship in the world. Her only possible challenger was the *Kaiser Wilhelm der Grosse* which, although built in the same shipyard, had experienced none of the machinery and vibration problems which damaged the *Deutschland's* reputation, but went serenely on her way in a seemingly endless succession of fast passages.

That fortune smiled upon her had been dramatically demonstrated on June 30 1900, when a fire which broke out at the Norddeutscher Line's piers in Hoboken, New York, spread so rapidly that within minutes four of the company's liners berthed alongside—*Bremen, Kaiser Wilhelm der Grosse, Main* and *Saale*—were swept by the flames. Although towed away by tugs, the *Bremen, Main* and *Saale* were extensively damaged—the last-named eventually sank with the loss of 109 lives. The *Kaiser Wilhelm der*

The *Umbria* of 1884, sister ship to the *Etruria*—the first Cunard Blue Riband 'pair' and the last two single-screw big passenger liners built for North Atlantic service. (*John McRoberts*)

The *Etruria*, like the *Umbria*, was fitted to carry sail as shown on this unusual photograph of her at sea. A distinctive feature of this pair was their enormous and not particularly handsome funnels. (*John McRoberts*)

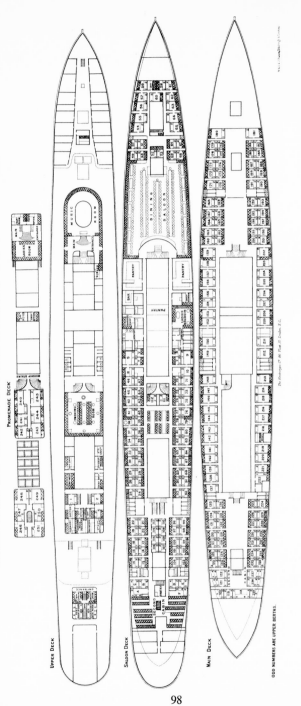

CUNARD ROYAL AND UNITED STATES MAIL STEAMSHIPS "UMBRIA" AND "ETRURIA"

PROMENADE DECK

UPPER DECK

SALOON DECK

MAIN DECK

ODD NUMBERS ARE UPPER BERTHS.

The *Umbria* and *Etruria* might fairly be said to have inaugurated the concept of the 'floating hotel' which was to become an obsession with the competing shipping lines on the Atlantic ferry. Velvet, brocade, stained glass and heavily carved tables and chairs epitomised Victorian luxury.

CUNARD LINE.

ESTABLISHED 1840.

ROYAL MAIL STEAMERS TO
NEW YORK AND BOSTON.

1888.		FROM LIVERPOOL.		FROM QUEENSTOWN.		STEERAGE PASSAGE MONEY.	INTERMEDIATE PASSAGE MONEY.
ETRURIA	For New York	Sat.,	March 31	Sun.,	April 1	Full in Steerage	7 & 8 Guineas
CEPHALONIA	For Boston	Thur.,	April 5	Fri.,	,, 6	Four Pounds	Seven Guineas
SERVIA	For New York	Sat.,	,, 7	Sun.,	,, 8	Five Pounds	7 & 8 Guineas
SCYTHIA	For New York	Tues.,	,, 10	Wed.,	,, 11	Four Pounds	7 & 8 Guineas
CATALONIA	For Boston	Thur.,	,, 12	Fri.,	,, 13	Four Pounds	Seven Guineas
UMBRIA	For New York	Sat.,	,, 14	Sun.,	,, 15	Five Pounds	7 & 8 Guineas
BOTHNIA	For Boston	Thur.,	,, 19	Fri.,	,, 20	Four Pounds	Seven Guineas
AURANIA	For New York	Sat.,	,, 21	Sun.,	,, 22	Five Pounds	7 & 8 Guineas
GALLIA	For New York	Tues.,	,, 24	Wed.,	,, 25	Four Pounds	7 & 8 Guineas
PAVONIA	For Boston	Thur.,	,, 26	Fri.,	,, 27	Four Pounds	Seven Guineas
ETRURIA	For New York	Sat.,	,, 28	Sun.,	,, 29	Five Pounds	7 & 8 Guineas
SAMARIA	For Boston	Thur.,	May 3	Fri.,	May 4	Four Pounds	Seven Guineas
SERVIA	For New York	Sat.,	,, 5	Sun.,	,, 6	Five Pounds	7 & 8 Guineas
SCYTHIA	For New York	Tues.,	,, 8	Wed.,	,, 9	Four Pounds	7 & 8 Guineas
CEPHALONIA	For Boston	Thur.,	,, 10	Fri.,	,, 11	Four Pounds	Seven Guineas
UMBRIA	For New York	Sat.,	,, 12	Sun.,	May 13	Five Pounds	7 & 8 Guineas
CATALONIA	For Boston	Thur.,	,, 17	Fri.,	,, 18	Four Pounds	Seven Guineas
AURANIA	For New York	Sat.,	,, 19	Sun.,	,, 20	Five Pounds	7 & 8 Guineas
GALLIA	For New York	Tues.,	,, 22	Wed.,	,, 23	Four Pounds	7 & 8 Guineas
BOTHNIA	For Boston	Thur.,	,, 24	Fri.,	,, 25	Four Pounds	Seven Guineas
ETRURIA	For New York	Sat.,	,, 26	Sun.,	,, 27	Five Pounds	7 & 8 Guineas
PAVONIA	For Boston	Thur.,	,, 31	Fri.,	June 1	Four Pounds	Seven Guineas
SERVIA	For New York	Sat.,	June 2	Sun.,	,, 3	Five Pounds	7 & 8 Guineas
SCYTHIA	For New York	Tues.,	,, 5	Wed.,	,, 6	Four Pounds	7 & 8 Guineas
SAMARIA	For Boston	Thur.,	,, 7	Fri.,	,, 8	Four Pounds	Seven Guineas
UMBRIA	For New York	Sat.,	,, 9	Sun.,	,, 10	Five Pounds	7 & 8 Guineas
CEPHALONIA	For Boston	Thur.,	,, 14	Fri.,	,, 15	Four Pounds	Seven Guineas
AURANIA	For New York	Sat.,	,, 16	Sun.,	,, 17	Five Pounds	7 & 8 Guineas
GALLIA	For New York	Tues.,	,, 19	Wed.,	,, 20	Four Pounds	7 & 8 Guineas
CATALONIA	For Boston	Thur.,	,, 21	Fri.,	,, 22	Four Pounds	Seven Guineas

CHILDREN UNDER 12 YEARS, HALF-FARE: INFANTS UNDER 12 MONTHS, 10s,

INTERMEDIATE PASSAGE TO NEW YORK - - SEVEN and EIGHT GUINEAS.
DO. TO BOSTON - - SEVEN GUINEAS.
Children under 12 years, Half-price. Infants under 12 months, One Guinea each. Passengers in this Class mess apart from the Steerage, and have an excellent Scale of Diet. Comfortable Beds, Bedding, and all necessary utensils provided by the Company. FIFTEEN CUBIC FEET MEASUREMENT OF PERSONAL LUGGAGE CARRIED FREE OF CHARGE FOR EACH ADULT.

Passengers booked through from NEW YORK to PHILADELPHIA without extra charge.

NEW YORK.—Passengers going to New York by the Saturday and Tuesday Steamers will be landed at Castle Gardens, a Depôt arranged by the Government for the reception of Emigrants. Representatives of the Cunard Company, speaking all the languages, are stationed at the Depôt to tender all requisite assistance and information. Passengers' Baggage is conveyed from the Steamer to the Railway Cars free of expense.

BOSTON.—Passengers by the Thursday Steamers to Boston will be landed at the Company's Wharf, where they will be received by the Company's Representatives and forwarded to their various destinations. Those who wish to go to New York will be sent to the former Port free of charge. The journey occupies about ten hours. The Cunard Company have an Emigrants' Home on their Wharf at Boston, where Passengers have free accommodation ; and as trains for all parts of the Union make a stop at a Platform attached to the Home. Passengers with their baggage are transferred to the Railway Carriages without trouble, expense, or anxiety. The attendance of Passengers is specially directed to this arrangement.

BERTHING.—Each Passenger will be provided with a separate Berth; Married Couples are berthed together with their Children in the same rooms; Single Females will be put in rooms by themselves; and Single Men together in rooms apart from all others. During the day there is no separation—all can be together.

OUTFIT.—Passengers will have to provide themselves with a Plate, Mug, Knife, Fork, Spoon, and Water-can, as also Bedding; all of which can be purchased for a few shillings.

LUGGAGE.—Passengers will please take notice that they must get their bedding, which may be required on the Voyage or of their boxes before going on board. A box is the most convenient article for carrying what is required during the voyage. Ten cubic Feet is the measurement of Personal Luggage will be carried free for each Adult, and in consideration thereof, the Company limit the liability for Luggage to the sum of Ten Pounds. Steerage Passengers must take charge of their own Luggage, which they should bring with them.

STEERAGE BILL OF FARE.—Each Passenger will be supplied with Three Quarts of Water daily, and with as much Provisions as can be eaten, which are all of the best quality. The Provisions are examined and put on board under the inspection of Her Majesty's Emigration Officers, and are cooked and served out by the Company's Servants:—

Breakfast at Eight o'Clock,—Coffee, Sugar, and Fresh Bread and Butter, or Biscuit and Butter, or Oatmeal Porridge and Molasses.

Dinner at One o'Clock,—Soup, Beef, Pork, or Fish, with Bread and Potatoes, and on Sunday Pudding will be added.

Supper at Six o'Clock,—Tea, Sugar, Biscuits and Butter. Oatmeal Gruel supplied when necessary.

The Company reserve the right of rejecting any person who may be found to be deaf, dumb, blind, maimed, or having symptoms of infectious disease.

All Intermediate and Third Class Passengers must present themselves at the Office of the Agents, at the port of embarkation, not later than Eight o'Clock in the Evening of the day before sailing, to receive embarkation instructions. Passengers failing to embark at the appointed time will forfeit their Passage-money.

All Passengers will have strictly to conform to the Rules laid down by the Company. In order to meet the requirements of the Government Emigration Officer, the Contract Ticket will be dated for the day previous to the advertised date of sailing.

☞ **THROUGH BOOKING.**—Passengers Booked Through to and from all parts of the United States and Canada, including Manitoba and the North-West Territories. Tickets can be purchased from any of the Cunard Agents.

Passages can be secured by sending a Deposit of One Pound for each Berth to the undersigned, with particulars of Name and Age of each Passenger.

Each Steamer carries an experienced Surgeon. Medicines and Medical attendance Free.
Drafts issued on New York and Boston free of charge.

Apply to

THE CUNARD STEAM SHIP COMPANY, LIMITED,
LIVERPOOL

31/3/88.

Time table and fare table issued by Cunard for sailings in 1888. The reverse of this schedule carries the menu for intermediate passengers bearing the appetizing announcement that 'Gruel' was to be served at 8 pm every day.

The *City of New York (III)*, first of the two large and fast liners ordered in 1887 by the newly-formed Inman and International Line to 'eclipse anything afloat'. (*John McRoberts*)

Grosse escaped serious damage, being towed to the comparative safety of the Cunard pier across the river.

The Norddeutscher Line board had every reason to be proud of their famous ship—and to be thankful for her lucky escape. However, the failure of the *Kaiser Friedrich* had meant that the *Kaiser Wilhelm der Grosse* was upholding the company's prestige single-handed. To that extent the service was unbalanced and to rectify this, an order was placed with the Vulcan Shipyard, Stettin, for a companion ship. Named *Kronprinz Wilhelm* she was launched on March 30 1901 and began her maiden voyage from Bremen and Southampton to New York on September 18 of that year.

Her principal dimensions were: length 637 ft; beam 66 ft; depth (to upper deck) 43 ft; gross tonnage 14,900. Passenger accommodation: first-class 593; second-class 362; third-class 696. The machinery installation comprised two sets of six-cylinder quadruple expansion engines of 33,000 indicated horsepower to give a designed speed of 23 knots. With her four funnels (again arranged in pairs), two pole masts, straight stem and counter stern, the *Kronprinz Wilhelm* closely resembled the *Kaiser Wilhelm der Grosse* in exterior appearance. But, as was to be expected, the opportunity had been taken to provide more facilities and more luxury especially for passengers in the first-class accommodation. They included a re-arrangement of the planning of the public rooms involving a reading room, in addition to the library and writing room; installation of several cabins on the boat deck (previously reserved exclusively for the master and officers); more suites comprising sitting room, bedroom and bathroom; more rooms with adjacent private bathrooms. One contemporary comment on the luxuries provided was: 'There seems no limit to the magnificence which rich Americans demand and will pay for in this direction'.

Undoubtedly the most notable feature of the *Kronprinz Wilhelm* was the extensive use made of electricity. It was, of course the principal means of lighting throughout the liner, even down to electric cigar-lighters in the first-class smoking room. But there were other and much more useful adaptations as instanced in the special device by which all clocks in the ship were synchronised with that in the chartroom and the elaborate telephone system extending 'from the bridge to each engine room, to the crow's nest, to the forecastle head and to the after bridge'. For the first time, telephones had been installed in the staterooms (first-class) enabling passengers to get into direct touch with the stewards' department. Again, electric fans had been installed to perfect the ventilation system.

One new development which delighted technical experts visiting the ship was located in the wheelhouse. This was a large plan of the lower decks showing the bulkhead arrangements. 'Wherever there is a watertight door, a little ring of brass with a centre of glass appears,' wrote a correspondent, 'on touching a handle some of these little circles become illuminated with electric light, whilst others remain dark. Thus it is at once shown which of the bulkhead doors may be open and which are shut. Should it be desirable or necessary to close them all, the gear for closing them can be actuated from the spot, and the electric device instantly shows how the mechanism far below has responded.'

F

The *Kronprinz Wilhelm* also carried a wireless telegraphy installation as did her companion ship the *Kaiser Wilhelm der Grosse*—the first North Atlantic passenger liner on the New York run to be so fitted.

After successful trials in the North Sea, during which she achieved an average speed of 23.34 knots, the *Kronprinz Wilhelm* took a party of German business executives on a short sea passage to Bergen. Then she crossed to the Firth of Forth, lying to anchor of Leith where, on September 10, the master of the liner and the owners entertained a large number of British business men, travel agents and other guests.

On her maiden voyage, starting from Bremen on September 17, the liner arrived at Southampton the following day, where she berthed at the Ocean Quay to embark passengers—she carried a full complement—before proceeding to Cherbourg, finally clearing the French port at 8 pm. The speed the *Kronprinz Wilhelm* had achieved during her trials—when her engines were not fully extended—had given rise to high hopes that she would prove faster that the *Deutschland* and become the Blue Riband holder on her first voyage. As it turned out, Captain L. Stormer, her master, was more concerned with coping with a North Atlantic at its worst than with driving his ship to new record heights. As a result he completed his first outward passage from Cherbourg to New York (Sandy Hook) in six days ten hours 15 minutes, at an average speed of 19.74 knots—in the circumstances a creditable performance. Homeward the weather was more kind, the passage from New York (Sandy Hook) to Plymouth (Eddystone Light) was completed in five days nine hours and 48 minutes at an average speed of 23.1 knots—the fastest eastbound voyage ever recorded.

An unusual, if not unprecedented, feature of the voyage was that the Norddeutscher Lloyd board, always aware of the need to keep the company well in the public eye, had put a cameraman on board, his job being to take a film record of the entire voyage. One Saturday afternoon at the end of November, the company took over the Alhambra Theatre, London, for a special showing of the film to invited guests. Among those present was a correspondent of the *Marine Engineer* who, reporting on the occasion, had this to say: 'The Norddeutscher Lloyd's biograph exhibition at the Alhambra was a very distinct success. The whole of the seats in that large building were occupied, the lower parts of the house containing many people of importance in the shipping and journalistic worlds, and the upper seats being thoughtfully allotted to a number of boys from the Greenwich Hospital who very much appreciated the proceedings.

'The managers of the show were certainly to be congratulated on having an audience containing so many businessmen whose Saturday afternoon is their only chance of relaxation. It needed something special to induce such people to come to an entertainment which however interesting savoured somewhat of the shop.

'The views depicted included some 31 scenes involving the use, it is said, of upwards of 180,000 separate pictures and some miles of film. They dealt not only with the experiences of the great and noble liner whose first voyage they commemorated but with a number of scenes which are familiar to the passenger to New York.

'Thus to begin with, we were shown the arrival of the NDL special trains from Bremen to Bremerhaven. Then there was the departure and the receding pierhead. Next there was the call at Southampton and then came the pictures of the life at sea. We saw steerage passengers usefully employed in helping the ship's staff to prepare their food, and on the promenade deck there were the long lines of chairs back against the deck houses with their fair occupants tucked in and sheltered from the breezes, whilst the never-ending promenade of men went on in the open space before them. Then there was the service of the 11 a.m. cup of beef tea, which is so much appreciated by the always hungry voyager.

'These little touches of everyday life were of course appreciated by those who had seen the real thing. But what was of interest to all were the numerous pictures which showed the angry Atlantic at its best. They will, I fancy, appeal to one more strongly when viewed a second or third time.

'Altogether the exhibition was a great success and both the Steamship Company and the photographer are to be congratulated on the suggestion and the way it was carried through.'

Viewed in retrospect, the Norddeutscher Lloyd Line were deserving of special congratulations in deciding to retain and show the scenes of 'the angry Atlantic at its best'—by no means the best way of inducing prospective passengers to make a Western Ocean voyage. Perhaps they were anxious to demonstrate the sea-going qualities of the *Kronprinz Wilhelm*.

Their confidence in the ship was fully justified and she proved in every way a worthy rival to the *Deutschland*. The keen competition between the two liners for the Blue Riband honours gave rise to a dispute in June 1902 after the *Kronprinz Wilhelm* claimed to have completed an eastbound voyage from New York at an average speed of 23.53 knots, compared with an average speed of 23.51 knots achieved by the *Deutschland*. This claim was challenged by the Hamburg Amerika Line, the resultant wrangle lasting several weeks before the Norddeutscher Lloyd Line conceded that a mistake had been made in the bridge calculations during the *Kronprinz Wilhelm's* voyage. Prestige was restored to the *Deutschland*, but not for long. In September 1902 the *Kronprinz Wilhelm* made a record passage from Cherbourg to New York (Sandy Hook) in five days 11 hours 57 minutes at an average speed of 23.09 knots and honours were even. The fractional margins in the speed performance of the two ships continued, but the *Kronprinz Wilhelm*, not troubled by the vibration problems which plagued the *Deutschland*, was always the more popular liner.

Despite their rivalry on the North Atlantic route the Hamburg Amerika and Norddeutscher Lloyd Line always maintained a mutual and close interest in their business relations—an arrangement which now was to serve them in good stead. It was at this period in the history of the Atlantic Ferry that Mr J. Pierpont Morgan, the American banker, was busily forming the International Mercantile Marine Company with the object of establishing a huge shipping combine which would absorb all the major Atlantic shipping lines. In 1902 his grandiose scheme had made considerable progress, including negotiations for the purchase of the White Star Line and overtures to the Cunard Company.

The two German lines, while remaining aloof, were fully aware of the combines implications and, if successful, the tremendous effect it would have on North Atlantic passenger and cargo trade. To offset this threat the Hamburg Amerika and Norddeutscher Lloyd companies came to a special ten-year agreement with Pierpont Morgan and the other IMM promoters under which, while the German companies would continue to operate independently, they would work in conjunction with the American combine. By so doing they could look to the future with greater equanimity.

One effect of the agreement was that it enabled the Norddeutscher Lloyd Line to go ahead with plans to safeguard their leading position on the North Atlantic by placing orders with the Vulcan shipyard, Stettin, for two large and fast liners which would also ensure that the Blue Riband remained in German keeping. Named *Kaiser Wilhelm II and Kronprinzessin Cecilie,* they were not only larger and faster than the *Kronprinz Wilhelm* and *Deutschland,* but incorporated in their design improvements on the many features which had contributed to the successful operation of these two record-breakers. The newcomers were also notable for the fact that they were built with a view to rapid conversion to auxiliary cruisers for service with the German Navy—a development in which the Kaiser took a keen personal interest. Four-funnelled ships, fitted with three pole masts, the main dimensions of both liners were almost identical: length overall 706.5 ft; depth 52.5 ft; gross tonnage 19,361. Propelling machinery consisted of two sets of six-cylinder quadruple expansion engines, indicated horsepower was 40,000 and designed speed 22 knots. Accommodation was provided for 775 first-class passengers; 343 second-class and 770 third-class. As was now becoming commonplace, ostentatious luxury was the keynote of the first-class public rooms and staterooms, declining to utilitarian in the second-class and 'seven large dormitories' for emigrants travelling steerage.

The *Kaiser Wilhelm II* was the first to be laid down. She was launched in July 1902, an occasion attended by the German Emperor and, completed in eight months, began her maiden voyage from Bremerhaven to New York via Southampton on April 14 1903. In August of the same year she deposed the *Kronprinz Wilhelm* by voyaging from Cherbourg to New York (Sandy Hook) in five days 15 hours ten minutes at an average speed of 22.6 knots; homeward she crossed from New York (Sandy Hook) to Southampton (the Needles) in the splendid time of five days ten hours 42 minutes at an average speed of 22.73 knots.

There was an unusual time gap between the commissioning of the *Kaiser Wilhelm II* and the *Kronprinzessin Cecilie*; launched in 1906, the latter ship did not enter service until August 6 1907. In some respects it was unfortunate because she was a lovely ship and might easily have outpaced her companion ship and gained the Blue Riband but, overtaken by developments in the North Atlantic shipping scene, she was never given a chance to demonstrate her powers of speed.

During the time of her building at the Vulcan yard, there had been increasing tension in Britain over the threat to national security and trade posed by the new active International Mercantile Marine Company. The absorption of the White Star Line into American ownership and the known fact that the Cunard Line were not uninterested, gave rise to anxiety about Britain's future representation on this important international trade route. To avert what was considered to be a national disaster, the British Government entered into long negotiations with the Cunard Line which was in no financial position to place orders for large and fast liners to put an end to the German domination of the Atlantic ferry. The outcome was that the Government agreed to advance to the Cunard Company £2,600,000, repayable in 20 years at 2.75 per cent interest per annum, which would enable the company to order two steamers capable of maintaining a speed of 24.5 knots on the North Atlantic. For their part the Cunard Line agreed, among other provisions, to remain a British company while the two proposed ships were in commission and also to devote all its other tonnage to Government service in time of national emergency. Before the agreement could come into operation it had to have approval from both Houses of Parliament. It was given by the House of Commons at 11 pm on August 13 1903.

Eight
1903—1907

The incomparables

Lusitania and *Mauretania*
Part one
Conception and commissioning

NOW THAT THE Government agreement with the Cunard Line had been passed by Parliament, it was up to the company's directors to implement the conditions they had promised to fulfil. It was a challenging prospect, the more challenging because the directors were well aware that they could not fail the British public who now looked to the Cunard Line to put into service liners which would not only wrest the Blue Riband from the German record-breakers, but which would remove the threat of an American stranglehold of the Atlantic ferry resulting from the formation of the giant Morgan combine.

The task confronting the company was to design two liners capable of maintaining an average speed of 24.5 knots and in which there would be sufficient passenger accommodation to make their voyages profitable. However, with the promised government loan taking care of building costs, the directors were in the comfortable position of being able to go ahead with plans already on the drawing board for two liners which in size, speed and luxury would prove the 'right' ships for the job.

To achieve the hitherto unknown speed on the Atlantic run of 24.5 knots meant that considerable space would be required for the machinery needed to provide the necessary power. Again, to offset the cost of the machinery installation, it was essential that the passenger accommodation should be on a scale far exceeding that already provided in liners operating on the North Atlantic. A third factor, which posed many problems, was that in determining the dimensions of the liners (length, breadth and particularly depth) account would have to be taken of the facilities for manoeuvring and docking the ships at their terminal ports, Liverpool and New York.

In their deliberations, the Cunard Company received every assistance and co-operation from the three shipbuilding firms who at the outset had been asked to tender for the ships. They were Swan Hunter and Wigham Richardson, Newcastle-upon-Tyne, Vickers Son and Maxim, Barrow-in-Furness, and John Brown and Company, Clydebank. Simultaneously with the model and other experiments being carried out by these firms, the Admiralty placed the government experimental tank at Hasler at the disposal of the company.

At this tank invaluable data was obtained after a long series of experiments and demonstrations carried out by Dr R. E. Froude in association with Sir Philip Watte KCB, Director of Naval Construction. As a result of these experiments the dimensions of the two ships were determined at 760 feet between perpendiculars (790 feet overall) by 88 feet beam and a depth from keel to shelter deck of 60 feet 6 inches. These dimensions were greater than those proposed in the original specifications and made it impossible for Vickers to put forward a final tender because of limitations in docking facilities at the Barrow shipyard. In consequence final tenders were received only from John Brown and Company, Clydebank, and Swan Hunter's at Newcastle-upon-Tyne.

There still remained another problem. This concerned the type of propelling machinery to be installed. The tank experiments had conclusively shown that for ships of the dimensions proposed to cross the Atlantic at an average speed of 24.5 knots, an indicated horsepower of 68,000 would be necessary. Up to July 1903 specifications had provided for this power to be achieved by reciprocating engines. This type of engine had been installed in Atlantic liners for many years, and in fact was a feature of the record-breaking German liners. Many marine engineers considered that at that stage there was no alternative and saw no reason why the question of any alternative type of machinery should be considered. There was, however, a growing body of opinion which favoured the system of turbine engines invented by the Hon Charles A. Parson, a system which had progressed considerably since that spectacular demonstration by the launch *Turbinia* at the Jubilee Naval Review at Spithead in July 1897.

One disadvantage was that the steam turbine was to a great extent still in the experimental stage. The number of vessels so equipped could almost be counted on the fingers of one hand. They included three torpedo boat destroyers, two Clyde ferry steamers—the *King Edward* (1901) and the *Queen Alexandria* (1902)—and two new cross-Channel steamers—the *Queen* engaged on the Dover/Calais run, and the *Brighton* on the Newhaven/Dieppe run, both of which had been completed in June 1903. Only one vessel fitted with turbines had, as yet, crossed the Atlantic. She was the steam yacht *Emerald* built for Sir Christopher Furness. The Allan liners, *Victoria* and *Virginian,* the first Atlantic passenger liners in which turbine engines were installed, were then being built for service to Canada.

It was admitted that the turbine system had proved successful in all the ships so fitted, and in the case of the Clyde ferry and the cross-Channel steamers had added greatly to the steadiness of the ships and hence the comfort of the passengers, but the gulf between the dimensions of these small vessels and the projected Atlantic 'giants' was immense, and if it was essential that to meet their obligations the Cunard Company should investigate every possible form of ship propulsion, it was equally essential that they should make no mistake. By the performances of the ships they would stand—or fall.

In September 1903, the Cunard Company took the unprecedented step of inviting a group of men, all expert marine engineers or men with long and practical experience of ship operation and shipbuilding, to form a commission to investigate the problem. Mr James Bain, General Superintendent of the Cunard Line, was appointed chairman of the commission. The other members were Engineer Rear-Admiral Oram, CB, engineer-in-chief of the Navy; Mr J. T. Milton, Chief Engineer Surveyor of Lloyds; Sir William H. White, late Chief Naval Instructor to the Admiralty and now a director of Swan Hunter & Wigham Richardson; Mr Andrew Laing of the Wallsend Slipway and Engineering Company; Mr Thomas Bell of John Brown and Company; the Hon Charles A. Parsons, inventor of the turbine engine; and Mr H. J. Brode of the shipbuilding firm of Denny Brothers of Dumbarton—a company which had practical experience in building ships fitted with turbine engines.

For six months this commission devoted much time and energy to the problem. They heard and considered all arguments for and against the turbine, they investigated data and studied the performances of turbine engines in shore installations as well as at sea; they weighed up such vital factors as vibration and the saving of machinery space, and against the mounting evidence in favour of the turbine they had to weigh the one unknown factor; if turbine engines were installed in the two ships, would they do the work required of them? There was no real precedent to guide them.

By March 1904 their investigations were complete. The balance sheet was drawn up and the experts unanimously recommended the adoption of the turbine. The final decision then rested with the Cunard board. They accepted the verdict of the committee and, as if to show their confidence in this decision, it was decided that turbine engines should also be installed in the 20,000-ton liner *Carmania,* the keel of which was about to be laid at John Brown's, Clydebank.

Swiftly following the settlement of this major problem came news of the contracts for the building of the two great liners; one vessel to be named *Lusitania* was entrusted to John Brown and Company at Clydebank; the other to be named *Mauretania* to Swan Hunter and Wigham Richardson, Newcastle-upon-Tyne.

Construction of the *Lusitania* began at Clydebank on September 20 1904. No time was lost and by June 1906 she was ready to be launched. This event took place in fine weather on June 7, the naming ceremony being performed by Mary, Lady Inverclyde, widow of Lord Inverclyde who, as chairman of the Cunard Company, had been in the forefront of the negotiations with the Government which had led to the agreement to build the two liners. His death on October 8 1905, at the early age of 44, was a great loss to the Cunard Company in particular and the shipping industry in general.

The launching of the great ship was regarded as a great national occasion. As the *Daily Mail* put it, 'At no previous launch of a merchant ship had there been a gathering of so many people distinguished in the scientific and maritime world. They came from all parts of Britain and the colonies, while Naval and Mercantile Marine representatives from France, Germany, Italy, Japan and Russia were also present.' The shipyard, divided up into platforms and balconies, contained about 20,000 persons, the ladies dressed in gaily coloured summer clothing, while every vantage point for miles around was crowded with spectators who cheered as the vessel took the water.

'The most elaborate precautions had been made for the operation,' reported one technical newspaper. 'That this was necessary may be gleaned from the fact that the launching weight of the leviathan was 16,000 tons— by far the heaviest weight ever carried on a cradle down the ways. The actual launching apparatus consisted of two hydraulically operated cams, and two electrically driven machines at varying distances apart.

'After all the timber shores had been removed from the hull, the tide being favourable and the river traffic having been previously stopped, Mr David McGee, works manager of the builders, pressed an electric bell giving the signal for the launching ceremony to begin. The time was 12.30 pm. Then Mary, Lady Inverclyde pressed an electric button which released the bottle of wine suspended by ribbons from the liner's forecastle and named the ship *"Lusitania"*.

'A few moments intervened before the hull showed any signs of responding, but soon the significant creaking of the timber that bore her was heard, and as this sound pressed along the whole line of her keel, the noble ship began her descent into the Clyde. Majestically she moved to the cheers of tens of thousands of people gathered on both sides of the stream and to the strains of a splendid band in the shipyard, gathering way as she glided down she finally made the graceful bow always taken by ships launched in this way, the moment the forefoot is clear of the ways, and altogether waterborne. On her way down she had broken loose from the temporary 'stops'—the dozen wire cables shackled to her side as checks. When the ship was afloat these cables, pair by pair, were brought into action finally stopping her career.

'Thus tethered to 16,000 tons of chain cable in a dozen heaps, the greatest specimen of naval architecture that ever floated was held in view of the admiring crowd at the river's edge of the yard.' The ship had been waterborne in two minutes 42 seconds; the actual time taken from her first movement down the ways was 28 seconds. The launching operation from land to water had been effected so smoothly that 'against anticipation the wash was slight and did little more than gently rock the five tugs standing by to take the great hull in charge and bring it to a safe berth in the adjacent fitting-out basin which had been specially lengthened to accommodate the ship'.

After the launching ceremony, some 600 guests gathered for luncheon in the builder's moulding loft which had been specially decorated for the occasion. Sir Charles MacLaren MP, chairman of John Brown and Company, presided. Among the guests were: Mr Charles E. Ellis (managing director, Brown & Co Ltd), Mr John G. Dunlop (director, Clydebank Works), Col J. G. S. Davies, Captain Tresfoder, CMG and Mr John Sampson (directors, John Brown and Co Ltd), Mr William Watson (chairman, Cunard Co), Sir William B. Forwood (deputy chairman), Right Hon Lord Inverclyde, Messrs E. H. Cunard, M. E. Maxwell, James H. Beazley, Sir Thomas Royden (directors, Cunard Co), A. D. Mearns (secretary), James Bain, RNR (general superintendent), Captain G. H. Dodd, RNR (marine superintendent), Mr Leonard Peskett (naval architect of the Cunard Company), Messrs David McGee, Thomas Bell, and W. J. Luke (local directors John Brown & Co Limited), Sir Alfred L. Jones (chairman, Elder Dempster Line) who travelled up from Liverpool with a special party, Mr G. B. Hunter (chairman), Mr William Denton (director), and Mr Stephenson (yard manager) of Messrs Swan, Hunter and Wigham Richardson Limited, Wallsend-on-Tyne (builders of the *Mauretania*), Admiral Sir Digby Morant, CMG, Lord Overtoun, Sir William Plowden, Sir William White, KCB (late Director of Naval Construction), Sir John Durston, KCB (engineer-in-chief to the British Navy), Colonel Hughes, the Lord Provost of Glasgow, Mr A. Piers (steamship manager, Canadian Pacific Railway), Sir Francis Evans, the Bishop of Glasgow, the Bishop of Ripon, Hon C. A. Parsons, Mr A. Earle, Mr A. W. Bibby (director, Pacific SN Co, etc), Professor Bryce, Mr Malcolm Dillon (Palmer's Shipbuilding and Iron Co Ltd), Right Hon W. J. Pirrie, PC (Harland and Wolff), Mr John Keppie, Captain Jujii (Japanese Navy), Mr James Gilchrist (Barclay Curle and Co), Colonel S. Saxton White, Sir John Luscombe and Mr Henry Wortley (Ocean Steamship Co).

Proposing the toast, 'The *Lusitania* and her owners', Sir Charles said he was certain there was no person present, even though he might in a sense be considered a competitor or rival, who was not gratified by what had been achieved on this occasion. The ship which had just been launched so successfully was by far the largest vessel that had ever been put into the water. In length, breadth, depth and capacity she exceeded any other vessel that had ever been designed, whilst her engine power would be such as to send her across the Atlantic at a speed never yet accomplished, except by a torpedo-boat destroyer. A vessel of such interest and magnitude was a thing of which any firm might be justly proud, and the Cunard Company had undoubtedly placed itself far in advance of any other shipowning firm in the world. He hoped that this enterprise would be justified, and that the great and growing traffic between America and this country would keep the ship filled on all her voyages. Sir Charles went on to say he hardly thought that this enterprise was one which should have been left to the initiative of any one private firm, and he was glad to think that its importance was so fully recognised by His Majesty's Government that they had taken a part in it and had contributed so largely in financing the undertaking. He was pleased that, in consideration of this support which had been extended to the directors of the Cunard Company, this vessel was really the latest addition to the reserves of His Majesty's Navy. It might be made with very slight alterations the fastest and most powerful cruiser in the world. The Government were well justified in standing at the back of an enterprise of this kind.

Considering the important national issues at stake there was something in acquiring distinction, and he felt that no one present would be satisfied that, for capacity and speed of Atlantic liners, the record should be held by Germany. Britain was the mistress of the seas; we had always been in the lead in marine construction, and there was not a Briton who ought not to feel proud that this launch had once more placed Great Britain in the forefront of marine architecture.

On behalf of his company, he would mention that all its members had felt the difficulties and risks of the ship's construction. It had not been undertaken lightly or without the fullest and closest scientific investigation; it was not until it was felt not only that the company could build the ship, but that it could also construct turbine engines of sufficient capacity and economy to produce the desired results, that the task was essayed. The first chapter had now been completed, but in about 12 months' time he hoped that the vessel would be in the possession of the Cunard Company. He was confident that, when that time arrived, she would run her trials with unqualified success. (Cheers.)

Mr William Watson (chairman of the Cunard Company), in responding, expressed keen regret that the late Lord Inverclyde had not been spared to see the successful accomplishment of the first stage of an enterprise which he had so greatly at heart. The Cunard Company was really supplying a vessel that could be used as the very fastest armed cruiser. It was not fair to expect any one firm to undertake that responsibility, and the Cunard Company was being paid for what they were providing. This had been called a subsidy; it was a payment for services rendered, and nothing else. They had been told that they were going into a wild speculation, but it would be well understood by scientists, shipbuilders, engineers and others that before going into that great operation, they had carefully deliberated and obtained the most expert evidence in the world, and he believed that they would find that the builder would give them what they asked for. The Cunard Company had had its good and its bad times; they had lain fallow a little some years before, but they had started a strong progressive movement, led by the late chairman who braced them up to a spirit which would not be allowed to deteriorate and to a policy which would not be abandoned.

Little over three months later, on September 20, the *Lusitania's* sister ship, the *Mauretania,* was launched from Swan Hunter's shipyard into the waters of the Tyne. Again the weather was kind and again vast crowds made their way to the shipyard to cheer the liner—the largest ship ever built on Tyne-side—as she was waterborne. The river was crowded with shipping, although in front of the yard and for a considerable distance east and west a clear space was maintained for a long time before the launch. The great Cunarder had been built in covered ways reaching from end to end of the ship and, as she lay there in preparation for her first plunge into the water, her tremendous proportions were an impressive sight.

The naming ceremony was performed by the Dowager Duchess of Roxburgh, sister-in-law to Lord Tweedmouth, First Lord of the Admiralty.

Guests on the launching platforms included the chairman of the Cunard Company, Mr William Watson, Sir William Forwood (vice-chairman), Mr Alfred Booth (director), Mr Ernest H. Cunard (director), Mr M. H. Maxwell, Mr A. D. Mearns (secretary), Mr James Bain (general superintendent), Mr A. P. Moorhouse (general manager), Mr L. Peskett (naval architect), Mr Thompson (superintending engineer), Captain Dodd and other representatives of the company, Mr G. B. Hunter (chairman of the building company), Mr Wigham Richardson (vice-chairman), Mr W. Denton, Lady and Miss Furness, Sir Fortesque and Lady Flannery, Sir John and Lady Glover, Mr J. L. Griffiths, Mary, Lady Inverclyde, Sir Alfred Jones, Sir John and Lady Jackson, Lord Angus Kennedy, Mr Francis and Lady Anne Bowes-Lyon, the Bishop of Newcastle and Miss Lloyd, Sir Riley and Lady Lloyd, Lady Mabel Lindsay, Lady McDonald, Sir John and Lady Milburn, Sir Ralph Moor, Sir Charles MacLaren, MP, Sir William Matthews, Sir Michael Nairn, Sir Isambard and Lady Owen, Mr R. and Mrs Oliver, Lord Eustace Percy, the Ladies Victoria and Mary Percy, Sir Charles Mark Palmer, MP and Lady Palmer, the Hon C. A. Parsons, Mrs and Miss Parsons, Sir G. H. Philipson, Sir Walter and Lady Runciman, Lord Rosse, Lord and Lady Ravensworth, Sir Horace Tozar, Major Villiers and Lady Victoria Villiers, Sir William, Lady and Miss White, the Hon C. H. Wilson, MP and Lady Marjorie Wilson, Vice-Admiral G. T. H. Boyes, Director of Transports, Admiral H. F. Cleveland, Rear-Admiral T. Macgill, CB, Captain Superintendent of contract-built ships, Engineer Rear-Admiral H. J. Oram, CB.

Prior to the launching, Lord Tweedmouth, accompanied by a director of the building company, walked round the ship and, to quote a contemporary newspaper report, 'had explained to him all the mechanism of the launching and all the thousand-and-one things that had to be foreseen and provided for and provided against.

'Threading his way amidst great trees of timber that shored up the hull, clambering over huge wedges and giant cables curled round armour plates that were to act as checks, Lord Tweedmouth saw all the preparations for the launch. Gangs of workmen round the sides knocked the great dog-shores away one by one with huge battering rams fitted with handles, and the sound of their working 'chanty' which they sang in chorus mingled with the incessant hammering that went on under the keel of the ship between the two ways where hundreds of carpenters who could not be seen were working by the light of torches.

'Ambulance men were posted all around the ship, and their presence gave a hint of the anxiety that lay behind the ceremony that made this day a holiday for the northern town. Now and then one of the huge dog-shores would fall in an unexpected direction and scatter the 50 workmen who had knocked it out of its place.

'At 4.15 p.m., after an hour's wait for the tide—for the ship is as long as the Tyne is broad—and had to be launched obliquely—a telephone message from the yard foreman below to those on the launching platform announced that all was ready. A bell rang sharply, then the Dowager Duchess, naming the ship, pressed the button which took off the last detaining touch that kept the *Mauretania* on land, and the liner began her passage to the water. The water foamed high at her stern, the great cradles fell away from her, and the Tyne seethed with the wreckage and with the first foam churned up by the ship. Then the cables tightened and the great vessel, a dead thing suddenly called to life was as suddenly killed and she showed all her shape in the water. Six tugs came fussing up to soothe and nurse her after such a violent baptism and tow her to the fitting out berth, which had been dredged for her. The launch was over. It had taken 70 seconds.'

Because of the comparatively late hour of the launching, the feasting and speech-making which, if a little smug and self-congratulatory, were typical of their Edwardian day and age, was held before the actual ceremony.

Mr G. P. Hunter, Chairman of Swan Hunter and Wigham Richardson, presided. He opened the proceedings by reading a cablegram from Lord Grey, Governor General of Canada. It read, 'Congratulations; hope you will soon build finest steamships for shorter route across Atlantic to Canadian ports'. Whether intended or not the message was an apposite reminder to the assembled guests that it was to a Canadian, Samuel Cunard, the owners owed the genesis of the company.

Proposing the toast of 'The *Mauretania* and the Cunard Company', Sir William White (late Director of Naval Construction) referred to the difficulties and problems which had had to be overcome and that there were people who declared that the high speed now obtained would never be maintained. He knew something about ship construction and in his judgment there had never been an undertaking of this nature which had attracted more attention from those capable of giving an opinion, which had been more thoroughly worked out, and would be brought to a successful conclusion by the achievement of a cross Atlantic speed hitherto unheard of, by the *Mauretania* and her sister ship *Lusitania*.

Sir William went on to say that from the first the Cunard Line was an Imperial Company, conceived and worked out in an Imperial spirit; and now that this crisis of high speed had arisen and a solution was to be attempted, they must all agree it could not have fallen into more fitting hands than those of the directors of the Cunard Company.

In his reply, Mr William Watson, the Cunard chairman, said so much money was to be spent on the *Lusitania* and *Mauretania* that a private firm could hardly undertake them; and as the Government required great ships and great speeds they had to give some assistance to private enterprise. That was the *raison d'être* of these ships and to their late chairman (Lord Inverclyde) belonged the credit of having conceived them and put them into being. They would go on doing the best they could to make the company successful, and he felt confident they would succeed. Without confidence there could be no success.

Lord Tweedmouth said it was true that he represented the Admiralty, and that therefore to some extent he might be considered a partner in the great concern of which Mr Watson was chairman, but his duty that afternoon was not to speak of the position of the Admiralty except to say that they hoped they would always be only sleeping partners in the Cunard Company and that God's blessing might prevent them from ever having to call on these magnificent vessels to serve in war.

While, however, they hoped they would not have to call upon them, they nevertheless felt that by having these vessels at their disposal they added a great strength to this great nation (hear, hear!)—that they were not only a great strength in their material force but that they were a great strength also from a sentimental point of view, because they linked together the navy and the mercantile marine. (Cheers.)

Speaking on behalf of his sister-in-law, the Duchess of Roxburgh, Lord Tweedmouth said she had asked him in the first place to associate her with all that had been said with regard to the great loss the Cunard Company had sustained by the death of their late chairman Lord Inverclyde. They all knew and recognised that it was due to Lord Inverclyde's great force of character, energy and tact that the possibility of building these great ships ever arose. Without his efforts the necessary negotiations would never have been carried through. He bridged the Atlantic Ocean and used the power that was in his hands to bring about the arrangement. (Cheers.) These were great services to the country and nation, services which he thought were recognised also on the other side of the Atlantic.

In a reference to the fact that turbine engines were to be the active power of the two liners, Lord Tweedmouth recalled that a little while ago he had seen HMS *Dreadnought* launched, but the ship they would see launched that day was a leviathan beside the great *Dreadnought,* the biggest of battleships. 'Anything connected with the sea must always be regarded with the greatest interest by the people of this country,' Lord Tweedmouth concluded, 'it is by the sea that we are united to our colonies and dependencies. It is by the sea that is brought the food to keep our people alive. It is by the sea that we bring the materials that our people use for their manufactures. It is by the sea that we have our greatest power of defence. Great companies like the Cunard deserve all the praise and all the encouragement that the population can give them.' (Cheers.)

While work on the two liners was proceeding, the Cunard directors were discussing with the Mersey Docks and Harbour Board arrangements for the berthing and docking of the ships when finally commissioned. The majority of liners sailing in and out of Liverpool berthed at the Princes Landing Stage to embark or disembark passengers. However it was found that there would not be a sufficient depth of water to permit the *Lusitania* and *Mauretania* with a loaded depth of 37 feet 6 inches to go alongside. So the port authority set to work and dredged over 20 square miles of the river bed abreast of the landing stage; it was a big job involving the removal of more than 200,000 tons of rock, clay and sand. The next job was to install on the landing stage itself baggage conveyors and movable elevated platforms from which gangways could be run out reaching to the great height of decks.

Nor was this the end of the plans made in Liverpool to receive the great ships. There was the important matter of facilities for drydocking. To enable this to be done safely, the port authority installed in the Canada Graving Dock, which the ships would use, blocks of sufficient strength to withstand the increased stresses to which they would be subjected. There was yet another problem which had to be sorted out. For many years, when waiting to dock or move alongside the Princes Stage, the Cunard ships had lain in a stretch of the river—abreast of Cammell Laird's Shipyard, Birkenhead—known as the Sloyne. Here were moored two buoys—

North Cunard and South Cunard. Although the ground mooring were strong, it was felt that they were not strong enough to hold a 30,000-ton liner with high deck erections, especially in times of stormy weather and strong winds. To overcome this a new buoy with ground moorings of exceptional strength laid in four legs was installed.

Meanwhile, work on the installation of machinery, fitting out and completion of accommodation on the two ships was proceeding rapidly. First to be ready was the *Lusitania* which, on July 27 1907, left her Clydebank birthplace for her trials, to be followed by a cruise around Ireland before proceeding to her home port; for the occasion the builders and prospective owners invited a large number of guests including representatives of the Admiralty and the Hon C. A. Parsons, who had a very special interest in the performance of the turbine machinery installed. It must have been a great relief to him when on her trial runs over the measured mile at Skelmorlie she achieved a speed of 25.6 knots—'thus giving good augury that she will succeed in maintaining the average speed of 24.5 knots in moderate weather which is required by the terms of the Cunard Company's contract with the Government', pontificated a correspondent of *The Times*.

Nine
1907—1929

The incomparables

Lusitania and *Mauretania*
Part two
Partners in peace and war

COMMANDED BY Captain J. B. Watt, Commodore of the Cunard fleet, with Mr Alexander Duncan as chief engineer, the *Lusitania* began her maiden voyage in the early evening of September 7 1907. It was a red-letter day for Merseyside. Over 200,000 people, it was said, made their way to the waterfront to watch embarkation scenes and the arrival of the special boat train from London at the Riverside Railway Station adjacent to the Prince's landing stage alongside which the great liner was berthed. The crowd cheered the ship heartily as she finally moved into midstream before heading down-river and so out to sea. As one contemporary newspaper said: 'Never before in the history of steam navigation had so much interest been excited'. And rightly so, for was not the *Lusitania* the world's largest, most beautiful and, it was confidently expected, fastest liner?

After leaving Liverpool, the *Lusitania* proceeded down the Irish Sea, putting into Queenstown to take on more passengers and mail. This done, the great ship headed for the North Atlantic, passing Daunt's Rock (Queenstown) at 12.10 hours on Sunday September 8. She arrived off Sandy Hook (New York) at 09.05 hours on Friday September 13, having completed the passage of 2,782 nautical miles in five days and 54 minutes at an average speed of 23.01 knots. She had failed to beat the record held

The *City of Paris (II)*, sister ship to the *City of New York (III)*. The two ships introduced a new era in exterior grace and interior luxury to the Atlantic Ferry. *(John McRoberts)*

The White Star liner *Teutonic* of 1889, and her sister ship the *Majestic*, were the first North Atlantic passenger liners specifically designed and built to serve as armed merchant cruisers in the event of war. (*John McRoberts*)

When commissioned in 1890, the *Majestic* carried a third (mizzen) mast. This was removed during her winter overhaul in 1902/03. The *Teutonic* and *Majestic* were the last 'pair' ordered by the White Star Line to capture the Blue Riband.

The first Cunard twin-screw steamers, the *Campania* and *Lucania,* brought new luxury to the North Atlantic. Here the *Campania* 'dressed overall' is lying in the Mersey prior to her maiden voyage. (*John McRoberts*)

Dressed in a different way, the *Campania* was purchased by the British Admiralty at the outbreak of the First World War and, as HMS *Campania,* was converted into a seaplane carrier. (*John McRoberts*)

The *Lucania* lying in the Mersey with the Cunard passenger and baggage tender *Skirmisher* alongside. Between them the *Lucania* and *Campania* held the Blue Riband for four years. (*John McRoberts*)

The Hamburg-Amerika liner *Deutschland* of 1900. Plagued by excessive vibration she was eventually converted into a cruise liner with reduced speed and renamed *Victoria Luise*. (*John McRoberts*)

by the *Deutschland,* to the great disappointment of the British public. Her daily runs (from Daunt's Rock) were:

Noon September 8 to noon September 9 — 556 miles
„   „   9 „ „   „   10 — 575 „
„   „   10 „ „   „   11 — 570 „
„   „   11 „ „   „   12 — 593 „
„   „   12 „ 09.05 hrs „ 13 — 483 „

Her best day's run of 593 miles exceeded that achieved by the *Kaiser Wilhelm II* by 11 miles, but it was eight miles less than the record day's run of 601 miles set up by the *Deutschland.* Taking the weather into account, the *Lusitania* had done well. During her voyage there had been foggy conditions for three days out of the five she was at sea, as a result of which Captain Watt had considered it prudent at times to reduce speed.

Commenting on the *Lusitania's* performance the technical journal *Marine Engineer* said: 'It is not right to compare her mean speed on her first voyage with the 23.15 knots of the record-breaking *Deutschland.* It were better to look at it in relation to the recent addition to the NDL fleet. Thus it will be seen that the *Kronprinzessin Cecilie* only attained a speed of 21.81 knots in her maiden trip (6.8.07) and was thus beaten by the *Lusitania* by 1.25 knots. It would seem to all reasonable observers that the new ship has done as quite as well as anyone had a right to expect and certainly as well as it was advisable for her to do so. Great speed on maiden voyages means constant trouble with machinery in later life.'

The paper continued: 'For all classes of passengers, the *Lusitania* offers the extremes of luxury and comfort. She is a floating hotel offering accommodation surpassing anything which any but perhaps one or two joint-stock palaces in wealthy cities can pretend to give. Of the hundreds of passengers who made a successful trip in her on this memorable maiden voyage, how many could truthfully say that they had ever had so luxurious a time in their lives? Probably it would be found that passengers of every class, even the cheapest, were enjoying unaccustomed luxuries and comforts.

'The size, the power, the luxury of the *Lusitania* no doubt appealed to the multitudes who welcomed her on her arrival at New York, and who followed with almost feverish excitement the publication of the Marconigrams which told how she was reeling off the miles of her long and arduous course, but to many of our readers and to many of the 200,000 persons who are computed to have witnessed her departure from the Mersey there is a deeper interest in her performance, a more sincere feeling of satisfaction that in her maiden trip she will assuredly, all being well, when the proper time comes surpass the performance of any vessel which has ever accomplished the Atlantic voyage.

'For the *Lusitania* is of British design and construction; she is owned and manned by our fellow countrymen. There has been much regret in many people's mind that for so long the palm of speed in the Atlantic, so long a British possession, has been enjoyed by vessels flying a foreign flag. But all that will be changed. The *Lusitania* has beaten the maiden voyage record; she has surpassed that of the latest German vessel (*Kron-*

prinzessin Cecilie) by over a knot, and more she was not asked to do. It would have been foolish indeed to have pressed her before her engines were settled, before the human element in the ship had got used to the vast and delicate machine from which they are eventually to extract the last fraction of a knot in speed. We may be sure that when she gets settled down and opportunity offers, the *Lusitania* will more than fulfil expectations and will prove as profitable to her owners as she is creditable to those who produced her.'

And possibly sooner than the experts, if not the public, had dared to hope the *Lusitania* fulfilled these 'expectations'. On her second westward voyage from Liverpool to New York, she regained the Blue Riband for Britain. Leaving the Mersey port on Saturday October 5, she made the coastal passage to Queenstown in ten hours at an average speed of 24 knots. Leaving the Irish port at 10.25 hours on Sunday October 6 she covered 41 miles to noon on that day. To noon on Monday her day's run was 590 miles; to noon Tuesday 608 miles, thus setting up a new record for a day's steaming. She improved on this performance by covering 617 miles at an average speed of 24.76 knots to noon on Wednesday. To noon on Thursday she steamed 600 miles, having to slow down slightly because of fog. At 01.75 hours on the Friday morning she was off Sandy Hook (New York), having voyaged 324 miles since the noon of the previous day. The voyage from Daunt's Rock (Queenstown) to Sandy Hook (New York) a distance of 2,780 miles had been accomplished in the record time of four days 19 hours 52 minutes at an average speed of 23.993 knots. By this achievement the *Lusitania* had secured for herself and regained for Britain the coveted Blue Riband of the Atlantic.

In a cablegram from New York dated October 11, *The Times*' own correspondent wrote: 'Everyone is delighted with the *Lusitania's* splendid run and Mr Gustav Schwab of the North German Lloyd handed the Blue Ribbon to the Cunard Authorities. The Germans are satisfied that she is a better boat and that turbines are satisfactory. Four German engineers went on board the *Lusitania* taking notes and photographs. The incident was referred to by the chairman at a concert on board. After speaking in complimentary terms of British engineers and declaring that British inventors had developed the turbine he said, "I believe our engineers are justified in their pride because we have the spectacle of our maritime rivals taking notes and photographs of interesting things and thus following all their derogatory opinions directed against the turbine engine."

'It is hoped that the *Lusitania's* time of sailing from Queenstown will be arranged earlier so that she may land her passengers on Thursday evening and letters on Friday morning.'

A Reuter's correspondent on board the liner had telegraphed on the Thursday evening how 3,000 passengers had crowded the rail when the *Lusitania* was passing the Nantucket Lightship. 'The greatest enthusiasm is displayed over the record-breaking trip. The engineers are making efforts to maintain a high rate of speed to the finish.' He continued: 'A concert which was given this evening developed into enthusiastic speechmaking. Several well-known Americans gave voice to sentiments congratulating England on regaining the mastery of the seas.'

In a further message from New York dated October 11 a Reuter's correspondent reported how, after her arrival at the Sandy Hook Light-ship, the great liner had lain to anchor until 07.12 hours when she crossed the bar 'and was brought carefully up the new and as yet uncompleted channel'. The *Lusitania* again dropped anchor off the quarantine station 'amid the blowing of whistles of all the steam craft in the vicinity. The medical examination lasted an hour, and the *Lusitania* then moved slowly and majestically up the harbour, replying with strident blasts from her siren to the salutes from the shipping.'

Mr Gustav Schwab, general manager in New York of the Nord-deutscher Lloyd Line, in an interview with newspaper correspondents, said: 'The *Lusitania* is undoubtedly a wonderful steamer and she has made a splendid record. I am going today to congratulate Mr Vernon Brown of the Cunard Company and, figuratively speaking, incidentally to hand him the Blue Ribbon of the Atlantic which the Norddeutscher Lloyd has held for several years. Of course it is with regret that the Nord-deutscher Lloyd parts with the ribbon which is the emblem of speed and superiority at sea, but in giving it up we have the consolation of knowing there is only one steamer in all the world which is faster than our *Kaiser Wilhelm II*. It is better to have held and lost the record than never to have held it at all. The *Lusitania* has made a record of which everyone should be proud, and we, above all others, because in order to gain the record she was obliged to defeat one of our steamers.'

Nowhere had the commissioning of the *Lusitania*, her teething troubles and her subsequent record voyage been more closely watched than on Tyneside where her sister ship *Mauretania* was nearing completion at the shipyard of Swan Hunter and Wigham Richardson. In their exterior dimensions and main plan of their passenger accommodation the two liners were identical. There were, however, differences in the design, decoration and layout of passenger accommodation which were always to be a source of friendly argument amongst patrons of the two ships; there were those who preferred the cool elegance of the white enamel paint relieved by gold ornamentation, a special feature of the *Lusitania,* to the carved oak and mahogany panelling in the *Mauretania*.

But these were only minor details. It was in their respective machinery installations that the major changes in detail lay. In the *Mauretania* the turbines had been fitted with more rows of blades than in the *Lusitania*. Again, in the second ship the diameter of the propeller blades was six inches greater than that of her sister ship. Only two main condensers had been installed in the *Mauretania* as compared with four in the *Lusitania,* but it was considered that the two condensers in the Tyne-built ship would prove equally efficient, being of great size and capable of condensing one million pounds of steam per hour. Then the *Mauretania's* 25 boilers were slightly less in diameter than those in the *Lusitania,* though they had more heating surface and more grate area.

These changes, it was hoped, would improve the *Mauretania's* perfor-mance when in service and incidentally go some way—if not all the way—to eliminating that bugbear of vibration, a complete solution to which had so far eluded all builders and marine engineers. Whether the *Mauretania* would succeed where others had failed was a hypothetical problem. Now the ship had been completed it was widely known that she was scheduled to leave the Tyne for Liverpool on October 22. It was therefore a mystified Tyneside which woke up one morning to find that overnight their beloved ship had disappeared from their midst, without any warning and without any indication of her destination.

The reason for this was that the builders and owners had decided to send the ship to sea, to carry out extensive trials to make sure that she would adequately meet the exacting tasks required of her. For five days the *Mauretania* carried out secret trials in the North Sea. Apart from those most concerned, nobody knew precisely where she had gone, indeed the master of any passing ship who chanced to sight the great four-funnelled liner being put through her paces must have been considerably astonished.

No official report was ever published as to the result of those critical five days. The story is told that on one day, when the ship was 'full out', much to the joy of the men in the engine room, a peremptory order was rung down from the bridge for speed to be reduced immediately. It was of course obeyed. When the disappointed engineers inquired discreetly why the 'old man' had given the order, the reply was brief and to the point. 'Because,' it stated, 'I was being shaken off my bridge.' True or not, the 'incident' emphasised the value of the secret trials in that steps were immediately taken to eliminate the trouble.

The value of the experimental trials was adequately proved in that, after her return to Swan Hunter's shipyard, the *Mauretania* was able to keep to the scheduled date for leaving her birthplace. On October 22 1907 the *Mauretania* officially left the Tyne for Liverpool—it was a proud day for Tyneside. Vast crowds lined the river banks to cheer their beloved *Mauretania* (after whom, it was said, babies were named) as she put to sea escorted by an armada of small ships. On arrival at Liverpool she went into the Canada graving dock where her hull was cleaned and final preparations were made for her official speed trials. She left Liverpool on November 3 and began her trials on November 5. These were quite exhaustive and fell into two sections. First of all there were the long-distance trials. The course chosen was between the Corswall Point Light on the Wigtownshire coast, Scotland, and the Longships Light off Lands End, Cornwall—a distance of 304 nautical miles.

The *Mauretania* was required to run this course twice in each direction, steaming continuously for 48 hours. On her first run south, despite a moderate gale with wind Force 7, the ship achieved an average speed of 26.28 knots. Steaming north, in calm seas with a light breeze astern, she did not do so well, averaging only 25.26 knots; the experts ascribed this disappointment partly to the fact that 'tide and currents were adverse'. Going south again, the *Mauretania* excelled herself by averaging 27.36 knots. On her last run north, during which the liner had to contend against headwinds and unfavourable tidal currents, she repeated her average speed on her first run north of 25.26 knots. Altogether she had covered 1,216 miles in 46 hours 44 minutes 30 seconds of continuous steaming, at an average speed of 26.04 knots. Her designed speed called for 25 knots. The experts were happy.

Then began the second stage of her trials. These took place over the Skelmorlie measured mile in the Clyde where she worked up a speed of

26.03 knots. Later she made two longer runs from Ailsa Craig to Holy Isle and back which she accomplished at an average speed of 26.17 knots. It was clear that the *Lusitania* would find a worthy rival in her sister ship which, having returned to Liverpool, was preparing for her maiden voyage. This began on November 16 and the world waited expectantly in the hope that on this, her first crossing of the North Atlantic, the *Mauretania* would wrest the Blue Riband from the *Lusitania*.

It was a cold and wet day but this did not deter a crowd of 50,000 from gathering on the Liverpool waterfront to cheer the departure of the liner. And a long wait they had. The special boat train from London was 50 minutes late in arriving at the Riverside Station adjoining the Prince's landing stage, and it was not until 19.30 hours that the *Mauretania*, commanded by Captain John Pritchard (chief engineer John Currie), moved away from the landing stage. In the darkness of that November evening her progress down-river, a blaze of light from stem to stern, presented an inspiring and unforgettable sight which amply repaid the faithful Merseysiders for their long and wearisome vigil.

Her passengers included a technical executive of the owners and builders, Admiralty representatives, newspaper correspondents and the inevitable groups of 'first voyagers' who had made sure of their passage by booking accommodation many months in advance. In addition, stowed away in a specially sealed compartment, the *Mauretania* was carrying a shipment of gold bullion valued at £2,750,000 consigned by the Bank of England to the US Treasury.

At the outset all augured well. The passage from Liverpool to Queenstown was made in good time and in smooth seas, the Irish Sea being on its best behaviour. The *Mauretania* arrived at Queenstown at nine o'clock on the Sunday morning. After embarking passengers and loading mail she put to sea at 11 o'clock to make her debut on the North Atlantic but, in contrast to the Irish Sea, the Western Ocean welcomed the new arrival most unceremoniously. Up to noon on Monday the *Mauretania*, despite steadily worsening weather, had covered 571 miles at an average speed of 23.75 knots, but by then the liner was pushing against a full westerly gale with high seas breaking over the forecastle to such effect that the spare anchor on the foredeck broke adrift to become the plaything of the sweeping seas. Captain Pritchard had no alternative but to turn his ship around and reduce speed to about three knots to enable his officers and deckhands to recover the anchor, gambolling in its dangerous freedom, and secure it safely. Precious hours had been lost, and by noon on Tuesday the liner had logged only 464 miles. The chances of a record voyage seemed remote.

But, having shown her worst side to the *Mauretania,* the Atlantic decided to calm down, and weather conditions began to improve. Although she was rolling heavily, the liner's run to noon on Wednesday reached 563 miles. That was more encouraging. Better still, from noon Wednesday to noon Thursday, 624 miles were logged—six more miles than the *Lusitania* had ever achieved in a day's run. Whatever might be the final outcome of the voyage, the *Mauretania* had set up a new record for a single day's run. Jubilant passengers began to have visions of landing at New York on the Friday morning, especially when the *Mauretania* was off Sandy Hook at 11.13 hours, but the weather decided otherwise. A blanket of fog suddenly enshrouded the ship and in a crowded sea lane Captain Pritchard decided to take no risks. He promptly brought his ship to anchor, and announced that he would not proceed until the fog had cleared.

The passengers, who by no stretch of imagination had enjoyed a particularly comfortable voyage, were not amused. News had reached the ship of a mounting depression in Wall Street, and a number of worried American businessmen discussed the possibility of forming a deputation which would proceed to the bridge to 'insist' that Captain Pritchard should get his ship under way. Fortunately for them, because they would most certainly have received short shrift from the master, the fog lifted as suddenly as it had fallen, and the *Mauretania* berthed alongside her New York pier at 18.15 hours. She had made the passage from Liverpool to New York in five days five hours ten minutes at an average speed of 22.21 knots. This was well below the *Lusitania* record but, if the general public had nothing to cheer about, at least it demonstrated the Cunard policy of putting the safety of passengers before all else.

The *Mauretania* began her homeward voyage from New York to Liverpool at 13.35 hours on Saturday November 30. Once again she was to be dogged by bad weather: on the Sunday she ran into fog which persisted for 30 hours. It was an anxious and wearisome time for Captain Pritchard and his officers. Whenever visibility improved speed was increased, but when the fog closed in again speed was reduced. In the circumstances, runs of 490 miles to noon on Sunday and 548 miles to noon on Monday were good, if not conducive to record making. The fog lifted to be succeeded by a westerly gale and heavy seas. On the Tuesday there came an historic moment in the lives of the two sister ships; the *Mauretania*, homeward bound, exchanged radio messages for the first time with the *Lusitania*, outward bound for New York. To Captain Pritchard in the *Mauretania* there may have been some consolation in the news that Captain Watt in the *Lusitania* was also experiencing a difficult voyage and was running behind schedule. To noon on Wednesday, assisted by a wind of 60 mph behind her and a following sea, the *Mauretania* logged 556 miles, giving her for the 23-hour day of the eastward run an average speed of 24.17 knots.

There was some excitement on the Friday afternoon, the last day of the passage, when the *Mauretania* overhauled the 23,000-ton White Star liner *Baltic* which had left New York on November 28, two days before the fast Cunarder. Although the *Baltic* had only a designed speed of 16.5 knots, it had not been expected that the *Mauretania* would pass her before reaching Queenstown. It was also some comfort to the passengers in the *Mauretania* to notice that the *Baltic,* which was renowned for her steadiness, was making very heavy weather of it. The *Mauretania's* voyage from New York to Liverpool was completed in five days ten hours 50 minutes at an average speed of 23.69 knots. However, her voyage from Sandy Hook (New York) to Daunt's Rock (Queenstown) had been accomplished in four days 22 hours 29 minutes at an average speed of 23.69 knots, beating the *Lusitania's* eastbound record by 24 minutes. It was a small enough margin, but large enough to enable the *Mauretania* to lay claim to the record. Nowhere was there greater rejoicing than on Tyneside—birthplace of the ship.

Commenting on the voyage, a correspondent of *The Times* wrote: 'The *Mauretania* dropped anchor at the Mersey harbour at five am on Friday and thus completed "on time" her first return journey across the Atlantic. The voyage both West and East was a complete success, and the latest addition to the Cunard fleet had more than justified the hopes of the company, of the builders, chairman Mr Hunter and of Captain Pritchard who does not conceal his delight with the command which crowned his career and of the many hundreds of passengers who enjoyed a notable experience.

'The *Mauretania* has been so fully described by naval and engineering correspondents of *The Times* that I am fortunately absolved from any technical account of her; but readers of what the experts have written may be looking for some notes on her maiden voyage from the point of view of the amateur or business wanderer for whom, subsidies apart, she is primarily intended, and on whose support her financial success depends.

'Some idea of the interest taken in the *Mauretania* and her sister *Lusitania* was given by the size of the crowd of 50,000, which gathered on a wet and windy night by the riverside quay Liverpool on November 16 to see her off. Americans have a reputation for taking a keen interest in anything which may be described as "the biggest in creation" and that this interest is not limited to their own numerous productions which come up to this standard was shown by the number of applications for passes to see over the ship. These came from a wide radius round New York and at least one party claimed to have come from California, mainly if not entirely with the object of seeing the *Mauretania*. A capital charge of 50 cents for Seamen's charities seemed to have no effect on the numbers.

'Unless, however, one is a naval architect or an engineer, the appearance of even the biggest liner in dock tells little of her capacities and conduct at sea. How far this conduct differs from that of liners of normal size and speed is what the general public will want to know. Comparing my own experience with that of men whose knowledge of ocean travel is larger and more varied, I am inclined to the conclusion that in calm weather or with a moderate breeze the *Mauretania* is steadier than would appear probable or possible in view of her speed. At the same time there is more vibration, especially on the promenade and boat decks than in a slower boat like the *Baltic* which has a special reputation for steadiness. Throughout the whole of one 25-hour day (westward clocks being advanced one hour), we averaged 25 knots making 624 knots for the day's run; and then it was not very easy to read and distinctly difficult to write anywhere except on the lower deck or in the cabins. On the other hand when we were going slowly through fog the vibration was scarcely perceptible.

'All this applies to moderate conditions of sea and wind. Fortunately we had the opportunities of noting the behaviour of the ship in a gale; for some 36 hours on the outward voyage there was a westerly wind of 50 to 60 miles and correspondingly high seas against us. During this period the *Mauretania* behaved like any other ship in a storm; her timbers "talked" loudly and she pitched with a vigour which finally disproved the prophecies of those who thought that her size would keep her steady. The discomfort might have been less if we had slackened speed; that we did not do so appreciably is shown by the fact that we made 464 knots in 25 hours of continuous gales, although during two of these hours we made practically no progress owing to the accident to an anchor.

'As regards rolling also the *Mauretania* is extremely steady in quiet weather but with a high sea she is capable of an immense but very slow roll—the sort of roll which sends palms in tubs clattering down the companionway, though it is too slow to compel any but the poorest sailors to follow them below. Intending passengers then may rest assured that under any conditions even stiff gales the *Mauretania* for her speed is as pleasant a vessel as any that cross the Atlantic; but a storm at sea in the *Mauretania* is not very different from a storm at sea in any other boat. One afternoon when a strong breeze was freshening to a gale, a passenger who was making his 40th westward Atlantic trip, and in whose company I was watching the pitch and toss of the bows from the boat deck, expressed astonishment at the deep plunging of so vast a ship, "who yet hath made the sea serve only in seeming" he quoted, and Swinburne's question may be commended to the attention of those who talk glibly of ocean hotels and an Atlantic ferry. At the same time it is fair to remember that gales are the exception rather than the rule, and it is the unanimous opinion of many experienced travellers whose opinion I ascertained that in ordinary weather no boats of anything like their speed can compare for comfort with the Cunard Company's new models . . . '

Commenting on the homeward run from New York, *The Times* correspondent said the three days' gales of the passage confirmed that the *Mauretania* rolled more heavily than was anticipated. 'Amid Kipling's "immense and contemptuous surges" she too feels something of "the heave and the halt and the hurl and the crash of the comber white-hounded". It is not impossible that some stiffening of the ship and alterations to the keel may have some effect; but it is fair to remember that she underwent a severe trial during the trip, and to assume that the roll will be less serious in more favourable conditions. Moreover the roll affects the speed but scarcely the passengers who seemed to be agreed that the new boat more than maintains the company's high standard of comfort. The only mishaps were of the trifling nature inevitable in first voyages which must always be to some extent experimental; a few broken windows, rather too much water here and too little there, some stained woodwork—the record of such things is evidence of the complete absence of serious incidents, and it was found that not a single rivet was loose.'

Concluding his comment, the correspondent added: 'As there seems little doubt that both the *Mauretania* and *Lusitania* will make even faster passages in the summer, the suggestion may be worth making that some means of "speeding up" the last lap of the six days' travel should be found. On Thursday the crossing was officially completed at 5.49 pm, the moment of reaching Daunt's Rock; but it was nearly 24 hours later that the majority of passengers reached London. It was pointed out on board that by landing at Queenstown passengers might have reached London at 9.05 on Friday morning, and that if the *Mauretania* had gone direct to Fishguard a special train might have brought passengers to London by Thursday evening. Moreover, although the first "Cunard Special" (from Riverside Station, Liverpool) reached Euston punctually at 2.50 pm on the Friday, the second and heavier section reached Euston at 5 pm—80 minutes late. Such a delay at least takes the edge off the satisfaction of beating the (Atlantic) record by 21 minutes.'

There was one feature of the maiden voyage of both ships which, although of little interest to the Press and general public, caused considerable relief in the Cunard boardroom. This was that the two liners consumed less coal than the 1,000 tons a day which had been estimated—an economic factor which materially affected voyage profit and loss accounts and a welcome physical relief to the 324 firemen and trimmers whose job it was to feed the hungry furnaces.

Figures for the maiden voyage of the *Mauretania* showed that when she set out from Liverpool for New York she carried 6,770 tons of coal. She arrived at New York with 1,350 tons of coal left in her bunkers. Before beginning her homeward passage she loaded 5,061 tons of American coal to give a grand total of 6,411 tons, and reached the Mersey with 1,020 tons to spare. Her coal consumption outward bound had worked out at 856.5 tons a day; homeward the figure was 917.13 tons. Despite difficult weather conditions, which had been of no help to her machinery performance, she had managed the round voyage at considerably less than the 1,000 tons a day mark. Chief engineer John Currie had every reason for pride in his Liverpool-Irish 'black squad' who had striven so mightily, at times to the point of physical collapse.

So now the battle for supremacy between the two ships was joined. The Cunard board might outwardly deplore the suggestion of any 'racing', although in private they may well have rejoiced in the fact that the liners had come up to all expectations and put the German record-holders 'well in their place', but for the public at large there were no reservations. Their pride in the *'Lucy'* and *'Maury'*, as they became affectionately known, was unbounded. Their voyages were a source of constant interest, and the subject of endless argument. Tyneside to a man supported the *Mauretania* as Clydeside did the *Lusitania*. On Merseyside partisanship depended largely upon which liner friends and relations served.

In their first years of service there was little to choose between the two ships, as the following passages show:

Queenstown (Daunt's Rock)—New York (Sandy Hook)

		Days	Hours	Mins	Average speed
1907	Lusitania	4	19	52	23.99
1907	Lusitania	4	18	40	24.25
1908	Lusitania	4	15	0	25.05
1909	Lusitania	4	11	42	25.85
1909	Mauretania	4	10	51	26.06

New York (Sandy Hook)—Queenstown (Daunt's Rock)

		Days	Hours	Mins	Average speed
1907	Lusitania	4	22	53	23.61
1907	Mauretania	4	22	29	23.69
1908	Lusitania	5	0	37	24.32
1909	Mauretania	4	20	27	25.20
1909	Mauretania	4	17	20	25.89
1909	Mauretania	4	13	41	25.61

Both ships experienced a certain amount of propeller trouble. For the *Mauretania* this reached a climax whilst outward bound for New York in May 1908 when one of her propeller blades dropped off; it was assumed she had struck a submerged object. She was not withdrawn from service, but for the remainder of the year had to make do with three propellers while a new set was being designed and cast.

On January 24 1909 the *Mauretania* sailed from Liverpool to New York with her new propellers. They marked a change from her original set in that the new design comprised a four-bladed propeller cut in one piece. To the delight of the technical experts the improvement was an immediate success. The *Mauretania* completed the westbound January voyage in five days two hours two minutes at an average speed of 23.71 knots, but she raced home in four days 20 hours 27 minutes at 25.20 knots, the fastest voyage so far recorded. The 14 round voyages she made during the rest of that memorable year she completed in under five days.

From that time onwards the *Mauretania* always had the slight edge on her sister ship when it came to speed records. The *Lusitania* might, and indeed did, make a faster passage but immediately the *Mauretania* went one better—if only by a matter of minutes. In the seven years they were to work together before the outbreak of World War I in August 1914, they were the glory of the Western Ocean and the admiration of the world, not only for their speed but for their freedom from trouble and the regularity of their voyaging.

As an instance, from the time of her return to service in January 1909 with her new propellers, the *Mauretania* was continuously in commission until the end of November 1911. During a period of virtually three years she was not withdrawn for a major refit. If anything needed to be done it was done during her brief stay in port either in New York or at Liverpool. In those three years she made 44 round voyages, in other words, 88 Atlantic crossings, covering approximately 264,000 miles. On 70 of these passages her average speed was over 25 knots; on 46 of these 70 passages she averaged 25.5 knots. Twice—in September 1909 and September 1910—she averaged 26.06 knots. On 15 passages her average speed was over 24 knots and on three voyages only she failed to reach an average of 24 knots. That was in January 1909, February and December 1910—not ideal months in which to come to grips with a vindictive North Atlantic which, on occasion, was no respecter of the world's largest passenger ships. As an example, the newspapers published on January 17 1910 carried reports of the arrival at New York of a weary, storm-battered *Lusitania*.

'On Monday night,' said one report, 'a huge wave struck the liner, burying her boats, surmounting the wheelhouse 80 feet above the waterline, and sweeping down the whole length of the ship. The pilot house was wrecked, the heavy plate glass windows being broken and the steel front bent in! the wheel was unshipped and the lights were extinguished. The men in the pilot house were overwhelmed by the water and were flung in all directions, receiving bruises and cuts. The officers' quarters were flooded and several boats were smashed. The ship was stopped and it was 40 minutes before the damage could be repaired sufficiently to enable her to get under way again.'

There was one rather curious aspect of the unceasing working life of the two ships. Whenever there was a 'special' voyage to be made the choice of ship always seemed to fall upon the *Mauretania*. This may have been due to the coincidence of sailing schedules, on the other hand it may well have been that the Cunard board had more confidence in the Tyne-built ship.

Thus, when in August 1909 the Cunard Company announced that plans had been completed for passenger liners coming eastward from New York to call at the Welsh port of Fishguard to enable passengers bound for London and the Continent to disembark instead of proceeding to Liverpool, so shortening the journey between America, London and the Continent, the *Mauretania* was chosen to inaugurate the service sailing from New York on August 25.

The voyage was a great personal triumph for the *Mauretania,* public excitement being intensified by the fact that the former record-holder *Kaiser Wilhelm der Grosse* had sailed from New York for Plymouth exactly 24 hours before the Cunarder. In the event the *Mauretania* arrived in Fishguard harbour on the afternoon of Monday August 30, having made a record passage from New York (Sandy Hook) to Queenstown (Daunt's Rock) in four days 14 hours 27 minutes at an average speed of 25.41 knots. The *Kaiser Wilhelm der Grosse* had arrived at Plymouth early the same day (August 30). Here she disembarked 22 passengers, 1,222 bags of mail and 257,026 dollars in gold specie. The passengers proceeded to London by a special train, reaching Paddington station at 12.15 hours.

The *Mauretania* dropped anchor in Fishguard harbour at 13.20 hours 'amid the cheers of crowds gathered on the cliffs and an informal gun salute from the Coastguard station'. Three tenders awaited the liner. Within 20 minutes, 897 bags of mail had been landed on one tender. At 14.00 hours the other two tenders were on their way to the landing stage, one carrying 240 passengers and the second with their baggage. Customs formalities were quickly completed and at 14.52 hours the first boat train was speeding on its way to London at 60 miles per hour to reach Paddington at 19.28 hours—24 minutes ahead of schedule. A second boat train left Fishguard at five minutes past three, arriving in London just before 20.00 hours. Passengers from the *Kaiser Wilhelm der Grosse* had arrived in London in time for luncheon; passengers from the *Mauretania* which had left New York one day later, arrived in London in time for dinner. Once again the *Mauretania* had shown what she could do.

Then, right on the heels of her sister ship's record-breaking eastward run, the *Lusitania* regained the westward record, arriving at New York on September 2 after a voyage of four days 12 hours three minutes, at an average speed of 25.88 knots. After leaving Queenstown on the Sunday she disembarked her passengers at her New York pier at 19.30 hours on the following Thursday evening—the first liner to discharge passengers in New York in four days from Queenstown.

That there was, in fact, little to choose between the two ships in the matter of speed was shown in statistical tables published in *The Times,* London, on February 21 1910. This report stated: 'Tables have been prepared at Liverpool showing the time taken last year (1909) by the *Mauretania* and *Lusitania* on their passages each way between the Liverpool Landing Stage and the Cunard Company's pier at New York.

'From these tables it appears that beginning with the departure from Liverpool on January 23 1909 the *Mauretania* made 15 round voyages, and, including the departure from Liverpool on December 16 1908, the *Lusitania* made 16 complete voyages.

'The shortest time taken by the *Mauretania* on the westerly passage is shown to have been five days one hour 30 minutes when the vessel left Liverpool at 11 pm on September 4th and arrived at the pier at New York at 12.30 am on the 10th (Greenwich mean time). The longest time taken was five days 21 hours and the average length of passage was five days 16 hours 58 minutes. Homewards the best passage made by the *Mauretania* was five days five hours when the liner left her New York pier on August 25th at 3 pm (GMT) and reached Liverpool Landing Stage at 8 pm on August 30. The longest time taken was five days 17 hours and the average length of passage was five days 12 hours 14 minutes.

'Outwards the best passage made by the *Lusitania* was five days seven hours when the vessel left Liverpool at 5 pm on August 28 and reached the Pier at New York at midnight on September 2 (GMT). The longest time taken was six days 18 hours when the liner left Liverpool on December 26 1908 and the average length of passage (pier to pier) was five days 21 hours 35 minutes. On the homeward passage the *Lusitania's* best time was five days 15 hours 30 minutes when the vessel left New York at 2.30 pm on July 28 (GMT) and reached Liverpool at 7 am on August 3. The longest time taken was five days 22 hours in January and the average length of passage is shown to have been five days 19 hours 22 minutes.'

The *Mauretania* made world news again when, in December 1910, it was announced she was to make a special Christmas round voyage from Liverpool to New York and return in 12 days—a schedule which many technical experts, including German shipowners, pronounced would be impossible, taking into account North Atlantic weather conditions at that time of the year.

The Cunard plan was that, outward bound, the *Mauretania* would carry home Americans resident in Britain and Europe in good time for Christmas, and on her return passage bring back Britons and West European people in time for the Yuletide festivities. The voyage schedule of 12 days gave the liner 48 hours to 'turn round' in New York; normally she stayed in New York for five days.

Commanded by Captain W. T. Turner, and with Mr John Kendall as chief engineer, the *Mauretania* moved away from the Liverpool landing stage at 17.43 hours on Saturday December 10. She had embarked 1,280 passengers (430 first-class, 250 second-class and 600 steerage). They included a score of newspaper correspondents whose job it was to keep an excited public informed by wireless messages of the liner's progress.

It proved an anxious voyage for Captain Turner, his officers and crew. Far from being in festive mood, the North Atlantic did its best to prevent the ship attaining her objective. Mr W. R. Holt, *Daily Mail* correspondent, summed it up tersely when he telegraphed: 'The voyage was eventful and tempestuous. Once the barometer fell as low as 28.18. The sea temperature was at freezing point one entire night, rising with a remarkable jump on entering the gulf stream the next morning. We passed through six snowstorms in one day. Many ladies present found it prudent to keep to their cabins for the greater part of the voyage . . . '

In spite of the serious delays caused by the head winds and tumbling seas involving a reduction in speed, the *Mauretania* steamed up New York harbour in the early hours of Friday December 15, a veritable 'Christmas' ship—coated from stem to stern with frost, her rigging heavily laden with icicles which 'shimmered and sparkled in the December sunshine'. There still remained the 'turn-around' problem—the 48 hours scheduled had been reduced to little over 30 hours. New York longshoremen, postal officials, Cunard dock workers, office staff and not least the liner's officers and crew took up the challenge and beat the deadline. At 18.00 hours on Saturday December 17, Captain Turner began the voyage home with the comforting prediction of fairer weather conditions awaiting him in mid-Atlantic. New Yorkers turned the departure of the liner into a gala occasion. Describing the scenes in a telegraphed report the *Daily Telegraph* correspondent said: 'On the stroke of six Marine Superintendent Roberts flashed from the lower and outer end of the pier a white electric light bulb. A man standing on the roof of the pier flashed a second white light signifying "all's clear". Captain Turner standing on the bridge with the pilot, pulled the handle of the telegraph apparatus which signalled Chief Engineer Kendall to start the engines, and the ship began to move out stern first. In the North river whither she had been assisted by a flotilla of tugs, she turned. An island of lights straightened out and paused as if to gather strength for the outward dash to John Bull's domain.

'Then with a gentle vibration from stem to stern the mighty engines began throbbing and the *Mauretania* leaped forward on the first stage of the long ocean flight. It was the noisiest send-off ever witnessed here. Thousands of people ashore cheered the Christmas vessel, and all the way down New York Bay, craft of all nations, with foghorns and steam sirens took part in speeding the departing liner.'

A wireless message received two hours after sailing said: 'All well and happy. Going full speed. Beautiful evening. Just had dinner. Madame Melba and the Russian Ambassador have the places of honour at the Captain's table. The band played the airs of Old England, the "Star Spangled Banner". Good-bye.'

By way of a change, good weather attended the ship throughout the voyage. She made the passage from Sandy Hook (New York) to Daunt's Rock (Queenstown) in four days 15 hours 57 minutes, at an average speed of 25.07 knots. After landing her 'Christmas' passengers and mails at Queenstown she proceeded to Fishguard, arriving at midnight on Thursday December 22. Here over 600 passengers disembarked, leaving by special trains for London. It had been a narrow squeak but once again the *Mauretania* had accomplished what she had set out to do—the first passenger liner to make the round voyage to New York and back in 12 days.

In June 1911, the *Mauretania* yet again rose to the occasion when she made a special 'Coronation' round voyage—this time from New York with Americans eager to be in London to take part in all the festival celebrations and excitement planned for the crowning of King George V and Queen Mary, in Westminster Abbey on June 22. The great ship sailed from New York on June 14 carrying 2,039 passengers, most of whom disembarked at Fishguard on June 19, after which the *Mauretania* proceeded to her home port, Liverpool. She left Liverpool on June 24, her passengers including a large number of returning Coronation excursionists, and landed them at New York on June 29 as she had promised to do.

The following December she was scheduled to make a second Christmas round voyage sailing from Liverpool on December 9, but during a strong southerly gale on December 7, she broke adrift from her moorings at the special Cunard Buoy in the Mersey and ran aground. The damage she sustained meant she had to go into dry dock for repairs. However, this did not lead to the cancellation of the much advertised Christmas voyage. The *Lusitania* stepped into the breach. She had arrived at Liverpool from New York on December 6, but was 'turned round' in less than 48 hours and kept her sister ship's sailing date.

The year 1911 had, in fact, proved outstanding for the Clyde-built liner. At the time of her arrival in the Mersey on December 6 she had completed during the 12 months no fewer than 16 round voyages between Liverpool and New York—a record of continuous voyaging never before accomplished, not even by the *Mauretania*. In achieving this record, the *Lusitania* had steamed well over 100,000 miles involving the consumption of about 160,000 tons of coal. Her average speed for the year was 24.67 knots outward bound and 24.66 knots on the homeward passage. Her best day's run was 654 miles westward and 608 miles on the eastbound voyage. Her fastest voyage from Daunt's Rock (Queenstown) to Sandy Hook (New York) was four days 13 hours 35 minutes at an average speed of 25.37 knots, and four days 15 hours 50 minutes at an average speed of 25.10 knots from Sandy Hook (New York) to Daunt's Rock (Queenstown).

To round off the record, the *Lusitania* had carried over 40,000 passengers—an average of 2,500 on each crossing—78,294 bags of mail and specie to the value of 6,820,000 dollars. There was little doubt, however, that her most triumphant performance of the year came at the end of August when, to make up time lost through a seamen's strike in the port of Liverpool, she made two complete round voyages to New York and back within one month. She left Liverpool on the first voyage on Monday August 28 and arrived at Fishguard on the completion of her second voyage on Monday September 25—an achievement unprecedented in North Atlantic passenger liner history. Her master, Captain J. T. W. Charles, his officers and crew had good reason to be proud of their splendid ship.

The sinking of the *Titanic* on her maiden voyage in April 1912 inevitably led to a reaction among a nervous section of the regular transatlantic travelling public against 'large and fast liners' and for a time passenger carryings in the *Lusitania* and *Mauretania* were lower than usual. The Cunard Company did everything possible to restore confidence in the two ships and, after the Board of Trade issued new regulations in respect of greater safety at sea, made certain that their passenger liner fleet complied with them.

The *Mauretania* had already been extensively overhauled in the first three months of 1912, but precautions to be taken in the event of an emergency were re-organised and more lifeboats were installed. At the end of the year the *Lusitania* was temporarily withdrawn from service for a complete refit and overhaul and did not resume sailings until August 1913. From then until the outbreak of World War I on August 4 1914, the two liners continued to maintain regular services between Liverpool and New York; the call at Queenstown by the two ships had been discontinued in 1913. No new records were attempted or set up for the very good reason that the public had temporarily lost faith in speed at sea— particularly on the North Atlantic run.

Nonetheless, wherever shipping men foregathered they spoke of the *Lusitania* and *Mauretania* as 'the Incomparables' and rightly so. Although now surpassed in size by the 45,000-ton *Olympic*, sister ship to the ill-fated *Titanic*, in the dignity of their external appearance, the elegance of their passenger accommodation and above all in the assured consistency of their voyages, combined with a reputation for prudent navigation, the two ships stood in a class apart from all other liners. The North Atlantic had always been noted for its outstanding 'pairs' of sister ships, but never had there been a 'pair' to equal the *Lusitania* and *Mauretania*, nor in those pre-war years did it seem that their supremacy would ever be surpassed.

The outbreak of World War I on August 4 1914 found the *Lusitania* and *Mauretania* going about their normal occasions. The latter ship, under the command of Captain James Charles, had sailed from Liverpool to New York on August 1. She was carrying a full complement of passengers including hundreds of Americans returning home from a Western Europe in which international tension was obviously reaching breaking point. Towards the end of the voyage, Captain Charles received wireless instructions to change course and proceed to Halifax, Nova Scotia, at all speed. That told its own tale. Britain and Germany were at war.

On August 5, the *Lusitania*, commanded by Captain Daniel Dow, began her homeward voyage to Liverpool. It was not to pass without incident. Within a few hours of clearing the port, the officers on watch sighted a German naval ship on the horizon. They also noted that she had changed course as if to intercept the great liner. Captain Dow at once deliberately set a course which would take the *Lusitania* into a bank of fog lying to the south, which he hoped would enable him to elude the warship. His manoeuvre proved successful and once his ship was fog-enshrouded, Captain Dow swung her round and proceeded northwards at full speed. Then he resumed his homeward run, navigating the *Lusitania* at night without lights, and so finally reached the safe waters of the Mersey and Liverpool.

Under the terms of the Cunard agreement with the Admiralty concluded in 1903, the *Lusitania* and *Mauretania* in the event of war were to be requisitioned as auxiliary cruisers and had been constructed with this in mind but, while the Government did in fact requisition various units of the Cunard fleet, including the new 45,000-ton *Aquitania* commissioned by Cunard on May 30 1914, no action was taken about the two record-breakers. One explanation given was that the Admiralty had taken note of the fate which had befallen the German former record-breaker, *Kaiser Wilhelm der Grosse*, which had been converted into an armed merchant cruiser. Whilst coaling off the port of Rio de Oro on the West Coast of Africa, the German ship had been taken unawares by one of Britain's oldest cruisers, HMS *Highflyer*, and had been unceremoniously sunk.

In their grandiose plans for using big fast merchant ships as cruisers in time of war, both the British and German naval authorities had overlooked one vital factor—the problem of coaling at 'out of the way' ports. The sinking of the *Kaiser Wilhelm der Grosse* while thus engaged had shown what could happen, and the British Admiralty were quick to take the hint. It was obvious that the operation of the *Lusitania* and *Mauretania* as auxiliary cruisers might well prove more of a hindrance than a help.

What was to be done with the two liners? While the Admiralty was trying to make up its mind the ships continued their normal role as unarmed Atlantic liners. The *Mauretania* made three more round voyages between Liverpool and Halifax, Nova Scotia. Then, at the end of October 1914, she was taken over by the Admiralty who stripped out her luxurious passenger accommodation, as they had done to the *Aquitania,* and promptly, again like the *Aquitania,* kept her idle in port. Both the ships might be wanted for Government service but when, and for what purpose, nobody really knew.

Meanwhile it had been decided to retain the *Lusitania* as a non-combatant ship on the Atlantic run. As was to be expected, passenger carryings had fallen away drastically. At the same time it was essential that there should be some fast links by sea with the United States, if only for the carriage of mails. It was arranged that the *Lusitania* should make one round voyage a month between Liverpool and New York and that her boiler power should be reduced by 25 per cent. The resultant saving in coal and labour, the Cunard board considered, would enable them to operate the liner without financial loss, even if there was no profit to be gained.

Accordingly, in November 1914, the *Lusitania* began a monthly sailing schedule from Liverpool with six of her 25 boilers closed down, reducing her maximum speed to 21 knots—which left her still the fastest liner on the transatlantic run. In February 1915, the *Lusitania,* on a homeward-bound voyage, had received a wireless message advising that German U-boats were known to be in the Irish Sea area. Her master, Captain Dow, also received instructions to fly a neutral flag. Carrying American mails and with 400 US citizens among his passengers, Captain Dow decided to hoist the American flag—a perfectly legitimate move. The *Lusitania* then crossed the Irish Sea at full speed, did not slow down to pick up a pilot at the Mersey Bar, and headed straight for Liverpool. Having once again brought his ship home safely, Captain Dow was given a deserved shore leave, his place as commander of the *Lusitania* being taken over by Captain W. T. Turner; because of the stresses and strains of voyaging in time of war, an assistant captain, J. Anderson, was also appointed.

From early in 1915 German consular officials and other German officials resident in America had carried out an assiduous campaign warning US citizens and citizens of neutral countries of the risks they were taking in voyaging in ships of nations with whom Germany was at war. This campaign reached a climax on Saturday May 1, the advertised sailing date of the *Lusitania,* when an official notice issued by the German authorities appeared in leading American newspapers. It read:

'Travellers intending to embark on Atlantic voyages are reminded that

The Norddeutscher Lloyd liner *Kaiser Wilhelm der Grosse*, first of the great German ships which from 1897 to 1907 dominated the Atlantic Ferry. (*John McRoberts*)

The *Kronprinz Wilhelm* of the Norddeutscher Lloyd Line setting out for New York, her foredeck crowded with emigrants. (*John McRoberts*)

The Norddeutscher Lloyd *Kaiser Wilhelm II* of 1903, the last of the German record-breakers which ruled the Atlantic shortly before the advent of the *Lusitania* and *Mauretania*. (*John McRoberts*)

The Cunard liner *Lusitania*, outward bound for New York, passing the Old Head of Kinsale, Eire. It was approximately at this point that, on May 7 1915, she was torpedoed without warning by the German submarine *U20. (John McRoberts)*

Five faces of a famous ship

Face one—the famous and well-beloved *Mauretania,* longest holder of the Blue Riband (1907-1929), outward bound from Liverpool.

Face two—in her World War 1 camouflage, while serving as a transport.

a state of war exists between Germany and her Allies and Great Britain and her Allies; that the zone of war includes the waters adjacent to the British Isles; that in accordance with formal notice given by the Imperial German Government vessels flying the flag of Great Britain or any of her allies are liable to destruction in those waters; and that travellers sailing in the war zone of Great Britain and her Allies do so at their own risk.

Imperial German Embassy
Washington D.C. April 22 1915.'

At noon on May 1 1915, the *Lusitania* cleared from New York with 1,959 passengers and a small cargo, including 4,200 cases of safety cartridges which, in the findings of an American Court of Inquiry in August 1918, 'could not have been exploded by setting them on fire in mass or bulk'.

At 14.15 hours on May 7 1915, while off the Old Head of Kinsale, Southern Ireland, the *Lusitania* was struck by a torpedo fired from the German *U-20* (Kapitan-Leutenant Schweiger). At 14.36 hours the great ship lifted her stern high and plunged to the bottom, taking with her 1,198 children, women and men. Captain Anderson went down with the ship; Captain Turner, who was thrown clear from the bridge, swam for three hours before being picked up by a small boat in search of the pitifully few survivors.

Thus, tragically, the *Lusitania* ended her sea-going life. Her name will always be associated with an infamous act of war. To that extent her remarkable pre-war career is overlooked. At the time of her commissioning in September 1907 she was the world's largest and fastest ship. She was the first quadruple-screw turbine-driven merchant liner; she was the first Atlantic liner to reduce the crossing to less than five days and she was the first liner to average over 25 knots during an Atlantic passage.

At the time the *Lusitania*, mortally torn apart, was plunging to the bottom of the Irish Sea, her sister ship *Mauretania*, commanded by Captain Dow, was proceeding through the Mediterranean, her decks crowded with 3,182 troops bound for Lemnos and the Dardanelles campaign. The Government at last had found a use for the great ship as a transport. In this guise she was to make two more voyages from Southampton to Mudros in July and August 1915, taking on each occasion over 3,500 Service personnel. '

As a troop carrier the *Mauretania* was a legitimate target for enemy attack. During one of her voyages through the Mediterranean she missed a similar fate to the *Lusitania* by the narrow margin of five feet; her escape was due to quick thinking by Captain Dow who, 'spotting' the track of a torpedo approaching the starboard bow, ordered the wheel to be spun 'hard-to-port' much to the consternation and physical discomfort of those on board.

The *Mauretania's* next war-time job was that of hospital ship, for which service she was refitted and equipped at Liverpool. She left Liverpool for Mudros in October 1915 carrying 283 medical staff, returning from Mudros to Southampton in November with 2,312 sick and wounded personnel. Altogether the *Mauretania* made three voyages to Mudros and returned with 2,307 medical staff and 6,298 sick and wounded. When the last troops had evacuated Gallipoli the *Mauretania* was paid off and returned to Liverpool.

Then, towards the end of 1916, she reverted to her role as a transport, making two voyages in October and November, bringing over 6,214 Canadian troops from Halifax, Nova Scotia, to Liverpool. Throughout the whole of 1917 the great ship lay idle on the Clyde but, with the entry of the United States into the war, she played a considerable part in ferrying American troops across the Atlantic. Between March and November 1918 she made seven voyages from New York with 33,610 officers and men. At the end of the war she found plenty to do in repatriating some 19,536 American and Canadian troops and it was not until May 17 1919 that she was finally demobilised and returned to her owners.

War Service

1915	Transport	Troops
May	Southampton to Lemnos	3,182
July	Southampton to Lemnos	3,630
August	Southampton to Lemnos	3,579
		10,391

1915	Hospital Ship		
October	Liverpool to Mudros	283	Medical staff
November	Mudros to Southampton	283	MS & 2,312 wounded
November	Southampton to Mudros	748	MS
December	Mudros to Southampton	283	MS & 2,012 wounded

1916	Transport	Troops
October	Halifax to Liverpool	3,087
November	Halifax to Liverpool	3,127
		6,214

1917-18	Laid up at Greenock

1918	Transport	Troops
March	New York to Liverpool	3,662
April	New York to Liverpool	4,932
June	New York to Liverpool	5,703
June	New York to Liverpool	5,129
July	New York to Liverpool	5,174
August	New York to Liverpool	5,226
November	New York to Liverpool	4,284
		33,610

September/October 1918   Laid up

1918	*Repatriating Troops*	*Troops*
November	Liverpool to New York	4,069
December	Southampton to New York	3,707
1919		
February	Southampton to New York	3,827
March	Southampton/Halifax/New York	3,946
		19,536

Government Service ended May 27 1919

Summary

	Troops	*Wounded & Medical Staff*
1915	10,391	8,605
1916	6,214	
1918	33,610	
November 1918/19	19,536	
	69,751	

After her release from Government service the *Mauretania* did not resume her normal Atlantic schedule for nine months. A great deal had to be done to refit and reinstall her passenger accommodation, and overhaul her machinery spaces. A major change was the decision to transfer her home port from Liverpool to Southampton, and it was from the southern port that, on March 6 1920, she began her first post-war sailing to New York, calling at Cherbourg *en route*.

It was with no great flourish of trumpets that the *Mauretania* made her debut on the Channel route. She made seven voyages that year and four only in 1921. On no single voyage did she average as much as 22 knots and on several voyages could only manage 20 knots. On one 'black' voyage she averaged only 17.81 knots. What had happened to those glorious record voyages which had made the *Mauretania* the wonder liner of the pre-1914 world? There were two reasons, shortage of good men in the stoke-hold and shortage of good coal. Outclassed in size and luxury by her companion ships and competitors on the Southampton run, the *Mauretania's* only claim to remaining amidst the company of her peers was in being the fastest merchant ship in the water. Without that blue riband pennant she would never hold her own. The sea travelling public was fickle and nowhere more so than on the North Atlantic route.

Obviously something had to be done, and it came about in quite an extraordinary way. Ironically enough it took a fire to solve a burning problem. At the end of July 1921 the *Mauretania,* while in port at Southampton, caught fire—an outbreak which gutted all the passenger cabins and E deck and damaged the deck above. There was no alternative but to cancel the next voyage. The liner was sent round to her builders' yard on the Tyne for repairs and, more important, conversion to an oil-burning ship, at a cost of £250,000.

143

In March 1922 she was back in service, and immediately it was evident that the conversion had proved a wise decision. In 1922 she made 11 voyages in nine months; in 1923, 12 voyages in ten months. Average speeds of 24 knots and over were again a feature of her passages. In August 1924 she crossed from New York (Ambrose Channel light vessel) to Cherbourg Breakwater in four days 19 hours at an average speed of 26.16 knots to set a new record on the Channel route, and once again the world acclaimed her triumph. It added zest to the news that the Norddeutscher Lloyd Line was planning a dramatic North Atlantic comeback by ordering two 50,000-ton super-liners which, when commissioned, would, it was claimed, sweep the *Mauretania* off the seas.

Ten
1929—1939
The last and glorious decade

THE FIRST OFFICIAL announcement that the Norddeutscher Lloyd Line, in fact, had placed orders for two 50,000-ton liners, which in speed and luxury would eclipse all existing tonnage maintaining the Atlantic Ferry, came in December 1926. The ships, it was stated, would be named *Bremen* and *Europa*.

The news created widespread interest and excitement. Twenty-one years had elapsed since the building of the last two Blue Riband liners—*Lusitania* and *Mauretania*. The latter still held the record. Would this famous and well-loved veteran prevail against the two German contenders incorporating in their machinery installation the many new developments in marine engineering?

There was more to this challenge of the Norddeutscher Lloyd Line than the deposing of the *Mauretania*. Since the end of World War I in 1918, the German company against all odds had made an outstanding 'come back' on the North Atlantic. This was reflected in the decision to order the *Bremen* and *Europa*—a decision which was to mark the beginning of an international contest for supremacy on the Western Ocean without parallel in shipping history.

These were boom years for the North Atlantic passenger liner business, characterised by a remarkable turn-about in the sources of traffic. The westward movement of thousands of emigrants from Europe, halted by the outbreak of World War I in August 1914, had never regained its impetus; it had declined still further when, in May 1921, the United States Government had imposed an immigrant quota system, followed in July 1924 by the more restrictive Immigration Law. Left with vast empty spaces in third-class accommodation, the liner companies had introduced a new 'class'—tourist-third—aimed directly at the American market. It proved an instant success. Thousands of Americans took advantage of the cheaper tourist-class fares to visit Europe, adding substantially to the numbers of their more prosperous fellow citizens travelling 'first-class' who demanded the utmost luxury and comfort and speed, and were prepared to pay for it.

It was estimated that Americans comprised 80 per cent of North Atlantic passenger traffic. Their discovery of Europe followed two set patterns. There were those who voyaged to Southampton to explore London and Britain before crossing to the Continent, returning home from Genoa or Cherbourg. There were others who preferred to visit the Mediterranean countries and the Continent first and finish their tour in Britain, returning home from Southampton. In the circumstances it was inevitable that the French and Italian shipping companies engaged in transatlantic services should be eager to capitalise on this tourist boom. So it came about that the traditional Blue Riband rivals, Britain and Germany, found themselves joined for the first time by France and Italy.

As a result, within the space of seven years, six magnificent super-liners all Blue Riband contenders, were to make their appearance on the Atlantic shipping scene. Germany was represented by the *Bremen* (1929) and *Europa* (1930), Italy by the *Rex* (1932) and *Conte di Savoia* (1932), France by the *Normandie* (1935) and Britain by the *Queen Mary* (1936). With the exception of the *Queen Mary,* the ordering of all these liners would not have been possible without financial aid in one form or another from the governments of the countries concerned. It was only in 1934, as a result of the world economic blizzard, that the British government stepped in with financial aid to ensure completion of the *Queen Mary.*

The Norddeutscher Lloyd Line awarded the contract for the *Bremen* to the A. G. Weser shipyard, Bremen; the order for the *Europa* was entrusted to Blohm and Voss, Hamburg. Construction of both liners began simultaneously in June 1928. This, in itself, was an unusual shipbuilding event. With German thoroughness it was probably so arranged to provide an added incentive to the labour force in the two shipyards to work 'full out'.

They were not identical sister ships, the *Bremen* was slightly larger than her consort. Principal dimensions were:

	Bremen	Europa
Length (overall)	932 ft 8 ins	936 ft 9 ins
Length (between perps)	888 ft 1.75 ins	888 ft 1.75 ins
Breadth	101 ft 9 ins	102 ft 1 in
Depth (moulded)	48 ft 2 ins	48 ft
Gross tonnage	51,656	49,746
Machinery	Single reduction / geared turbines	Single reduction / geared turbines
Boilers	21 watertube	24 watertube
Propellers	4	4
Designed speed	27.5 knots	27.5 knots
Funnels	2	2
Decks	11	11
Total passengers	2,000	2,000

	Bremen	Europa
First-class	600	600
Second-class	500	500
Tourist-class	300	300
Third-class	600	600
Crew	960	960

In their external appearance both ships were similar. As the owners had predicted, the ships brought to the Atlantic an unprecedented outward design as far removed from that of existing liner tonnage as those liners in turn had been removed from the record-holders at the turn of the century. Great power linked with great speed was the dominating impression. The cut-away stem was slightly raked; below the waterline it flared out into a bulbous shape. This unusual development had been agreed after numerous tank experiments and proved a complete success, giving the ships greater ease of movement, especially in heavy weather. If of no great concern to passengers, another innovation which created wide interest in the shipbuilding industry was that the hull plates overlapped forward instead of aft (the more usual procedure). The idea was that, as the ships cut their way across the Atlantic, the water running along the ships' sides would meet a series of blunt edges which in fact resulted in a fractional increase in speed.

Both ships were fitted with two masts and two great funnels. Here there was a difference. The funnels installed in the Bremen were pear-shaped, while those in the Europa were oval. At the outset there was considerable trouble in keeping the decks clear of smuts, a problem which was only cured by adding another 15 feet to the funnels. A publicity gimmick which delighted the public was the display at night of the ships' names in lights on the port and starboard sides of the sundeck. Outstanding amongst the safety provisions was the installation of motor-powered lifeboats for all passengers. A special feature in the Bremen, when first commissioned, was the catapult aeroplane on the aft deck with the object of saving time in delivery of 'flying' the mails off the ship when nearing the end of a voyage.

In planning the passenger accommodation the owners sought to anticipate the demands of the most exacting luxury-loving, pleasure-seeking passengers. Swimming pools, sports arena, ballroom, cinema, shopping centres—all were to find a place in the liners and, if there were not too many innovations compared with the facilities in the larger but slower 'giant' liners, travellers who patronised the Bremen and Europa were happy in the knowledge that lay-out, furnishings and decorative features of the accommodation reflected the trends and fashions of the late 1920s and, when it came to 'keeping up with the Joneses', that was all that really mattered.

From the time of laying the keel plates, construction of both liners continued without interruption, and with such precision that their launching dates coincided. Obviously the owners and their guests could not arrange to be in two shipyards at the same time. The problem was solved by arranging that the Europa should be launched on July 15 1928, and the Bremen on the following day, July 16—an event attended by the President of the Reichstag, Paul Von Hindenburg. The next stage of the schedule was fitting-out and commissioning. At that time there was every indication that the two ships would make a joint Atlantic debut in July 1929. Hopes of such a sensational double event were not to be realised. While fitting out in her Hamburg shipyard, the *Europa* was swept by fire and extensively damaged. It took eight months to effect repairs.

Temporarily bereft of her consort, the honour of introducing the new German image on the Atlantic scene fell to the *Bremen*. Completed in June 1929, she put to sea from Bremerhaven for extensive trials. On June 22, while steaming off Bishop Rock, Cherbourg, she sighted the *Mauretania* which had just cleared the French port in the course of a scheduled voyage to New York. For the officers and crews in both liners it was a dramatic chance encounter which heightened speculation as to the future holder of the Blue Riband. The issue was soon to be decided.

To the strains of bands playing on the quayside and the cheers of widely excited crowds, the *Bremen*, commanded by Captain Ziegenbaum, left Bremerhaven on July 16 at the outset of her first voyage to New York. Three days earlier, on July 13, the *Mauretania*, commanded by Captain McNeil, had sailed from Southampton. It was her 220th voyage in normal Atlantic service. The three days' gap between the departures of both liners obviously ruled out any ideas of a 'race'. The *Mauretania* berthed at New York early on July 19, completing the passage in five days one hour one minute at an average speed of 25.53 knots—a normal voyage.

Meanwhile, in good weather conditions, the *Bremen* was making rapid progress. From radio reports of the voyage sent by press correspondents on board the *Bremen*, it soon became clear that, barring accidents or a sudden change in the weather, the great ship had the Blue Riband in her grasp, and so it proved. The *Mauretania's* crew, preparing their ship for the homeward voyage, were left in no doubt of the issue as they heard the sounds of the traditional New York harbour welcome to a new liner intensified to a deafening crescendo, in honour of the arrival in the port of the first new Blue Riband holder for 22 years. The *Bremen* had made the passage from Cherbourg breakwater to New York (Ambrose Channel Light vessel) in the record time of four days 17 hours 42 minutes, at an average speed of 27.9 knots. The *Mauretania's* fastest passage over the same route had been achieved in September 1928 when she crossed in four days 18 hours 38 minutes at an average speed of 25.27 knots. If there was little difference in the actual times of their respective passages, the margin of over two knots between their respective average speeds was conclusive of the *Bremen's* superiority—a triumph acknowledged by Captain McNeil when he made a courtesy visit to Captain Ziegenbaum to congratulate him on behalf of the *Mauretania* on the *Bremen's* Blue Riband victory.

On her homeward run the *Bremen* made doubly sure of the record by crossing from New York (ACLV) to Plymouth (Eddystone Light) in four days 14 hours 30 minutes at an average speed of 27.92 knots—and all Germany rejoiced at her outstanding maiden voyage achievement, never before recorded in Blue Riband history.

Although the *Bremen's* speed had put the prospect of recapturing the Blue Riband far beyond the *Mauretania's* capability, the veteran liner astounded and delighted the world by setting up a new personal record the following month. On August 3 1929 she left Cherbourg for New York and completed the passage in four days 21 hours 44 minutes at an average speed of 26.85 knots. Homeward she made the voyage from New York to Plymouth (Eddystone Light) in four days 17 hours 50 minutes at an average speed of 27.22 knots. Then, with a final flourish, she accomplished the short run of 106 miles from Plymouth (Eddystone Light) at an average speed of 29.7 knots—a fantastic achievement for this 22-year-old veteran which, for Britain at least, took some of the edge off the *Bremen's* success.

No people were to hail the triumph of the *Bremen* with greater delight than those of German origin resident in the United States. This was instanced in the bronze plaque presented to the owners and given a place of honour in the liner. It bore the inscription: '*Bremen*, Queen of the Seas, 27 July 1929, presented to the Norddeutscher Lloyd Line by the Association of German Societies in New York.'

Content to rest for the time being on her Blue Riband laurels, the *Bremen* did not attempt any new records while awaiting the commissioning of her companion ship the *Europa*. This latter event took place on March 25 1930 when she began her maiden transatlantic voyage and immediately demonstrated that she was a worthy consort by making a record passage from Cherbourg (Bishop Rock) to New York (ACLV) in four days 17 hours six minutes at an average speed of 27.91 knots, in so doing capturing the westward record from the *Bremen*.

For the next three years these two proud ships were to dominate the Atlantic Ferry and take the cream of the passenger traffic in much the same way as their distinguished predecessors had done at the turn of the century, and, as had previously happened with record-breaking 'pairs', the *Bremen* proved marginally the faster. This she conclusively proved when, in June 1933, she made a westbound voyage from Cherbourg (Bishop Rock) to New York (ACLV) in four days 16 hours 15 minutes at an average speed of 28.51 knots.

Meanwhile the economic recession which, beginning in the United States, had become world-wide, was having a drastic effect on transatlantic passenger carryings. Traffic carried by all passenger lines in 1929—the year the *Bremen* had entered service—totalled 1,069,000; in 1930 it had decreased to 1,002,000. One year later the figure was down to 685,000. The times were certainly not propitious for the building and commissioning of large, record-breaking liners. One immediate consequence of the recession had been that the construction of the Cunard *Queen Mary*, the contract for which had been placed with John Brown & Company, Clydebank in December 1930, as shipyard Number 534, was suspended. Work continued, however, on the French Line's challenger *Normandie* and on the two Italian contenders *Rex* and *Conte di Savoia*.

Commissioned in 1932, the *Rex* and *Conte di Savoia* were at that time the largest merchant ships ever built in Italian shipyards, and the first Italian liners designed to capture the Blue Riband. They were not sister ships and in fact were ordered by separate owners, the *Rex* in December 1929 by the Navigazione Generale Italiana, Genoa, and the *Conte di Savoia* in October 1930 by the Lloyd Sabaudo Line, Turin. From the outset both companies received substantial financial help from the Italian government who saw in the commissioning of the two liners an immense 'boost' to Italian prestige, this apart from the additional American tourist passenger traffic which would accrue. However, on November 11 1931, the Minister of Communications announced that, as from January 2 1932, the two companies, together with the Cosulich Line, would be merged into one company to be known as the 'Italia' Line, and it was under the 'Italia' houseflag and new funnel colours (white with narrow red, white and green bands at the top) that the two ships began their sea careers.

The keels of both liners were laid down in 1930. The *Rex*, the larger of the two, was built at the Soc Anon Ansaldo shipyard, Sestri Ponenti, and the *Conte di Savoia* by the Soc Anon Cantieri Riuniti dell'Adriatico, Trieste. As with the *Bremen* and *Europa*, construction of the ships proceeded simultaneously and without loss of time to enable the commissioning schedule to be maintained. The main dimensions of the liners were:

	Rex	*Conte di Savoia*
Length overall	880 ft	815 ft
Length (between perps)	834 ft	786 ft
Breadth	97 ft	96 ft
Depth	47.3 ft	32.4 ft
Gross tonnage	51,062	48,502
Machinery	single reduction/ geared turbines	single reduction/ geared turbines
Boilers	14	10
Propellers	4	4
Designed speed	27.5 knots	27 knots
Funnels	2	2
Decks	10	10
Passengers	2,024	2,060
First-class	378	360
Interchangeable	378	—
Tourist	410	778
Third	866	922
Crew complement	810	750

A special feature of the *Conte di Savoia* was the installation of gyro-stabilising equipment with the object of reducing 'rolling' at sea to a minimum. The installation—the first of its kind to be fitted into a large passenger liner—comprised three big Perry gyroscopes of equal dimensions. Each had a flywheel weighing 175 tons and making 910 revolutions a minute. The total weight of the equipment was 750 tons; the horsepower absorbed was 2,000. Results obtained during the liner's sea trials proved satisfactory, and there seems little doubt that, when the *Conte di Savoia* entered service, the operation of the equipment in heavy weather added greatly to the comfort of her passengers.

Ordered as they had been by separate owners, the *Rex* and *Conte di Savoia* differed considerably in exterior appearance. The *Rex*, the larger and longer ship, had a counter stern, while the *Conte di Savoia* was fitted with a cruiser type stern. The latter ship, with her beautiful streamlined hull, was accounted by many experts to be the most handsome of the super-liners commissioned in the post-war years. Again, with long experience of the Mediterranean route to and from Genoa and New York, the original owners of the two ships were fully aware of passengers' requirements, and designed and furnished the public rooms and private accommodation accordingly.

The most splendid room in the *Rex* was the ballroom forward of the main hall. Two decks in height and occupying a floor area of 7,250 square feet, this room was one of the largest ever to be installed in a ship. The pride of the *Conte di Savoia* was the Colonna Hall, named after the gallery of the 17th century Colonna Palace, Rome. Running to a height of 24 feet and occupying an area of 5,918 square feet, this magnificent, if slightly bizarre room was decorated with marble pilasters, classical sculptures and friezes in the style of the 17th century. The ceiling was notable for a reproduction of a painting by Luchessini of the Battle of Lepanto, the original of which was executed for the Colonna Palace. Taking full advantage of the more southerly course maintained by the liners, it was possible to build an open-air swimming pool into each ship.

Both ships were laid down in 1930, the *Rex* on April 27 and the *Conte di Savoia* on October 4. Building proceeded rapidly, enabling the *Rex* to be launched on August 1 1931, and the *Conte di Savoia* on October 28— a quite remarkable performance. First to be completed, the *Rex* left her birthplace for preliminary trials in September 1932, when she delighted her owners and builders by achieving a speed of 28.9 knots during a nine-hour run. On September 27 1932 she left Genoa at the outset of her maiden voyage to New York, calling at Naples and Gibraltar. It was not an auspicious beginning as she developed turbine trouble when off Gibraltar and was delayed whilst repairs were effected.

The *Conte di Savoia* ran her preliminary trials in the Adriatic in September 1932, after which she went to Venice for drydocking and returned to her builders' yard in Trieste for adjustments to be made. On November 3, she finally sailed from Trieste for Genoa her home port. During this passage she carried out full trials when she exceeded the trial run speed of the *Rex*, by attaining an average speed of 29.5 knots over several 'runs'. On November 30 1932 this loveliest of all Italian Atlantic liners began her maiden voyage from Genoa to New York, calling at Naples and Gibraltar. Like the *Rex*, the *Conte di Savoia* developed engine trouble and was delayed when some 800 miles from New York, owing to a broken valve in a turbo-generator.

Teething troubles overcome, both liners settled down to a regular, steady schedule, and in so doing secured considerable patronage amongst transatlantic passengers. It was unfortunate that neither fulfilled the promise of the average speeds they reached during speed trials, but in August 1933, the *Rex* shook the complacency of the *Bremen* by completing a voyage from Gibraltar (Tarifa Point) to New York (ACLV) in four days 13 hours 38 minutes at an average speed of 28.92 knots, the fastest passage so far recorded for the westward run. For the first and only time the Blue Riband was held by Italy: a record eastbound run always eluded the *Rex*. The *Conte di Savoia* never figured in the official records of Blue Riband holders, although in 1933 she crossed from Gibraltar (Tarifa Point) to New York (ACLV) at an average speed of 27.53 knots—at that particular time a better average speed than that subsequently achieved by her companion ship, but not equal to the record set up by the *Bremen*. In fact, the

Rex was to hold the westward record until the entry into service of the French liner *Normandie* in May 1935. For this reason the Italian liner holds the unusual and permanent distinction of being featured on one of the four enamelled panels on the Blue Riband Trophy presented by Mr Harold Hales, British Member of Parliament for Hanley, to be awarded to the current record-breaking Atlantic liner. The trophy—which the Cunard Line refused to recognise—was not completed until 1935, by which time the *Rex* had been deposed by the French ship. Nonetheless, the *Rex* was designated to be the first holder.

The keel of the *Normandie* had been laid down at the Penhoet Shipyard, St Nazaire, on January 26 1931. Seven weeks earlier, on December 1 1930, John Brown and Company, Clydebank, had begun work on the Cunard liner *Queen Mary*. The name of the ship was in fact kept a closely guarded secret and, up to the actual moment of launching, she was always known by her number on the Clydebank books—number 534. Simultaneous with their building, port authorities in Southampton, Cherbourg and New York began work on the construction of new piers, baggage and customs sheds, and the deepening of approach channels in readiness for the day when the two great ships would enter service. At Southampton, the facilities to be provided included a new drydock some 1,200 feet long with a width of 135 feet and depth of 48 feet. Estimated cost of the dock, to be ready by the summer of 1933, was £1.5 million.

Although completely different in exterior appearance, type of propelling machinery and the layout and decor of public rooms and passenger accommodation, the dimensions of the *Queen Mary* and *Normandie* were virtually the same.

	Queen Mary	Normandie
Length (overall)	1,018 ft	1,029 ft
Length (between perps)	1,004 ft	963 ft
Beam	118 ft	119 ft
Depth (to promenade deck)	100 ft	97 ft
Gross tonnage	81,237	83,433
Propelling machinery	single reduction geared turbines	turbo-electric
Boilers	27	29
Propellers	4	4
Designed speed	28.5 knots	29 knots
Decks	12	12
Passengers	2,139	1,972
First	776	848
Tourist	784	670
Third	579	454
Crew complement	1,050	1,345

They were the largest and fastest liners ever planned for service on the Atlantic Ferry and world-wide interest in the two liners was stimulated by the fact that they were being built at the same time and were both scheduled to enter service in 1933. Throughout 1931 the labour force in both shipyards worked unceasingly, and rapid progress was made in the building of the ships. Outwardly there seemed no reason why the planned commissioning schedules should not be fulfilled, but the economic recession which had been affecting the world industrial scene in general, and the United States in particular, grew in intensity. Passenger and cargo traffic on the North Atlantic continued to fall, and there seemed no likelihood of any recovery in the foreseeable future.

The Cunard Line, which had already spent £1.5 million on Number 534, found it impossible to continue financing construction of the ship out of their own resources. An approach to the British government for assistance failed. As a result, on December 11 1931 work on Number 534 was suspended. For 27 months the uncompleted hull was to lie deserted on her shipyard stocks. In Britain her very desolation was to become symbolic of the great recession which had thrown thousands of people out of work.

Financed from the outset by the French government, work on the *Normandie* continued without interruption, despite the fact that her owners, like the Cunard Line, were operating Atlantic services at a considerable loss. On October 29 1932, amidst scenes of tremendous national enthusiasm, the great ship was launched from her Penhoet shipyard, St Nazaire, in the presence of M Lebrun, President of the French Republic, the naming ceremony being performed by Mme Lebrun. The event was to be perpetuated by the French postal authorities who issued a special commemorative stamp, to the delight of philatelists throughout the world.

Completion of the liner was delayed as a result of labour disputes in the shipyard, and government financial problems stemming from the economic depression, which made it difficult to meet the cost of building and fitting out, estimated at £8 million. The cumulative effect was that the commissioning of the *Normandie* ran well behind the original schedule. It was not until April 1935—two years late—that she put to sea for her trials during which she attained a speed of 31.9 knots, and an admiring world acclaimed her revolutionary appearance and the exotic splendours of her passenger accommodation—the like of which had never been seen on any of the oceans of the world.

This universal paean of praise was well deserved. To the design and construction of the *Normandie* had been brought all the skills and genius of French naval architects and marine engineers: over 2,000 tests on embryo models were carried out in the experimental tank at Penhoet before agreement was reached on the hull form. The final result was to be evidenced in the clipper-type raked stem with a semi-bulbous forefront, the rounded turtle-back foredeck, under which deck machinery and capstans were concealed, stretching to a strong V-shaped breakwater to prevent heavy seas breaking over the upper decks. At the after end of the great ship the passenger decks were stepped down in terraces so that all passengers, no matter in which class of accommodation they voyaged, could have a clear view over the wide Atlantic ocean. The three enormous, streamlined, red and black-topped funnels fell away progressively in height; the aftermost funnel was a dummy used as a kennels for passengers' dogs. The two rather short pole masts were slightly raked.

The *Normandie's* machinery installation was of special interest to marine engineers. The power needed to drive the ship across the North Atlantic in four days and in all weather conditions, involving an average speed approaching 29 knots, was supplied by 29 Sulzer mono-tube oil-burning boilers, providing steam for four sets of steam turbo-generators, which in turn would generate electricity for the driving power of four electric motors coupled to the four propeller shafts. This particular system had never been introduced into a ship of so great a size and the outcome was awaited eagerly.

As with the hull and machinery, the passenger accommodation in the *Normandie* set revolutionary standards in layout and decoration. At the time of her commissioning, it was said that the planning and furnishing of her public rooms and private staterooms was the embodiment of Gallic wit and elegance. Certainly the Atlantic Ferry had never seen such magnificence as instanced in her Grand Hall, her Salon—three decks in height, the walls of which were covered in panels of painted glass depicting the story of ships through the ages—her chapel decorated in Byzantine style, her grill room, theatre, indoor swimming pools, private suites and dining salons. 'The ultimate,' the critics chorused, 'had been reached in sea-going luxury and splendour'.

On May 29 1935 the *Normandie* made her grand entry into North Atlantic service when she began her maiden voyage from Havre and Southampton to New York. When it came to speed, she realised the hopes of her owners, her builders and France by completing the passage from Cherbourg (Bishop Rock) to New York (Ambrose Channel Light Vessel) in four days three hours 14 minutes at an average speed of 29.94 knots. Her best day's run (noon to noon) was 754 miles at an average speed of 29.92 knots; at one moment in this triumphant day she touched 31.37 knots. New Yorkers in their thousands celebrated the arrival of the new record-holding mistress of the seas in traditional fashion.

Homeward bound, the *Normandie* put her claim to hold the Hales Blue Riband Trophy beyond doubt by crossing from New York (ACLV) to Cherbourg (Bishop Rock) in four days three hours 25 minutes at an average speed of 30.35 knots. This first experience of North Atlantic seaway conditions when voyaging at speed had indicated that the *Normandie* —like many previous record-holders—was troubled with vibration problems, but this was eliminated by a change in the type of her propeller blades. On her first six round voyages the *Normandie* steamed 38,753 nautical miles at an average speed of 28.55 knots. In every way this sophisticated, luxurious and speedy liner had proved worthy of the honour she had brought to France for the first time.

There was little doubt that the *Normandie* presented a formidable challenge to the British contender, Number 534, which, after long months of idleness, was now being completed at Clydebank, the Government having agreed to provide the necessary money to enable work to be resumed. This agreement had been reached after protracted negotiations between the Cunard Company and the Treasury, in which Mr David Kirkwood, Member of Parliament for Clydebank, had played an active part. The negotiations had not been easy, nor had they been helped by a continuing decline in transatlantic passenger carryings—642,000 in 1932; 467,000 in 1933 which, in fact, was to culminate in an all-time 'low' of 460,000 in 1934.

Another hurdle which had to be overcome was the sharp divergence of opinion among shipping experts, industrialists and leading financial houses on the question as to whether one 'big ship', like Number 534, would prove as economic to operate as two smaller 30,000-ton liners. This argument, supported by facts and figures, had led in turn to the Government setting up a special committee of inquiry under the chairmanship of Lord Weir, to examine the position. The outcome of this inquiry was that the committee came down in favour of the 'big ship' and, at the end of December 1933, an agreement was reached.

One unexpected condition of the agreement was the merging of the North Atlantic assets of the Cunard and White Star Companies, which were to be transferred to a new company to be called Cunard-White Star Limited, effective from January 1 1934. The Cunard Company was to be credited with 62 per cent of the share capital of the new company and the Oceanic Steam Navigation Company (White Star) with 38 per cent. For their part the Treasury agreed to advance £4.5 million to enable Number 534 to be completed and, in addition, £5 million if it was decided to build a second ship (eventually the *Queen Elizabeth* [*I*]). These loans were subsequently paid in full.

On Tuesday April 3 1934—the previous day (Easter Monday) having been a public holiday—some 4,000 men streamed through the shipyard gates at Clydebank to resume work on Number 534. Her keel had been laid as a Cunard contract; she was to be completed for new owners, Cunard-White Star Ltd. No time was lost at the shipyard and, on September 26 1934, a day of incessant torrential rain, about 200,000 people made their way to Clydebank to welcome King George V, Queen Mary and the Prince of Wales, in his capacity of Master of the Merchant Navy and Fishing Fleets. It was the first time a British queen had launched a merchant ship and excitement was intensified by the fact that it was not until the Queen had graced the ship with her own name, *Queen Mary*, that a waiting world learned under what name Number 534 would begin her sea-going career.

Completion of the ship took ten months, and on March 24 1936 the *Queen Mary* finally left the shipyard in which she had been cradled for Southampton. Never before had so big a liner made the passage down the narrow Clyde channel, and world interest in the event was tremendous. As it was, there were one or two 'frightening' incidents during this journey, especially the moment when, off Dalmuir Light, the *Queen Mary* swung across the stream and lay aground for 13 minutes. But, under the expert direction of Clyde pilots, Captain Duncan Cameron and Captain John L. Murchie, with whom on the navigating bridge was Commodore Sir Edgar Britten, first commander of the *Queen Mary*, the voyage was safely accomplished, and at 2.23 pm (four hours 28 minutes after leaving her shipyard berth) she was lying to anchor off Greenock.

Later the same day, the *Queen Mary* proceeded to Southampton and entered the new King George V graving dock, where her launching cradles were removed and underwater hull cleaned and overhauled. On April 15 she left Southampton for the Clyde, where trials were carried out. These proved successful. No official figures were published and she returned to her home port where final preparations were made for her maiden voyage, scheduled for May 27.

During the months that the *Queen Mary* was being completed, King

George V had died and a new king, Edward VIII, reigned in his stead. On May 25 1936 the King, accompanied by the Queen Mother and his two nieces, Princess Elizabeth (Queen Elizabeth II) and Princess Margaret, made a special visit to Southampton to inspect the liner.

It was a proud ship the Royal party toured—a ship as British in her hull form, machinery installation and the furnishing and decor of her passenger accommodation as her great rival, the *Normandie* was French. Passengers who voyaged in both liners were to find themselves crossing the Atlantic in two different worlds. If the *Normandie* brought Gallic wit to the Western Ocean, the *Queen Mary* brought a curiously British sturdiness, exemplified perhaps in the extensive use of woods, for the most part from Britain and the Commonwealth, in her public rooms, alleyways and staterooms. Pacific maple, Indian freywood, English oak and yew, chestnut and sycamore, Burma cedar, African cherry—over 50 varieties there were vying with each other in their loveliness. Leading British artists had been called upon to contribute paintings and wall panels for the public rooms and salons. So too it was with the carpets and cutlery and glassware. The *Queen Mary*, to the last detail, was a product of British skill and craftsmanship.

She began her maiden voyage from Southampton to New York on May 27 1936 and, as at the time of her launching, thousands of sightseers gathered along the waterfront to cheer the great ship as, with Captain Sir Edgar Britten on the bridge, she sailed down Southampton Water and headed for Cherbourg. She was in traditional Cunard colours, black hull, white superstructure, three massive, orange-red funnels with their three black rings and black tops, but from her mainmast there flew two houseflags, Cunard and White Star. Hopes were high that in this maiden voyage she would depose the *Normandie* and restore the Blue Riband to British ownership. These hopes were not to be realised although, at one stage in her voyage, it looked as if they might be, when from noon May 29 to noon May 30 she covered 766 nautical miles at an average speed of 30.64 knots —a record for a day's steaming on the westward route. In the event she arrived at New York on the morning of June 1—a glorious first of June indeed—to receive the traditional heartwarming welcome, described by a passenger in the liner. He wrote: 'As the sun climbed the cloudless sky so down the bay sped a convoy of cutters and launches, to greet the *Queen Mary*. On board this convoy were the official welcoming party—civic leaders in top hats and morning dress—port officials, customs and immigration officers, a fresh host of newsmen and photographers.

'From the *Queen Mary's* boat deck, some 90 feet above the water line, cockleshells the little boats looked as they ranged alongside, and pygmies looked the officials as they scaled the steel cliff which was the liner's hull, gratefully accepting the steadying hands of the quartermasters who brought them safely aboard, there to be welcomed by Captain Britten and Sir Percy Bates, the Cunard White Star chairman.

'Formalities over and the ship given her clearance—for even newly-arrived Queen liners must be subject to port regulations—we began our royal progress. By now the official launches had been joined by scores of other craft who ranged themselves along each side of the *Queen Mary* as, dressed overall, her white superstructure and three red and black

Face three—the *Mauretania* as a hospital ship during World War 1, standing out against the hills as she lies in Naples Bay.

Face four—the *Mauretania,* an elegant lady 'dressed' in readiness for another cruise.

Face five—July 1 1935: the *Mauretania* preparing to leave Southampton for the shipbreakers' yard at Rosyth after a glorious 28-year sea career. (*British Transport Docks Board*)

This artist's impression of a typical embarkation scene on the Mersey, prior to the departure of a transatlantic liner, was included in Cunard's birthday number in July 1929.

46

Germany stages an Atlantic 'come-back' in 1929 with the Norddeutscher Lloyd liner *Bremen,* which regained the Blue Riband for her country from the formidable *Mauretania.* The *Bremen* was joined in 1930 by her sister ship *Europa. (John McRoberts)*

The *Rex*, a superb and extremely luxurious liner commissioned in 1932 by Italia Lines and which brought the Blue Riband to Italy for the first time. (*Italia Navigazione*)

Companion ship to the *Rex*, the beautiful *Conte di Savoia* made several fast voyages but was never officially recognised as a Blue Riband holder. (*Italia Navigazione*)

The largest passenger liner ever built, the French liner *Normandie* regained the Blue Riband from the *Bremen* in 1935, being finally deposed by the *Queen Mary* in 1938. Here she is seen on June 3 1935 on the occasion of her triumphant arrival at New York at the end of her record maiden voyage. (*Cie Générale Transatlantique*)

June 12 1935. The *Normandie* flying a Blue Riband pennant from her mainmast sets out from New York on her return voyage. (*Cie Générale Transatlantique*)

R·M·S
'QUEEN MARY'

Mr T. E. Hughes

I t is with great pleasure that we welcome you on board "QUEEN MARY" on the occasion of her Maiden Voyage from Southampton via Cherbourg to New York, this 27th day of May, 1936, and we trust that your crossing will be in every way enjoyable and leave you with many happy memories.

May your life be long and successful as we this day wish our new vessel to prosper in her role of promoting international friendship particularly between the nations bordering the North Atlantic Ocean.

CUNARD WHITE STAR LIMITED.

COMMODORE

This certificate was presented to all passengers on the maiden voyage of the *Queen Mary* in May 1936.

topped funnels gleaming in the vivid sunshine, she moved slowly towards the harbour.

'The nearer we approached, the larger the escorting armada became. Ships seemed to come from nowhere, ahead, alongside and trailing astern, small boats, ferry boats and chartered ships crowded with passengers and listing perilously, the city's fireboats cascading their welcoming jets of water. The piers on the Hudson river were brave with flags and dense with people. Then a tumult of sound filled the air, the like of which waterfront men said had never been heard before. Merchant ships of all flags and all nations, berthed in the port, or going about their sea-going, sounded their welcome which the *Queen Mary* acknowledged with a single diapason blast on her whistle which sent the seagulls whirling and screaming high in the air, affronted by this new and awesome sound they were hearing for the first time. This was the *Queen Mary's* day and New Yorkers with their characteristic warm-hearted generosity made sure that it would be a day to remember.'

The *Queen Mary's* homeward voyage from New York began on Friday June 5. She called at Cherbourg early on Wednesday June 10 to disembark Continent-bound passengers and then proceeded to Southampton where she berthed later the same day. The times for her maiden voyage out and home were:

	Days	hrs	mins	Distance (miles)	Av speed (knots)
Westward					
Cherbourg to New York (ACLV)	4	12	24	3,158	29.133
Eastward					
New York (ACLV) to Cherbourg	4	15	15	3,198	28.74

Commenting on the voyage, Sir Percy Bates, Cunard White Star chairman, who had been a passenger, said he had been pleased at the liner's performance. He added that some day the company might try to find out what the *Queen Mary* could do, but he was 'not out to take any risks'.

Two months later, in August 1936, the *Queen Mary* made her first record crossing and with it gained the Blue Riband. Westward, she voyaged from Cherbourg (Bishop Rock) to New York (ACLV) in four days 27 minutes at an average speed of 30.14 knots; eastward she completed the passage from New York (ACLV) to Cherbourg (Bishop Rock) in three days 23 hours 27 minutes at an average speed of 30.63 knots.

It was the first time a passenger liner had crossed the Western Ocean from New York in less than four days and it was the first time an average speed of over 30 knots had been maintained west to east. These cumulative records entitled the *Queen Mary* to hold the Hales Trophy. The Cunard White Star directors would have nothing to do with it on the grounds that any implication of ocean 'racing' was not consistent with the company's policy.

In the event, the *Queen Mary's* tenure of the Blue Riband was brief. Quick to accept the challenge, the *Normandie,* under the command of Captain Pierre Thoreux, made record voyages in 1937. In the March she crossed from New York (ACLV) to Cherbourg (Bishop Rock) in four days six minutes at an average speed of 30.99 knots. She followed up this record average speed in July by making the passage from Cherbourg (Bishop Rock) to New York (ACLV) in three days 23 hours two minutes at an average speed of 30.58 knots, and completed the triple event in August when she voyaged from Cherbourg (Bishop Rock) to New York (ACLV) in three days 22 hours seven minutes at an average speed of 31.20 knots. These voyages were to be the crowning achievement of this magnificent French liner's sea-going career. They were to be eclipsed in 1938 by the *Queen Mary*. Leaving Southampton on August 3 under the command of Captain Sir Robert Irving, she completed the passage from Cherbourg (Bishop Rock) to New York (ACLV) in three days 21 hours 48 minutes at an average speed of 30.99 knots; on her homeward voyage, beginning on August 10, she made the run from New York (ACLV) to Cherbourg (Bishop Rock) in three days 20 hours 42 minutes at an average speed of 31.69 knots to gain for herself the distinction of being the world's fastest merchant ship.

Coincidence it may have been, but it was fitting that this triumph should have been achieved in the centenary year of the pioneer paddle steamer *Sirius* of 703 tons which had begun her maiden transatlantic voyage from London on March 28 1838 and, after a voyage lasting 18 days 12 hours, had arrived at New York in the early hours of April 23—St George's day.

In North Atlantic shipping history, the year 1938—the last full year of peace before the outbreak of World War II—occupies a special and memorable place in that it was to mark the 'finest hour' of the great armada of passenger liners maintaining the Atlantic ferry. Unchallenged by air liner services, they crowded the Western Ocean sea lanes, secure in the knowledge that they were the only means of transport between the continents of Europe and North America.

In the van were the magnificent six record-breaking liners: *Queen Mary, Normandie, Conte di Savoia, Rex, Europa* and *Bremen*. The trade recession of the early 1930s was fast becoming an unpleasant memory, passenger traffic was steadily improving; the *Queen Elizabeth (I)*, consort to the *Queen Mary*, was completing at Clydebank; the Norddeutscher Lloyd Line had announced plans for the building of a mammoth superliner to be called *Viktoria*; and the French Line was likewise busily planning a companion ship, to be named *Bretagne*, for the *Normandie*. Despite mounting tension in Europe following the signing of the Munich Pact in September 1938, never had the future of North Atlantic passenger liner services seemed more assured, nor the prospect of intensified competition for Blue Riband honours more exciting.

Then, on September 1 1939, Hitler invaded Poland. Within days Europe was involved in a war, the consequences of which were as disastrous as they were appalling. One immediate effect was the disruption of North Atlantic passenger liner services. Liners still in port were ordered temporarily to remain there. They included the *Normandie* at New York, the *Rex* and *Conte di Savoia* in Genoa and the *Europa* at Bremen. The master of the *Bremen*, which was homeward bound from New York, was instructed by radio to set a northerly course and proceed to the port of Murmansk. The *Queen Mary* which, on August 30, had sailed from Southampton with a record complement of 2,332 passengers—the majority of them Americans—was ordered to remain at New York on arrival until further orders. On Sunday September 3, within a few hours of Britain declaring war on Germany, the Donaldson passenger liner *Athenia*, which had left Liverpool for Montreal the previous day, was torpedoed and sunk without warning.

And, for the second time in 25 years, the great Brotherhood of the Sea was to be lost in bitterness and hate and, upon the North Atlantic, there fell a darkness in which Blue Ribands had no place.

Eleven
1952—1973

The 'forgotten' record

THE ENDING OF World War II and the dawn of peace brought with it the gradual release from National Service as transports or in other capacities those North Atlantic liners which had survived the conflict. One by one they returned to their owning companies for refit, involving virtual reconstruction of passenger accommodation. Losses by sea and air attack had been heavy. Many liners which, in the pre-war years, had been familiar figures on the Western Ocean, never came back. They included four of the six Blue Riband ships.

The *Normandie,* laid up at her berth in New York since September 3 1939, had been taken over by the United States Government after the collapse of France. In December 1941, after the Japanese attack on Pearl Harbour and the entry of the United States into the war, it was decided to convert the *Normandie* into a troop-carrier, to be named *Lafayette.* This work began on December 12 1941. Rapid progress was made until February 9 1942 when, as if affronted by the indignities committed upon her, this proud and most elegant liner caught fire. The floods of water, estimated at 80,000 tons, poured into her by zealous firemen proved too much for the *Normandie* to bear. Top-heavy, she suddenly heeled over and sank. Salved in 1943 at an estimated cost of 4.5 million dollars she was found after survey to be beyond economic repair. For three years the desolate charred hulk, which was once the *Normandie,* lay rusting at her berth until, in September 1946, she was sold for scrap for £50,000, and for that purpose was towed to Port Newark, New Jersey.

After being extensively damaged during an air raid on Bremen on March 18, 1941, the *Bremen* had been broken up. A similar fate had befallen the *Rex,* bombed and sunk at Capodistria, Northern Italy, on

September 9 1944. The *Conte di Savoia*, sunk in shallow waters off Venice two days later on September 11 1944, was salved only to be sold for scrap. Only two of the 'magnificent six' had survived the war—the *Europa* and *Queen Mary*.

The *Europa* escaped with minor damages during air raids on Bremen. In 1946, under the War Reparations Scheme, she was handed over to France and after an extensive refit was operated by the French Line under the name *Liberté*.

Of the six, only the *Queen Mary* saw continuous active service as a transport. In this work she had been joined in 1941 by her consort *Queen Elizabeth (1)* which had yet to make a normal North Atlantic commercial voyage. Up to May 31 1945, the two 'Queen' liners between them had transported 1,243,538 Service personnel to and from the various theatres of war. On the North Atlantic, running between New York and the Clyde (Greenock), they had carried 869,694 troops eastbound and 213,008 westbound, of whom a large percentage comprised American service men and women—a fact which the US Government had duly noted.

The remarkable contribution to the war effort by these two big and speedy liners—one the fastest merchant ship in the world, the other yet to win her North Atlantic spurs—fitted as they were to carry 15,000 troops in a single voyage, was to have an important bearing on the post-war North Atlantic passenger liner scene. It was, in fact, one of the main factors which caused the US Government to agree to the building and commissioning of a liner which, primarily, could be rapidly converted into a transport in the event of war and which would also be fast enough and luxurious enough to take a fair share of the rapidly increasing transatlantic passenger traffic which, since their return to commercial service, the *Queen Mary* and her companion ship were virtually monopolising.

Perhaps because the main intention was to put into service a troopship which could also serve as a liner—a reversal of the usual procedure— the American government turned a 'blind eye' to the very significant fact that competition from air lines engaged in North Atlantic services was becoming a very real challenge. Up to September 1939, air competition was non-existent. After the war it was a dramatically different story. North Atlantic traffic statistics, published by the International Air Transport Association in June 1952, showed that member lines had carried 252,864 passengers in 1948; 272,637 in 1949; 317,164 in 1950; and 341,523 in 1951. In other words, over the four years 1,184,188 passengers had preferred to save time by travelling by air rather than by sea. In ever-increasing numbers they continued to do so.

Despite this clear 'message' from the air, the American Government persisted in the 'big ship' project. In this it had the active support of President Truman, who had expressed the opinion that he saw no reason why the two 'Queen' liners should earn over 50 million dollars a year for Britain in that most of the North Atlantic passenger traffic comprised American tourists. There was every prospect that the value of the tourist trade by passenger liner could reach 17 billion dollars a year to be shared by all nations operating passenger liner services in which the United States was a virtual absentee.

On February 8 1950, in a drydock specially built by the Newport News

Shipbuilding and Drydock Corporation, the keel of the largest merchant ship ever built in the United States was laid down with due pomp and ceremony. To be named *United States,* the estimated cost of this troopship/liner was put at 77 million dollars, of which the United States Lines, who were to operate the ship on the Atlantic Ferry, were to contribute 32 million dollars, while the US Government would absorb 45 million dollars.

Plans for the liner were drawn up by the firm of Gibbs and Cox, New York, naval architects with long experience in the design of tonnage for the US Navy and passenger liners for American owners. Because of the proposed dual role for the *United States,* all plans, drawings and specifications had to be approved by the US Navy before work could begin. Throughout her construction a veil of secrecy enshrouded the dockyard. No information was released about the *United States* and there were no periodic tours of the ship while she was under construction.

It was not until June 23 1951, the day of the official 'floating' ceremony in her drydock birthplace—a ceremony attended by President Truman and Mrs Truman who named the liner *United States*—that officially invited spectators could obtain any impression of what the liner would be like when she entered service. Gathering information about the ship was not unlike putting together pieces of a jig-saw puzzle. From the sparse details available it became known that the *United States* would be 990 feet long and 101 feet in width. Her draught was never given, but it was known that she had been designed to make the passage through the Panama Canal if ever called upon to do so. Her gross tonnage was variously given as 53,329 and 50,924 (US measurement). Propelling machinery comprised double reduction geared turbines, installed in separate water-tight compartments so that, in effect, there were two engine rooms. Four propellers were fitted and her designed speed was said to be 30-33 knots.

The passenger accommodation for 1,962 passengers—882 first-class, 525 cabin and 555 tourist-class—if it did not match up to the high standards of the *Queen Mary* and *Queen Elizabeth (1)*—was quite luxurious if on a modified scale, which was to be evidenced in the patronage she obtained when commissioned. Great emphasis was laid on the need for the liner to be virtually fireproof. For this reason light metal and aluminium was used in the furniture and other decorative features. Again to save weight, aluminium largely replaced steel in the liner's superstructure and in such feaures as the two funnels, single mast and lifeboats. The entire concept was governed by the basic fact that the *United States* had been envisaged as a troopship/liner and that in a national emergency she could be withdrawn from her peaceful sea-going occasions and speedily converted into a transport in which 14,000 service personnel could be embarked.

Any ideas Americans may have entertained that the *United States* would bring a new post-war image to the North Atlantic liner scene were doomed to disappointment. When she put to sea for trials in June 1952, it was evident that in her exterior appearance at least she conformed to tradition. With her slightly raked stem, long sleek hull, single short mast and two large funnels (red with a white band topped by a narrow blue cowl) she was as pleasing as she was graceful. In a curious way she seemed to have more in common with the White Star liner *Oceanic* at the turn of the century than with the mid-century Blue Riband holders, but with it all she gave the impression of the great power and great speed which she was to demonstrate conclusively on her maiden voyage.

On July 3 1952, under the command of Captain Harry Manning, Commodore of the United States Lines' fleet, the *United States* left New York at the outset of her maiden voyage to Havre and Southampton. Among her full passenger complement was Miss Margaret Truman, daughter of the President. In the early hours of July 7 she passed the Bishop Rock; she had completed the passage from the Ambrose Channel Light Vessel in three days ten hours 40 minutes at an average speed of 35.59 knots; homeward from Southampton she steamed from Cherbourg (Bishop Rock) to New York (ACLV) in three days 12 hours 12 minutes at an average speed of 34.51 knots. To those speeds the *Queen Mary* had no reply. For that matter neither had the *Queen Elizabeth (1)*, although she never attempted a record voyage. The Cunard White Star directors adhered to their often expressed policy of no interest in 'Blue Ribands' and were quite content for the two 'Queen' liners to maintain between them a regular service between Southampton, Cherbourg and New York for which they had been specifically designed in the 1930s, replacing the three ships then needed for such a service.

The triumph of the *United States* was hailed with delight by American citizens all over the world. For the first time in 100 years an American-built passenger liner had won the Blue Riband of the Atlantic. The previous American-built holder had been the Collins' wooden paddle steamer *Arctic* of 2,850 tons which, in 1852, had deposed the Cunard paddle steamer *Asia* by voyaging from New York to Liverpool in nine days 17 hours 12 minutes at an average speed of 13.25 knots. It had cost £150,000 to build the *Arctic;* estimated cost of building the *United States* was £25 million.

The *United States* received her Blue Riband accolade—the Hales Trophy —on November 12 1952. The presentation was made by the Duke of Sutherland to Mr John M. Franklin, president of the United States Line, on board the liner berthed at her pier in New York. The trophy, which the Cunard-White Star directors refused to accept after the *Queen Mary* regained the record from the *Normandie* in August 1938, had been in safe keeping in a jeweller's shop in Hanley, Staffordshire.

For the next 17 years the *United States* was to maintain sailings on the Western Ocean. Happy in her maiden voyage record she never improved upon it,—although there were odd occasions when she showed herself capable of doing so. During two days of voyage in August 1966 she touched average speeds of 33.5 knots and 33.2 knots and in September 1968 she crossed from New York (ACLV) to Cherbourg Rock in three days 17 hours 11 minutes at an average speed of 33.68 knots. There were times, especially in the summer season, when she carried full complements of passengers, but her owners, like other shipping companies maintaining North Atlantic passenger liner services, found themselves operating at a loss, overwhelmed by the soaring success of airliner services. From 1958 there had been a rapid decline in passenger liner traffic. One million passengers had crossed the North Atlantic by sea in 1957; by 1965 the total had dropped to 650,000. Over the same period, passenger traffic by air had increased from one million to four million a year. The Atlantic Ferry had taken wings. The day of the 'Blue Riband' ships was ending.

At a press conference held in London on May 8 1967, Sir Basil Smallpeice, chairman of the Cunard Company (the 'White Star' interests had been disposed of in 1959), announced that over the next two years there would be a 'phased withdrawal' of the *Queen Mary* and *Queen Elizabeth* (*1*). Every effort had been made to keep the ships in service, but results had shown that, even when engaged in cruising during the winter months, the ships were not paying their way. They were each losing about £750,000 a year. Sir Basil went on to express regret that the two ships would shortly come to an end of their working lives, holding as they did 'a unique position in the history of the sea and in the affections of sea-faring people everywhere'.

The *Queen Mary* left Southampton on her last voyage to New York on September 16 1967—it was her 1,000th Atlantic crossing. She left New York on September 22 and arrived at Southampton on September 27— the day after the 23rd anniversary of her launching. She then made two short cruises, finally berthing at Southampton on October 19.

Sold to the City of Long Beach, California, who paid 3,450,000 dollars (£1,232,000) for her, the liner left Southampton on October 31 1967. The voyage to her final berth took the form of a long cruise by way of the South Atlantic and Cape Horn, the liner being manned by Cunard personnel. She arrived at Long Beach on December 9 where she was given a great welcome.

The *Queen Elizabeth's* final transatlantic voyage took place in 1968. She left Southampton on October 20 1968, arriving at New York on October 25. She then sailed from New York on October 30, berthing at Southampton on November 4. An unexpected and deeply appreciated royal gesture was the visit by the Queen Mother when she said goodbye to the great ship she had launched on September 27 1938.

Like the *Queen Mary,* the *Queen Elizabeth* (*1*) ended her Cunard career with a short cruise, leaving Southampton on Friday November 8 and returning home on Friday November 15. She sailed from Southampton for the last time on November 29, for Fort Lauderdale, Florida.

Of all the famous ships which had held the Blue Riband, only the *United States* remained. The inevitable question was, how long would she continue in service? It was soon to be answered. Rumours of her impending withdrawal persisted but, under the command of Captain John S. Tucker, this great record-breaking liner kept to her Atlantic Ferry schedule. Then, on November 15 1969, the centenary year of the maiden voyage of the pioneer US paddle steamer *Savannah,* it was announced that the United States Line had decided that, for economic reasons, the *United States* should be laid up. For nearly four years she was to remain idle until, on February 10 1973, came the news that she had been purchased by the US Maritime Administration. The price paid for this, the last, fastest and most costly record-holder was 4.6 million dollars.

The Blue Riband of the Atlantic, to become an honoured memory, had passed into shipping history.

Tugs take charge of the imposing *Queen Mary* at Southampton.
(*British Transport Docks Board*)

October 31 1967. The *Queen Mary* outward bound from Southampton on her last voyage from the port. (*Skyfotos*)

The 35-knot Blue Riband holder, *United States*, passes her companion ship, the *America*, in mid-channel. (*Skyfotos*)

The glory is departed. The final Blue Riband holder, the *United States*, outward bound from her home port, New York.

Appendix one Record passages 1929—1952

Westbound

Year	Month	Ship	Owners	Course	Distance (nautical miles)	Time D h m	Av speed (knots)
1929	July	Bremen	Norddeutscher Lloyd	Cherbourg (Bishop Rock)—New York (ACLV)	3,164	4.17.42	27.83
1930	March	Europa	”	”	3,157	4.17. 6	27.91
1933	July	Bremen	”	”	3,199	4.16.15	28.51
1933	August	Rex	'Italia'	Gibraltar—New York (ACLV)	3,181	4.13. 8	28.51
1935	May	Normandie	French Line	Cherbourg (Bishop Rock)—New York (ACLV)	2,907	4. 3. 2	29.98
1936	August	Queen Mary	Cunard-White Star	”	2,906	4. 0.27	30.14
1937	July	Normandie	French Line	”	2,907	3. 2.32	30.58
1938	August	Queen Mary	Cunard-White Star	”	2,906	3.21.48	30.99
1952	July	United States	US Lines	”	2,906	3.12.12	34.51

Eastbound

Year	Month	Ship	Owners	Course	Distance (nautical miles)	Time D h m	Av speed (knots)
1929	July	Bremen	Norddeutscher Lloyd	New York (ACLV)—Plymouth (Eddystone)	3,084	4.14.30	27.92
1935	June	Normandie	French Line	New York (ACLV)—Cherbourg (Bishop Rock)	3,015	4. 3.28	30.31
1936	August	Queen Mary	Cunard-White Star	”	2,939	3.23.57	30.63
1937	March	Normandie	French Line	”	2,978	4. 0. 6	30.99
1937	August	Normandie	”	”	2,936	3.22. 7	31.20
1938	August	Queen Mary	Cunard-White Star	”	2,938	3.20.42	31.69
1952	July	United States	US Lines	”	2,942	3.10.40	35.59

Appendix two

The Blue Riband ships
Post-record careers

Commissioned

1840—*Britannia, Acadia, Caledonia, Columbia*—Cunard

The *Britannia* and *Acadia* were sold to North German Confederation Navy in 1849. The *Britannia* was renamed *Barbarossa* and in 1852 was transferred to the Prussian Navy in which she served until 1880, when she was sunk when acting as 'target' ship during experiments with early forms of torpedoes. The *Acadia* was renamed *Erzherzog Johann*. After dissolution of the German Confederation Navy in 1852, was bought by the German Line, Bremen. Renamed *Germania,* she maintained sailings between Bremen and New York—first voyage August 3 1853. Chartered to British government for transport service in Crimean War. Returned to owners. Sold to shipbreakers 1858 and scrapped in Thames Yard.

The *Caledonia* was sold to Spanish Navy in 1850 for conversion into a frigate. Wrecked near Havana in 1851.

The *Columbia,* while still in Cunard service, ran aground near Seal Island, Halifax, NS, on July 2 1843 and became a total loss. No lives were lost.

1850—*Atlantic, Arctic, Baltic, Pacific*—Collins Line

After Collins Line had gone into liquidation in 1858, the *Atlantic* was laid up until 1860 when she made one round voyage between New York and Southampton in the service of the newly-formed American company, the North Atlantic Steamship Company. In 1861 was taken over by Federal government for transport service in the American Civil War. In 1866 she was purchased by the North American Lloyd Line (New York-Southampton-Bremen) and in 1867 for the New York and Bremen Steamship Company (same owners). Sold for breaking up 1871.

The *Arctic,* while still in Collins' service, sank after collision with French steamer *Vesta* on September 27 1854 while on voyage from Liverpool to New York. The *Baltic* was laid up until 1861 when she was used as a transport during the American Civil War. In 1867 was purchased by the North American Lloyd Company and later by the New York and Bremen Steamship Company. Converted into a sailing ship in 1870, she was operated by a German company until sold for scrap in 1880.

The *Pacific* was 'lost without trace' on a voyage in Collins' Line service from Liverpool to New York beginning January 23 1856.

1856—*Persia* (3,300 gross tons)—Cunard Line, R. Napier, Glasgow

Held Blue Riband 1856-62. Requisitioned as troopship in 1861 at time of *Trent* crisis. Remained in Cunard service until 1868 when sold for £10,000. Scrapped in Thames Yard 1872.

1862—*Scotia* (3,871 gross tons)—Cunard Line, R. Napier, Glasgow
Held Blue Riband 1862-67. Last voyage Cunard service May 29 1876. Sold to the Telegraph Construction Maintenance Company 1879. Converted into twin-screw cable ship, one funnel removed; wrecked at Guam, Ladrone Islands, 1904.

1866—*City of Paris I* (2,556 gross tons)—Tod & MacGregor, Glasgow
Held Blue Riband 1866-69. Remained in Inman service until 1883. Sold to French shipping company 1884, renamed *Tonquin*, lost in collision off Malaga, March 1885.

1867—*Russia* (2,960 gross tons)—Cunard Line, J. and G. Thomson, Clydebank
Held Blue Riband 1867 (one voyage). Sold by Cunard to Red Star Line, Antwerp, 1878, renamed *Waesland*. Sank off Anglesey, North Wales, March 7 1902 after collision with steamer *Harmonides*.

1869—*City of Brussels* (3,081 gross tons)—Inman Line, Tod & McGregor, Glasgow
Held Blue Riband 1869-72. Remained in company's service. Sank on January 7 1883 at entrance to River Mersey, Liverpool, after collision with steamer *Kirby Hall*.

1871—*Baltic* (*I*) (3,707 gross tons)—White Star Line, Harland & Wolff, Belfast
Held Blue Riband (eastbound) 1873. Chartered to Inman Line 1883 and 1885-6. Last White Star voyage May 3 1888, sold to Holland America Line for £32,000 in 1888. Renamed *Veendam*. Lost after striking derelict object in North Atlantic February 6 1898.

1872—*Adriatic* (*I*) (3,888 gross tons)—White Star Line, Harland & Wolff, Belfast
Held Blue Riband (westbound) 1872. Remained in White Star service until November 1897. Sold for scrap. Arrived Preston, February 2 1899.

1874—*Britannic* (*I*) (5,004 gross tons)—White Star Line, Harland & Wolff, Belfast
Blue Riband (westbound and eastbound) 1876. Boer War transport 1899-1902. Returned Belfast for refit. Plan abandoned. Sold to German shipbreakers for scrap 1903 for £11,500. Left Belfast in tow for Hamburg August 11 1903.

1875—*City of Berlin* (6,004 gross tons)—Inman Line, Tod & McGregor, Glasgow
Blue Riband holder (west and east) 1875. Last Inman voyage Liverpool-New York, March 1 1893, taken over by American Line 1893. Renamed *Berlin*, operated on Southampton-New York route. Purchased by US government for service as transport ship 1898 and renamed *Meade*. Scrapped 1921.

1875—*Germanic* (5,008 gross tons)—White Star Line, Harland & Wolff, Belfast
Blue Riband westbound 1876; eastbound 1877. Capsized New York pier February 13 1899, due to weight of ice on decks; refloated. American Line service 1904, sold Dominion Line 1904—renamed *Ottawa*. Laid up

1909. Sold Turkish government 1910; renamed *Gul Djemal;* Turkish transport World War I; sunk by British submarine in Sea of Marmora—later salved, operated by Ottoman-American Line, Constantinople-New York 1920-21; service in Black Sea as *Gulcemal* 1929. Store ship at Constantinople 1949; floating hotel 1950; scrapped at Messina November 16 1950.

1879—*Arizona* (5,147 gross tons)—Guion Line, John Elder, Glasgow
Blue Riband (westbound and eastbound) 1879. Remained in Guion Line service until liquidation of company in 1894; laid up in Gareloch, River Clyde 1894-6; taken over by original builders, John Elder & Co, Glasgow, and refitted for San Francisco-Japan-China service; bought by US government in 1898 for transport service in Spanish-American War and renamed *Hancock;* transport in World War I. Sold for scrap 1926.

1882—*Alaska* (6,932 gross tons)—Guion Line, John Elder, Glasgow.
Blue Riband (westbound and eastbound) 1882; remained in Guion Line service until liquidation of company in 1894. Laid up in Gareloch, Clyde, 1894-6. Chartered to the Spanish Compania Transatlantica for transport service during the Cuban Rebellion 1897, renamed *Magallanes.* Sold for scrap 1899. Bought by Barrow Shipbuilding Company for use as workmen's hostel. Finally scrapped 1902.

1883—*Oregon* (7,375 gross tons)—Guion Line, John Elder, Glasgow
Sold to Cunard 1884. Blue Riband (westbound and eastbound) 1884. Requisitioned by British government as armed merchant cruiser 1885. Returned to Cunard service. Sunk after collision with schooner *Charles Morse* off Fire Island, New York, March 14 1886. All passengers and crew rescued by Norddeutscher Lloyd steamer *Fulda.*

1884—*America* (5,528 gross tons)—National Line, J. and G. Thomson, Clydebank
Blue Riband 1884, single westbound voyage; requisitioned as armed merchant cruiser 1885; returned to National Line service; sold 1887 Italian navy and renamed *Trinacria.* Employed as cruiser, transport, royal yacht, exhibition ship. Scrapped 1925.

1884—*Umbria* (7,718 gross tons)—Cunard Line, John Elder & Co, Glasgow
Blue Riband, westbound 1887; eastbound 1883. Although no longer record-holder, speed improved with service; transport Boer War. Scrapped 1910.

1885—*Etruria* (7,718 gross tons)—Cunard Line, John Elder & Co, Glasgow
Blue Riband westbound 1885, eastbound 1887. Like her sister ship *Umbria,* speed improved with service. Scrapped 1909.

1888—*City of New York (III)* (10,499 gross tons)—Inman and International, J. & G. Thomson, Clydebank
Blue Riband westbound 1889, eastbound 1892. Transferred to America Line and US Registry 1893—name shortened to *New York.* Requisitioned by US government as transport Spanish-American War 1898—renamed *Harvard;* returned to Atlantic service, US transport World War I, 1917-19, renamed *Plattsburg.* Last voyage American Line 1920. Sold to Polish Navigation Co 1922. Scrapped 1923.

1889—*City of Paris (2)* (10,479 gross tons)—Inman and International, J. & G. Thomson, Clydebank
Blue Riband eastbound and westbound 1889. Transferred to American Line and US Register 1893—name shortened to *Paris.* Requisitioned by

US government as transport Spanish-American War 1898—renamed *Yale*. Returned to service. Stranded Manacles, Cornwall, 1899; returned to service after refit, renamed *Philadelphia;* US transport World War I, 1917-19, renamed *Harrisburg;* last sailing America Line (*Philadelphia*) 1920; sold to New York-Naples SS Company 1922. Scrapped Genoa 1923.

1889—*Teutonic* (9,984 gross tons)—White Star Line, Harland & Wolff, Belfast

Blue Riband westward 1890. Took part Diamond Jubilee Naval Review 1897. Transferred White Star Dominion service 1911 (Liverpool, Quebec, Montreal). Armed merchant cruiser World War I, purchased by Admiralty 1915; operated as troopship. Laid up 1921; sold to German shipbreakers and scrapped at Emden 1921.

1890—*Majestic* (9,965 gross tons)—White Star Line, Harland & Wolff, Belfast

Blue Riband westbound voyage 1891. Transport during Boer War. Returned to White Star and remained in service until 1914. Sold for scrap 1914.

1893—*Campania* (12,950 gross tons)—Cunard Line, Fairfield Shipbuilding & Eng Co, Glasgow

Blue Riband eastbound 1893, westbound 1894; speed improved in service; sold to shipbreakers 1914. Purchased by British Admiralty 1914; converted into aircraft carrier, sunk in Firth of Forth after collision with naval vessel November 5 1918.

1893—*Lucania* (12,952 gross tons)—Cunard Line, Fairfield Shipbuilding & Eng Co, Glasgow

Blue Riband westward 1893, eastward 1894. Speed improved in service. Damaged by fire Huskisson Dock, Liverpool, August 14 1909 and sold to shipbreakers for scrapping.

1897—*Kaiser Wilhelm der Grosse* (14,350 gross tons)—Norddeutscher Lloyd, Vulcan, Stettin

First four-funnelled Atlantic liner. First German liner to win Blue Riband, eastbound 1897; westbound 1898. Outbreak of World War I converted into armed cruiser; sunk by HMS *Highflyer* off Rio de Oro, West Africa, August 27 1914.

1900—*Deutschland* (16,703 gross tons)—Hamburg Amerika, Vulcan, Stettin

Blue Riband eastbound and westbound 1900. Converted into cruise liner 1910, renamed *Victoria Luise*. World War I depot ship at Hamburg; left in German ownership 1918; renamed *Hansa* 1922. Scrapped 1925.

1901—*Kronprinz Wilhelm* (14,900 gross tons)—Norddeutscher Lloyd, Vulcan, Stettin

Blue Riband westbound 1902 (single voyage). World War I German armed merchant cruiser, very successful. Interned by US government at Norfolk, Virginia, April 1915; taken over by US in 1917 and converted into transport *Von Steuben*; laid up after war. Scrapped 1923.

1903—*Kaiser Wilhelm II* (19,361 gross tons)—Norddeutscher Lloyd, Vulcan, Stettin

Blue Riband westbound 1904, eastbound 1906. Laid up New York World War I. Taken over by US government 1917, converted into transport, renamed *Agamemnon*. After war, sailed as the *Monticello* for US Shipping Board; scrapped at Baltimore 1940.

1907—*Lusitania* (30,396 gross tons)—Cunard Line, John Brown & Co, Clydebank
Blue Riband westbound, eastbound 1907; sister ship *Mauretania*, remained Cunard service World War I; torpedoed and sunk off Old Head of Kinsale, Ireland, on May 7 1915 while on voyage New York-Liverpool carrying 1,959 passengers and 702 crew; 1,198 lost, 1,463 saved, including master, Captain W. J. Turner.

1907—*Mauretania* (31,938 gross tons)—Cunard Line, John Brown & Co, Clydebank
Blue Riband 1907-1929, longest period of all Blue Riband holders. Sister ship *Lusitania*. Requisitioned by Admiralty World War I—transport, hospital ship; released Government service May 1919; returned Cunard service Southampton-New York 1919; lost Blue Riband to *Bremen* July 1929; personal speed record August 1929; remained Cunard service North Atlantic, cruising until October 1934; sold to Metal Industries for breaking up April 1935; left Southampton for shipbreaking yard Rosyth July 1 1935.

1929—*Bremen* (51,656 gross tons)—Norddeutscher Lloyd Line, A. G. Weser, Bremen
Won Blue Riband (west and east) from *Mauretania* July 1929; World War II extensively damaged during air raid on Bremen March 18 1941; broken up for scrap, 1941.

1930—*Europa* (49,746 gross tons)—Norddeutscher Lloyd Line, Blohm & Voss, Hamburg
Blue Riband 1930 westbound (single voyage). Companion ship to *Bremen*; World War II laid up at Bremen; slight damage in air raids on Bremen. Post-war handed over to France under War Reparations Scheme 1946; operated by French Line as the *Liberté*, scrapped in Italy 1961.

1932—*Rex* (51,062 gross tons)—'Italia' Lines, Cantiere dell Adriatico, Trieste
Blue Riband (Gibraltar-New York) 1933. World War II—sunk during air raid on Capodistria, near Trieste, September 9 1944; salved but sold for scrap 1947. The companion ship to the *Rex*, the *Conte di Savoia* (48,502 gross tons), although a fast ship, never made an official Blue Riband voyage.

1935—*Normandie* (83,433 gross tons)—French Line, Penhoet Shipyard, St Nazaire
World's largest passenger liner. Won Blue Riband westbound and eastbound from *Bremen* May 1935; after entry of Cunard White Star *Queen Mary* into Atlantic service in May 1936, keen rivalry between two liners for Blue Riband honours finally held by *Queen Mary* August 1938. Outbreak of World War II September 1939, *Normandie* laid up at New York; taken over by US government 1941 for conversion into troopship *Lafayette*; caught fire while fitting out, sank at berth February 9 1942; salved but beyond repair; sold for breaking up at Port Newark, New Jersey, September 1946.

1936—*Queen Mary* (81,235 gross tons)—Cunard White Star, John Brown & Co, Clydebank
Keel laid for Cunard Line December 1930; work suspended December

11 1931, world trade recession; work resumed April 1934 under new ownership Cunard White Star Ltd; commissioned May 1936; won Blue Riband from *Normandie* west and east August 1936; keen competition between the two liners; *Queen Mary* finally regained Blue Riband August 1938. Taken over by British government World War II; served as transport until 1946; returned Cunard White Star service; reverted to Cunard ownership 1959. Withdrawn from service October 1967. Sold to City of Long Beach, California; left Southampton for Long Beach October 31 1967. Now highly successful exhibition ship and maritime museum. (The *Queen Elizabeth (1)*, consort to the *Queen Mary*, never attempted a record voyage and never held the Blue Riband of the Atlantic.)

1952—*United States* (53,329 tons)—United States Lines, Newport News Shipbuilding and Drydock Co

Last holder of the Blue Riband of the Atlantic which she gained from the *Queen Mary* on maiden voyage in July 1952 with unsurpassed record speeds of 35.59 knots eastbound from New York and 34.51 knots westbound from Southampton. Held Blue Riband unchallenged for 17 years until withdrawn from service in November 1969. Laid up Norfolk, Va; bought by US Maritime Administration February 1973 for 12 million dollars. Offered for sale to US citizens. Bids opened in Washington January 1974. Highest bid received was $30,700,000.

Appendix three

RMS *Mauretania*
Speed records

It was on November 16 1907 that the *Mauretania* began her maiden voyage from Liverpool to New York, via Queenstown, and within a short time of her commissioning beat all existing speed records.

Here are some of her outstanding voyages:

November 16 1907—Daunt's Rock (Queenstown) to Ambrose Channel Light Vessel (New York), five days five hours ten minutes. Average speed 22.21 knots.

November 30 1907—Ambrose Channel Light Vessel (New York) to Queenstown, four days 22 hours 29 minutes. Average speed 23.69 knots.

March 5 1909—Daunt's Rock (Queenstown) to Ambrose Channel Light Vessel (New York), four days 12 hours six minutes. Average speed 25.55 knots.

June 16 1909—Ambrose Channel Light Vessel (New York) to Daunt's Rock (Queenstown), four days 17 hours 21 minutes. Average speed 25.88 knots.

August 25 1909—Ambrose Channel Light Vessel (New York) to Fishguard, four days 14 hours 17 minutes. Average speed 25.41 knots.

During 1909 the *Mauretania* made 15 westbound voyages which averaged 25.39 knots; her eastbound passages averaged 25.48 knots.

September 10 1910—Daunt's Rock (Queenstown) to Sandy Hook (New York), four days ten hours 41 minutes. Average speed 26.06 knots.

September 15 1910—Ambrose Channel Light Vessel (New York) to Daunt's Rock (Queenstown), four days 13 hours 41 minutes. Average speed 25.61 knots.

August 9 1924—Cherbourg to Ambrose Channel Light Vessel (New York), five days three hours 20 minutes. Average speed 25.6 knots.

August 20 1924—Ambrose Channel Light Vessel (New York) to Cherbourg, five days one hour 49 minutes. Average speed 27.03 knots.

September 5 1928—Ambrose Channel Light Vessel (New York) to Eddystone Light (Plymouth), four days 23 hours ten minutes. Average speed 25.41 knots.

September 15 1928—Cherbourg to Ambrose Channel Light Vessel (New York), five days two hours 34 minutes. Average speed 25.26 knots.

August 3 1929—Cherbourg to Ambrose Channel Light Vessel (New York), four days 21 hours 44 minutes. Average speed 26.90 knots.

August 16 1929—Ambrose Channel Light Vessel (New York) to Eddystone Light (Plymouth), four days 17 hours 50 minutes. Average speed 27.22 knots.

These were not world records. The *Bremen* had gained the Blue Riband of the Atlantic during July 1929.

Other Mauretania Records

Highest day's run westbound—August 5 1929, 887 knots—average speed 27.48 knots.

Highest day's run eastbound—August 21 1929, 636 knots—average speed 27.65 knots.

Record Speed—Plymouth to Cherbourg, August 1929. 106 knots at average speed of 29.7 knots.

Record Christmas turn round—On December 9 1910 the *Mauretania* left Liverpool for New York, arriving there on Friday December 16. Leaving New York at midnight on December 18, she landed her passengers at Fishguard on December 22. She thus accomplished the remarkable feat of twice crossing the Atlantic in little over 12 days, which included the 'turn round' at New York.

Four trips in one month—In 1931 the *Mauretania* accomplished a record feat of crossing the Atlantic four times in one month, a total distance of over 12,400 miles.

At one period in her career the *Mauretania* made 27 consecutive runs across the Atlantic at an average speed of 25½ knots.

On July 19 1933, the *Mauretania* left Havana during a cruise and up to noon on July 20 had travelled 603 miles, at an average speed of 27.78 knots. The best rate of steaming was between Carysfort Reef Lighthouse and Jupiter Inlet Lighthouse, 112 miles, at an average speed of 32 knots, or 36.84 land miles per hour.

Appendix four

Table of distances, published 1896

Liverpool to New York

		North track Miles	North track Total distance from Liverpool Miles	South track Miles	South track Total distance from Liverpool Miles
Liverpool (Rock Light)	to Bar Lightship	11	11	11	11
Bar Lightship	to Skerries	50	61	50	61
Skerries	to Tuskar	94	155	94	155
Tuskar	to Conningbeg Lightship	19	174	19	174
Conningbeg Lightship	to Ballycotton	50¼	224¼	50¼	224¼
Ballycotton	to Queenstown (Roche's Point)	11	235¼	11	235¼
Queenstown (Roche's Point)	to Old Head of Kinsale	16	251¼	16	251¼
Old Head of Kinsale	to Fastnet	42	293¼	42	293¼
Fastnet	to Fire Island Lighthouse	2,699	2,992¼	2,778	3,071¼
Fire Island Lighthouse	to Sandy Hook Lightship	30	3,022¼	30	3,101¼
Sandy Hook Lightship	to Sandy Hook	6½	3,028¾	6½	3,107¾
Sandy Hook	to New York	15½	3,044¼	15½	3,123¼

New York to Liverpool

		North track Miles	North track Total distance from New York Miles	South track Miles	South track Total distance from New York Miles
New York	to Sandy Hook	15¼	15¼	15¼	15¼
Sandy Hook	to Sandy Hook Lightship	6½	22	6½	22
Sandy Hook Lightship	to Fire Island	30	52	30	52
Fire Island	to Fastnet	2,726	2,778	2,813	2,865
The Fastnet	to The Old Head of Kinsale	42	2,820	42	2,907
Old Head of Kinsale	to Queenstown (Roche's Point)	16	2,836	16	2,923
Queenstown (Roche's Point)	to Ballycotton	11	2,847	11	2,934
Ballycotton	to Conningbeg Lightship	50¼	2,897¼	50¼	2,984¼
Conningbeg Lightship	to Tuskar	19	2,916¼	19	3,003¼
Tuskar	to Skerries	94	3,010¼	94	3,097¼
Skerries	to Bar Lightship	50	3,060¼	50	3,147¼
Bar Lightship	to Liverpool (Rock Light)	11	3,071¼	11	3,158¼

187

New York to various ports

		North track Miles	North track Total distance from New York Miles	South track Miles	South track Total distance from New York Miles
New York	to Fire Island	52	52	52	52
Fire Island	to Bishop Rock Lighthouse (Scilly Isles off Cornwall)	2,860	2,912	2,939	2,991
Bishop Rock Lighthouse	to Falmouth	67	2,979	67	3,058
" " "	to Plymouth	96	3,008	96	3,087
" " "	to Needles (Isle of Wight)	194	3,106	194	3,185
" " "	to Southampton	215	3,127	215	3,206
" " "	to Cowes (Isle of Wight)	208	3,120	208	3,199
" " "	to Havre	255	3,167	225	3,246

Various ports to New York

Distance to Bishop Rock Lighthouse
(Scilly Isles off W Cornwall)

From	Miles
Havre	255
Cowes	208
Southampton	215
Needles	194
Plymouth	96
Falmouth	67

	Total distance to New York	
	North track	*South track*
From	*Miles*	*Miles*
Havre	3,141	3,213
Cowes	3,094	3,166
Southampton	3,101	3,173
Needles	3,080	3,152
Plymouth	2,982	3,054
Falmouth	2,953	3,025
Bishop Rock Lighthouse	2,886	2,958

Bibliography

THE WRITING OF this history of the Blue Riband of the Atlantic inevitably involved considerable research and recourse to the numerous books and wealth of documentary material which, since the beginning of steamship voyages across the Western Ocean, have dealt in one form or another with this fascinating subject. Among the more rewarding and informative books were the following:

The Atlantic Ferry, Arthur J. Maginnis (Whittaker, London, 1893)

North Atlantic Steam Navigation, Henry Fry (Sampson, Low, Marston & Co, London, 1895)

The History of Steam Navigation, John Kennedy (Chas Birchall, Liverpool, 1903)

Recollections of a Busy Life, Sir William Forwood (Henry Young & Sons, Liverpool, 1910)

A Century of Atlantic Travel, Frank C. Bowen (Sampson, Low, Marston & Co, London, 1933)

Pioneer Shipowners, Sir Clement Jones (Chas Birchall, Liverpool, 1934)

Atlantic Ferry, C. R. Benstead (Methuen, London, 1936)

Ships of the North Atlantic, A. G. Horton-White (Sampson, Low, Marston & Co, London, 1936)

A Short History of Naval and Marine Engineering, Eng Capt Edgar C. Smith (Cambridge University Press, 1937)

Mauretania, Humphrey Jordan (Hodder & Stoughton, London, 1937)

Steam Conquers the Atlantic, David Budlong Tyler (D. Appleton-Century Co, New York, 1939)

Giant Liners of the World, Alan Cary (Sampson, Low, Marston & Co, London)

Transatlantic Paddle Steamers, H. Philip Spratt (Brown, Son & Ferguson, Glasgow, 1951)

Passenger Liners of the Western Ocean, C. R. Vernon Gibbs (Staples Press, London, 1952)

North Atlantic Seaway, N. R. P. Bonsor (T. Stephenson, Prescot, 1955)

White Star, Roy Anderson (T. Stephenson, Prescot, 1964)

Other invaluable sources of information were publications, some now defunct, concerned with maritime affairs, including *The Marine Engineer*, *The Shipbuilder*, *Sea Breezes*, *Shipping World*, and individual histories issued by North Atlantic liner companies. Finally, there were the personal records and press cutting books amassed over the past 50 years, without which the work involved in collating and selecting the material for this definitive history would have proved much more difficult.

Index

190

Abbreviations: C.S.A. *Cie Sud Atlantique;* C.W.S. *Cunard White Star;* Fr. Line *French Line;* G.W. *Great Western Steamship Co;* Hapag *Hamburg Amerika Line;* I.M.M. *International Mercantile Marine Co;* Nat. Line *National Line;* N.D.L. *Norddeutscher Lloyd Line;* O.S.N. *Ocean Steam Navigation Co;* S.G.S.P. *St George Steam Packet Co;* S.S.C. *Savannah Steamship Co;* T.S.C. *Transatlantic Steamship Co;* U.S. *United States Line;* Vand. *Vanderbilt;* W. Star *White Star Line.*